THE RISE AND FALL
OF
AMERICAN TECHNOLOGY

THE RISE AND FALL
OF
AMERICAN TECHNOLOGY

Lynn G. Gref

Algora Publishing
New York

Library of Congress Cataloging-in-Publication Data —

Gref, Lynn G.
   The rise and fall of American technology / Lynn G. Gref.
      p. cm.
   Includes bibliographical references and index.
      ISBN 978-0-87586-753-3 (trade paper: alk. paper)—ISBN 978-0-87586-754-0
(case laminate: alk. paper) 1. Technological innovations—United States. 2. Research,
Industrial—United States. I. Title.
   HC110.T4G74 2010
   338'.0640973—dc22
                              2009037641

Printed in the United States

To my family, who believed in me and made this book possible

Acknowledgments

This book is the result of all that I have experienced in my professional life. Thus, everyone with whom I have had a relationship has in some way influenced the arguments and findings contained herein. Bosses and mentors certainly had a major role shaping the experiences upon which I have relied so heavily. They include Dave Callender, Alan Schaffer, Sy Zeiberg, Albert Latter, William Spuck, Mal Yeater, and Rhody Stephenson. Colleagues Larry Delaney and Dick Montgomery played instrumental roles in my serving on the Army Science Board and participating on several studies of the Naval Studies Board of the National Academy of Sciences. I have been blessed to work with some of America's smartest and brightest scientists and engineers. I admit to having worked in a forest of giants. I owe each and every one of them a great deal. They will remain unnamed since the list is too long and I would undoubtedly leave someone very important off the list. Therefore, I must express my great appreciation to them as a group.

The idea of writing the book lies with several colleagues on the Army Science Board. They include John Cittadino, Phil Dickinson, Bob Douglas, and Gil Herrera. I was encouraged further in this direction by colleagues at the Jet Propulsion Laboratory, which was my employer at the time. They include Elliot Framan, Gerry Meisenholder, and Al Paiz. Without the suggestions and encouragement of these kind people, I would never have considered writing this book.

This book is itself truly a product of America's technology. The personal computer and its word processor has greatly facilitated the writing and editing. The internet has proved to be invaluable in researching information that I would have had little likelihood of finding in a traditional library. Even Wikipedia deserves special mention. Although it is not recognized as a scholarly research source, its articles provide useful background information and direct visitors to appropriate references in their bibliographies.

The encouragement of family and friends has been essential to the book's completion. My good friend Bob Canovitz has encouraged me from start to finish. Sally, my wife, has been my greatest fan and helpmate. She has read every draft, providing feedback on everything from English usage to the comprehensibility and flow of the ideas and concepts contained herein. Finally, I am deeply grateful to my reviewers, Charles Bridges, Gerri Caldwell, Gil Herrera, Jim Vlasek, and Sheldon Wettack, whose feedback and corrections of fact and grammar enhanced the final version considerably. It has indeed taken a community of supporters to produce this book. I am also grateful to Algora Publishing and their editing team for their essential role in completing the realization of this book. I am most honored and appreciative.

Lynn G. Gref
Topanga, California

TABLE OF CONTENTS

PREFACE

If one accepts the argument that a decline in American technology is occurring, then one has to know about how America got to where it is today and what the conditions were that made it all possible in order to understand the significance of a decline.

The purpose for this book is to encourage a discussion at the national level regarding the importance of technology-based innovation to the economic health of the United States and regarding the adequacy of current support for research and development. With this purpose in mind, the targeted readers are those who are not necessarily technologists or even technology literate but rather those who perceive that they have a stake in America's technology capabilities in one way or another. Certainly, technologists should have an inherent interest in the issues addressed in this book. Specifically targeted readers include managers and workers of both high-tech companies and companies that depend on technology in their products, services, or processes for a competitive advantage. The targeted readers also include the decision makers and their supporting staffs in Government. Community leaders, who consider the American standard of living important, comprise an important segment of the targeted readership. The prospective reader is anyone who has an interest in seeing that the United States remains the leading economic nation in the world. I would hope a few of those who largely disagree with the goals and arguments of the author would also read the book so as to contribute to a national discussion on American technology — where we have been, where we are, and where we should go.

A career spent in the world of advanced technology serves as a basis for the observations and the arguments presented herein. This fortunate experience provided the opportunity to participate in and witness close up the development of technologies and products that today dominate our lives — primarily communications and information technologies. This first hand experience shapes the arguments that are central to the book and supply some of the examples that illustrate the discussion.

1

My lack of direct involvement in the medical or biological sciences limits their treatment in this book. I have extracted and presented the basic funding data and trends for the medical and biological sciences from available sources. These data and trends together with the inclusion of an extremely limited number of examples and vignettes from the biological and medical sciences complete the story. This approach has kept ignorance of the biological sciences from being overly blinding in the pursuit of a line of reasoning. I discussed the basic arguments of the book with knowledgeable people in the biological sciences and received assurances that the biological sciences present no real disparities. In all cases, a greater awareness and discussion of a possible decline in America's technological prowess and its consequences fulfills the purpose of the book.

The story told in this book has come about slowly and the basic notion of a decline took hold during a series of briefings on the Department of Defense's research budget. As a member of the Army Science Board, I discussed some of the basic observations and sub-arguments with colleagues on the Board. Sometimes, these pronouncements would surprise them. Eventually I shared what would become the basic outline of this book with some of my Board colleagues and coworkers at the Jet Propulsion Laboratory. They provided the encouragement and impetus for writing the book.

The basic observations about technology development began early in my career at the Aerospace Corporation. I was involved in advanced ballistic reentry systems and advanced missile systems development and witnessed first hand the challenges of making things work and the winnowing of concepts, which never make it into deployed systems. While at R&D Associates, I participated in the transition of the ARPANET to the Defense Communications Agency. I was also involved in innovative methods for developing information systems. Later, while at the Jet Propulsion Laboratory (JPL) I had the pleasure of collaborating with a friend and colleague, Dr. William Spuck, on what we called the Rapid Development Method. This turned out to be a great refinement of my earlier primitive concepts. These efforts laid the groundwork for the discussions of the technology development cycle. Managing technology development efforts at JPL provided insights for related discussions in this book.

During the six-year saga of writing this book, I found the arguments became more focused and sharper. In addition, some new data sets became available that further support one or another argument. The process of writing the book has been one of discovery and comparable to that of a great journey, and it required significant research. This research together with considerable pondering brought to light some possibilities for solutions. The overall results have yielded many reasons for optimism.

I hope you find the story as interesting and intriguing as I have found it to be.

INTRODUCTION

Metaphors can be very useful for the explanation of concepts and remembering things. One might think of an automobile as a metaphor for a country's economy. In the case of the United States, it has been like a high-powered Indianapolis racecar since the Civil War. For most of the rest of the world, its economy has been like an underpowered economy car. Continuing the metaphor, technology has been the engine, engineers and scientists have been the pit crew, and the American spirit has been the fuel. Moreover, the United States has been burning up the track and its lead over the rest of the world has been daunting. Alas, Americans may have become complacent or have lost the thrill of the race. Worse yet, they may have turned against the race altogether because of guilt over the consequences of their past preoccupations.

Here are some facts behind the metaphor. Information workers comprise more than 45% of the U.S. workforce, largely due to the information technology revolution. The application of technology accounts for two thirds of the annual increase in worker productivity since 1995. Roughly, 6.5 million workers hold high-paying high-tech positions in America's businesses. More than 200,000 entrepreneurs open technology-based companies every year. Research and development (R&D) spending in the U.S. is at a record level, which has resulted in an exploding array of technology based products and services. That is great! However, we must try to assess what the future has in store and where America can go from here.

The quickening pace of technology and the explosive growth of technology comprise the theme of a number of books and articles. Information and modern communications technology has touched everyone in one way or another. New and improved products hit the marketplace at a dizzying rate. It would seem that everyone is familiar with Moore's Law, which states that the number of transistors on a chip will double about every two years. In fact, briefings by senior industry representatives assured the Army Science Board that they know how to proceed in the development of microprocessors for the next decade that will preserve Moore's Law.

For those who read annual reports of companies such as Intel, Microsoft, Motorola, Texas Instruments, IBM, Google, Oracle, VeriSign, Symantec, National Semiconductor, EMC, Cisco and Hewlett Packard it would seem that research and development expenditures are large and growing at a quickening pace. (Reports reflecting the impact of the current economic downturn may reflect a somewhat sobering view as companies cut costs to remain profitable or minimize losses.) To these readers it is clear that technology is the engine of America's economy and it would seem that the future could not be brighter.

Neither the present nor the immediate future afford any significant basis for concern, but rather the long-term future, decades from now, poses the real danger. It is too late to escape the adverse consequences of a decline in American technology when it becomes obvious to everyone, if the observations and arguments presented in this book are correct. Therefore, it behooves us to try to understand the underpinnings of a technologically driven economy, to identify where shortfalls may have developed, and to take steps to overcome them. This is precisely the underlying reason for attempting to stimulate discussions regarding America's technology future.

The main thesis of this book is that a decline in American technology has begun. The principle argument or path of reasoning depends on a number of sub-arguments or paths of reason, each of which rests on a collection of facts and observations. The material may be challenging to grasp at times, especially for those not steeped in the world of technology development. Thus, the use of vignettes to the extent possible makes the argument more apparent. Further complicating the discussions is the fact that key portions of the argument depend on the generalization of observations to which exceptions abound. However, the preponderance of the observations support the arguments presented. It certainly will provide some basis of conversation if the book establishes its main thesis. In some cases more information is provided than is necessary but the particular details are quite interesting and worthy of discussion.

Three main sections comprise the book. The first section consists of the first five chapters of the book and addresses all the nitty-gritty details involved in the development of technology-based products. The questions related to who, what, how, when and where of technology development are answered in the first four chapters. The fifth chapter is devoted to the finances of technology development.

Chapters six through ten comprise the second section. Peering through the lens developed in the first five chapters reveals the story of the rise through the beginning of a decline in American technology.

Chapters eleven through fifteen comprise the final section. A discussion of the impact that a decline in technology would have on America starts the section. An argument for the relevance of technology in America's current service economy follows. This leads to a consideration of opportunities for technology development. The section finishes with a discussion of some possible actions to stem a decline that go beyond throwing money at the problem,

There are many great stories to be told related to technology development in America. They also represent much of America's twentieth century great epic. Edison epitomizes Americana. There are stories of great competitions such as that between Tesla and Edison. Moreover, there are stories of friendship such as that between Edison and Ford. There are stories of conflict and controversy such as the one that enveloped the invention of the laser. There are stories of fabled success and those of abject failure. The transistor story is one of the most fabled success stories and the bubble memory is one of failure. The stories of technology developments clearly intertwine those of their developers.

Along the way of revealing the technology development story, we will uncover several underlying principles pertinent to the development of technology. First, decades are generally required to take a basic science discovery and exploit it in a brand new or a revised product. Second, the technology development cycle passes through a number of distinct phases in order to carry a concept from idea to an implemented product or service. Furthermore, the cost to complete a phase tends to be an order of magnitude more expensive than the cost to complete the previous phase. Third, generally different people and different organizations perform the various phases of the technology development cycle. Yet, the performers of one phase couple closely with those of the next phase. Some personnel from one phase will frequently participate in the next phase of development.

Our story traces the evolution of the technology development cycle from the modestly educated inventor working with a small team of assistants and craftsmen to today's highly educated professionals, who often have masters and doctor's degrees and work in sophisticated multi-million dollar laboratories and product development centers employing hundreds or thousands of similar researchers. Along with these changes, the funding picture has changed to that of Government sponsored research dominating the early phases and corporate funded product development dominating the last phases.

Although there is not a single explicit indicator and other indicators are only very indirect, sufficient evidence is present to conclude that a decline has begun in the earliest phases of the development cycle. America's economic growth has largely reflected the growth of its technology base. Recent productivity increases are a result of industry's adoption of information technology. If America cannot develop technologies, which will create new industries with good job opportunities, then most of the population will have to compete with the global work force and accept a lot less. In addition, Americans cannot count on finding high paying service jobs to replace the ones lost to outsourcing or lost because its companies can no longer compete in the world marketplace.

There is no lack of research and development opportunities as is evident by considering some of the larger R&D problems facing the globe at this time. Public health, the environment, and energy encompass a broad array of R&D opportunities. Fortunately, America has some very bright and capable people to pursue these challenges aggressively. Collectively, Americans need to want to do something about the future much more than satisfying their latest whim. America would benefit from taking a lesson from the cultural heritage of its Asian population and for once start thinking long range.

Unless Government takes some actions, the decline will only strengthen. Approaches for reversing the decline vary from increasing Government funding in the early phases of the technology development cycle to making changes in the patent laws that will incentivize industry to fund the early phases of technology development. The monetary costs for reversing the decline are modest since the early phases of the technology development cycle are relatively inexpensive. On the other hand, recruiting the gifted young people to pursue education and careers in research and engineering poses a greater challenge. This places challenges on both America's educational system and its culture. Respect, romance, excitement, and rewards need to be very apparent for those involved in these careers. Learning science and engineering cannot be boring. Education must be world class. Others have contributed and documented some very outstanding recommendations for achieving the educational goals. The discussion on education provides only brief summaries of these recommendations with the anticipation that those with an interest in improving technology related education would refer to the original source materials. The story of American technology ends with the hope that an awareness of the decline will result in appropriate actions being taken to stem it.

Chapter 1. The Technology Development Cycle

"In all things there is a law of *cycles*." — Publius Cornelius Tacitus

The world is full of cycles. The earth circles around the sun giving us the cycle of seasons. There are life cycles, economic cycles, and weather cycles. The technology development process has a cycle. One has a choice in the number of parts or phases into which one breaks it, as it is with a number of other cycles. For example, just two phases consisting of a new moon and a full moon could have defined the monthly moon cycle instead of the generally accepted four phases of the moon. Alternatively, in theory eight phases could work for the moon's cycle except for the somewhat awkward situation that each phase would be three and a half days long. The choice rests on convenience and utility. Dividing the technology cycle into four phases suffices for the purposes of this book. This number provides sufficient granularity to support the arguments and concepts that follow and it keeps the discussion of the details of the process to a minimum.

For many, primary school lessons provide the basis of their knowledge of the technology developers and their associated development methodologies. This includes the stories of Ben Franklin discovering with his kite flying escapades that lightening is really electricity. These primary school lessons provided visions of him having problems seeing and tinkering in his workshop to develop bifocal glasses. Similarly, these lessons retold the story about Thomas Edison and his trial and error approach to developing the light bulb in his workshop. Moreover, no one can forget about Alexander Graham Bell's, "Do you hear me?" question to Mr. Watson, his assistant in the next room. Unfortunately, these images are mere caricatures of reality. Exploring some examples of modern technology development will provide some insight into the technology development process.

The transistor provides a good example of modern technology development. Today, transistors permeate everything electronic including telephones, computers, cell phones, fax machines, microwave ovens, cameras, time clocks, radios, and televisions. They have found their way into some products that traditionally did not need them such as automobiles, furnaces, kitchen appliances, clothes washers, and dryers. Some have proclaimed the transistor to be the most important invention of the twentieth century. However, the story begins in the nineteenth century. A German physicist, Ferdinand Braun discovered in 1874 that crystals could conduct current in only one direction under certain conditions. He had discovered a new principle about crystals and electricity.

The transistor's development continued at Bell Laboratories, which American Telephone and Telegraph (AT&T) founded in 1925 to pursue research in communications and other technologies. One field of research was to follow up on the work of Braun and others on what was to become semiconductors. Numerous people contributed to developing the theoretical understanding of semiconductors in the 1920s and 1930s. Ironically, some researchers working in the area of radio communications made a startling discovery. Trying to overcome some limitations in the vacuum tube, which was the staple of electronic devices before the transistor took over, they discovered that silicon was comprised of two distinct regions distinguished by the way in which the region favored current flow. Impurities in the region determine the direction of flow. Furthermore, the researchers discovered just how to introduce the right impurities so that they could predict and control the direction of flow. These discoveries provided essential groundwork for the invention of the transistor.

In 1945 Bell Labs director, Mervin Kelly, initiated a "mini-Manhattan project" within the Labs to develop a replacement for the vacuum tube amplifier. He selected William Shockley, who was one of the important theoretical physicists of the 1930s, to lead it. Shockley recruited a world-class team of solid state physicists, laboratory technicians, and staff. Among its members was Walter Brattain, who was an experimental physicist and enjoyed a well-deserved reputation for being able to make anything work. Another member of the team was a noted theoretical physicist, John Bardeen. These three, Shockley, Brattain, and Bardeen became the inventors of the transistor.

Applying the tried and true technique of taking something that works in one situation and applying it to an entirely new one, the team attempted to do with semiconductors what worked with vacuum tubes. Shockley's first design of a solid-state amplifier failed. He assigned Brattain and Bardeen to find out why it failed. Those that seem to know have portrayed these three as very independent researchers. It then follows that Brattain and Bardeen did not focus on Shockley's failed design. Rather, Bardeen suggested experiments and interpreted the results while Brattain built the apparatus and performed the experiments suggested by Bardeen. In December 1947, Bardeen gained an historic insight that ran counter to prevailing theory. Without telling Shockley, Brattain and Bardeen changed the design and built the first successful solid-state amplifier, a "point-contact" transistor.

Shockley was furious at not being directly involved. He immediately went to work on his own design. In less than four weeks, he came up with the "junction or sandwich" transistor. It took another two years to build one that worked. His device proved to be more rugged and more practical than the point contact transistor.

Shockley's transistor is much easier to manufacture and is the basis of today's semi-conductor industry. This and the events that followed led to the breaking up of the Bell Labs team.

Amazingly, the invention languished for several years. Shockley saw the possibilities and founded Shockley Semiconductor in Palo Alto, California. He hired a brilliant staff but his personality had the effect of driving them off after awhile. Eight defectors established Fairchild Semiconductor. Bob Noyce and Gordon Moore, two of the eight, went on to form Intel Corporation. Thus was the beginning of Silicon Valley.

Commercial products exploiting transistors did eventually find their way into the marketplace. First, it was a trickle but rapidly it grew into a torrent of transistor-based products. Hearing aids were the first commercial devices to employ transistors in 1952. In 1954, Texas Instruments efforts led to the production of the first transistor radio in the United States. Bell Labs announced the first computer based on transistors in 1955. (The ENIAC, which employed vacuum tubes, began the modern computing era in 1946.) The UNIVAC Solid State Computer was the first successful "transistorized" commercial computer. Although the Air Force accepted the prototype in 1956, Remington Rand was not able to market a commercial version until 1959. IBM followed rapidly with its transistor based 7070 computer.

Japanese engineers Masaru Ibuka and Akio Morita founded Sony Electronics in 1946 and almost immediately recognized the impact of the invention of the transistor. They introduced their first mass-produced tiny transistorized radios in 1955. From this beginning and capitalizing on transistor based electronics, they built their dominating consumer electronics business. This brief review of the history of the transistor would not be complete without acknowledging that the three principal inventors — Shockley, Bardeen, and Brattain — received the Nobel Prize for physics in 1956.

The development of the transistor began with the discovery about crystals. The invention involved the work of both theoreticians and experimentalists. Replacing vacuum tubes in the amplifiers of transoceanic telephone cables provided the motivation for the invention of the transistor. It did not get immediate acceptance. It took people other than the inventors to develop it and incorporate it into products. Its applications have gone far beyond the motivating application. It took different players and organizations from the inventors to develop the applications. It spawned a completely new industry, the semiconductor industry.

A discussion of Bell Laboratories' achievements with regard to the transistor transitions very naturally into a discussion of the development of the laser. LASER is an acronym for Light Amplification by the Stimulated Emission of Radiation. A laser is a device that emits a coherent beam of light. Albert Einstein first suggested the existence of this phenomenon in his 1916 paper proving Planck's law of radiation. For a long time, researchers considered the idea odd and consequently it received little attention for several decades.

The laser was not a result of a direct quest such as the case of the transistor. The story of the invention of the laser begins with Charles H. Townes' graduation with a Ph.D. in physics from the California Institute of Technology in 1939. Bell Labs immediately hired him and soon put him to work on a radar bombing system. As with most people of his generation, World War II had a permanent impact on Townes life's work. The bombing systems that Townes worked on used 10-centimeter wavelengths. The military wanted to use 1.25-centimeter wavelengths to get greater accuracy. He feared that the water vapor in the atmosphere would absorb the electromagnetic waves. To make a long story short, Bell Labs built the radar and it did not work for this very reason.

After the war, Townes moved to Columbia University in 1948 and focused on molecular spectroscopy. Now, molecular spectroscopy involves the observing of how a molecule responds to the exposure of electromagnetic energy. This was a direct extension of his work on the radar and the reason for it not working. There was the belief that the amount of energy a molecule could radiate was limited by the Second Law of Thermodynamics, which crudely stated, says that losses are entailed in making energy conversions. While at a scientific meeting in Washington, D.C., Townes took an early morning walk in Franklin Park. Mulling over this dilemma he came to the realization, "... now wait a minute! The Second Law of Thermodynamics assumes thermal equilibrium. We don't have to have that!" One does not need to understand the physics here, but what is important is to realize that Townes had one of those "AHA!" moments just when he was stumped, mystified, or whatever you want to call it.

When Townes returned to Columbia, he recruited his graduate student, James P. Gordon, and hired H. L. Zeiger to assist in the project. There was little interest in the idea by other researchers. Townes and his team proceeded with their research at a rather leisurely pace. They demonstrated a working device in 1953 which Townes dubbed the maser. MASER stands for Microwave Amplification by Stimulated Emission of Radiation. A maser is similar to a laser but emits microwaves, which are at a lower frequency than light. Although a maser is similar to a laser, it is not a laser. Thus, the invention of the laser remained. However, the invention of the maser represented a major step towards the laser's invention.

The second player in the invention of the laser was Arthur L. Schawlow. He received his Ph.D. from the University of Toronto in 1949 and joined Townes at Columbia University. At Columbia, he encouraged Townes regarding his concept for the maser. However, he left Columbia to accept a position at Bell Labs where he worked on superconductivity and missed the entire development of the maser. The two scientists continued their collaborations and in 1955 co-authored the book *Microwave Spectroscopy*. Bell Labs offered Townes a consulting job in 1956. Townes realized that infrared light and visible light were better for spectroscopy than microwaves. He stopped by to see his old friend and now brother-in-law, Schawlow, and to discuss his ideas. It turned out that Schawlow had similar thoughts. Schawlow had the idea to arrange a set of mirrors, one at each end of a cavity, to bounce the light back and forth.

They began work in earnest on their concept in the fall of 1957. They pursued these efforts without interrupting their other duties to their respective employers. Townes worked on the theory and Schawlow worked on the device. After eight months of working in this mode and without actually producing a laser, they wrote a paper on extending the principles of the maser to the optical regime and applied for a patent through Bell Labs. Two years later, in 1960, they received a patent for the invention of the laser. Subsequently, Townes received the Nobel Prize for his fundamental work leading to the maser/laser and Schawlow received it for his contributions to laser spectroscopy.

Schawlow and Townes had not produced a working laser – an actual device that emitted a coherent beam of light. As one might expect, technology's great race to invent and demonstrate the first working laser was off and running. Bell Labs researchers put their all into it. The Defense Department's Defense Advanced Research Projects Agency (DARPA) funded a small company lavishly. Ultimately, the development, demonstration, and patenting of the first working laser was accomplished by yet another individual "out of left field" (West Coast versus the East Coast), Theodore Maiman. He was born in Los Angeles, California and educated at Stanford University where he received his Ph.D. in 1955. He went to work for Hughes Research Laboratories in Malibu and became interested in Townes' maser. He made a number of innovations in the maser that significantly increased its practicality. However, his management did not want him to work on his ideas for a laser. He persisted on his own and in May 1960, he demonstrated a laser employing a ruby crystal. Ironically, one of America's most prestigious physics journals refused to publish the results believing it was just another announcement on maser research.

Controversy adds a little spice to the history of technology and there is some here. Some historians have claimed that Gordon Gould was the first one to invent the optical laser rather than Maiman. Gould, who was born in New York City, idolized Edison. He graduated from high school during the Great Depression and could not afford to attend the school of his choice, Massachusetts Institute of Technology. He used his New York State scholarship to attend Union College where he attended lectures by General Electric (GE) researchers and visited GE's facilities. He got an MS in physics from Yale in 1943 and went to work on the Manhattan Project. After the war, he continued his graduate studies at Columbia University. Here he studied optical and microwave spectroscopy. Gould has said that his first ideas for the laser "came in a flash" one night in 1957. He wrote these down in a notebook entitled *Some rough calculations on the feasibility of a LASER: Light Amplification by Stimulated Emission of Radiation*. This was the first use of the acronym LASER and historians credit him with coining the term.

He had his notes notarized at the local drugstore the next morning. Based on the advice of an attorney, he believed that he had to have a working model of his LASER to file for a patent. As a result, it was not until 1959 that he filed for a patent and the patent office refused to grant it. In addition, his original patent application contained a number of different inventions. The patent office reviewer also believed that a graduate student who lacked any real credentials could not have made the invention. After nearly twenty years of legal battles Gould's perseverance paid off with the granting of two patents, one for optically pumped laser amplifiers and another for discharge excited laser amplifiers. (These are two different ways to increase the amount of light produced by a laser.) Gould's laser patents cover eighty percent of today's industrial, commercial, and medical applications of lasers.

Maiman's laser was only capable of pulsed output. (Pulsed output means that the laser emits light for a short period of time — pulse — followed by no output.) Yet another person made an important contribution to the "invention of the laser." Ali

Javan was born in Tehran, completed high school in Tehran, and attended Columbia University where he received his Ph.D. in 1954. He stayed at Columbia doing post-doctoral work for four more years. In 1958, he joined Bell Labs and convinced them to permit him to pursue his gas laser idea. (A gas laser is one in which the molecules, which are responsible for creating the laser light output, are in a gaseous state. Similarly, a solid-state laser is one in which the molecules which are responsible for creating the laser light output are a solid or in the form of a crystal. A semiconductor laser is a special case of a solid-state laser but happens to have its own category.) Two years and two million dollars later and shortly before Christmas of 1960, he and his team succeeded in demonstrating a continuous gas laser (i.e., a steady beam of light rather than the short bursts of light of the pulsed laser). In fact, his team transmitted a voice conversation using a laser beam the next day on December 13, 1960. One widespread use of the gas laser is in the scanners at the checkout counter at the store.

The introduction of yet another contributor is required to complete the story of the "invention of the laser." Robert N. Hall who was born in New Haven, Connecticut received his BS in physics from the California Institute of Technology (Caltech). After graduation, he joined General Electric's Research and Development Center in Schenectady, New York. He contributed to the World War II effort by designing systems that used continuous wave magnetrons to jam enemy radars. After the war, he returned to Caltech to earn a Ph.D. in nuclear physics. He then returned to GE's Research and Development (R&D) Center, where he spent the rest of his professional career. (These discussions of the people and the organizations at which they worked will be relevant to the discussions in later chapters.)

Hall first developed a technique to purify germanium. This led to the discovery of semiconductor devices called p-n diodes. (Diodes are electronic devices in which current can flow in only one direction.) In 1962, he attended a talk on highly emitting diodes. He realized that a very special variation of his p-n diode allowed for the highly efficient generation of coherent light from the semiconductor. Thus, the semiconductor injector laser came into being and Hall received a patent for it in 1967. All CD and CD-ROM players, all DVD players, all laser printers, and most fiber-optic communications systems employ solid-state lasers.

By this time, it was common to refer to the laser as an invention looking for an application. It was not for a lack of ideas. It was just very difficult to overcome all the problems that came up in trying to make an application work. For a time, it seemed as though laser applications were going to be the sole domain of science fiction writers in the form of killer beams and light sabers of Star Wars fame.

Although Gary Starkweather combined a laser beam with the xerography process to kludge together a laser printer out of a copier at Xerox's research facility in Webster, New York in 1959, it took until 1976 before anyone capitalized on the idea. Somewhat surprisingly, Xerox was not the first to introduce a laser printer into the commercial marketplace but rather it was IBM.

Optical communication applications have proved to be elusive despite Ali Javan and associates' demonstration of voice transmission over a laser beam one day after verifying their continuous laser. The atmosphere has proven to be very unkind to transmitting a laser beam through it for any great distance (e.g., causes attenuation and dispersion).

Finally, a full decade after the first laser based communications laboratory demonstration, researchers recognized that glass fibers were an efficient medium to "carry" a laser beam. Corning Glass became a global supplier of optical fiber for use in telecommunications. It took nearly seven more years to develop all the components needed for General Telephone and Electronics to establish the first fiber optic based telephone network in 1977. Fiber optics remains the primary means of laser communications.

Twenty years after the invention of the laser, Philips Electronics and Sony Corporation co-invented the compact disc in 1980. The first CD players and CDs were in the stores two years later. One might consider this the "killer application" by the size of the market for CD and DVD players.

Due to today's popularity of laser eye surgery it is worth noting that IBM researchers saw the potential of using the Eximer laser for surgery as early as 1982. It was not until 1987 that doctors performed the first laser eye surgery.

Some interesting observations come to mind regarding the development of the laser. The theorists got all the Nobel Prizes. The inventors of real working lasers got none. There is a real distinction between the theorists and the inventors or device builders. The likes of IBM, Corning Glass, Sony, and Phillips brought the applications to market.

Before getting into a discussion of the technology development cycle, let us review one last example, the history of the solar cell. It was in 1839 that a nineteen-year old French experimental physicist, Edmund Becquerel, discovered that certain metal electrodes placed in an electrolyte would produce small amounts of electricity when exposed to light. Scientists refer to this phenomenon of materials producing electrons when exposed to light as the photoelectric effect.

Thirty-four years later, in 1873, Willoughby Smith discovered the photoconductivity of selenium. (A material is said to be photoconductive when its ability to conduct electrons increases when exposed to light.) American inventor Charles Fritts constructed the first true solar cells in 1877. His solid-state cells were made of selenium wafers coated with an almost transparent layer of gold. These cells were less than one percent efficient. This limited the application of such devices to the detection and measurement of light. Hence, applications were limited and a primary application was in photography.

It was not until 1903 that Albert Einstein established the theoretical basis for solar cells in a published paper on the photoelectric effect. Thirteen years later, Millikan provided experimental proof of the photoelectric effect. Between 1918 and 1954, researchers made numerous advances in the growing of semiconductor crystals.

During the late 1940s and early 1950s work at Bell Labs by a team of researchers led by Gerald Pearson, Calvin Fuller and Daryl Chapin resulted in the discovery in 1954 of a 4.5 percent efficient silicon solar cell. Within a few months, they raised the efficiency to 6 percent. Western Electric, Bell Labs sister organization in the AT&T empire, began selling commercial licenses for silicon photoelectric technologies. Early successful applications included dollar bill changers and devices that decoded computer punch cards and tape. In the last half of the 1950s, Hoffman Electronics raised the efficiency of silicon solar cells to 14 percent. Commercial success eluded the manufacturers of solar cells because the cost remained extremely high in spite of this rapid technical progress. A one-watt solar cell cost approximately $300 in 1956 compared to 50 cents to build one watt of capacity for a commercial power plant. Consequently, applications were largely limited to novelty items such as toys and radios.

In the first days of the space program, satellite designers did not consider solar power a viable option. Chemical batteries for the near term and nuclear power for the far term comprised the primary options. In fact, the Navy considered solar cells as an untried technology and far too risky for its first satellite, the Vanguard, and decided to use chemical batteries. One of the space pioneers, Dr. Hans Ziegler, strongly differed with the Navy. He argued that within a very short time the chemical batteries would run out of power and turn a satellite worth millions of dollars into worthless space junk. In contrast, he argued that solar cells could power a satellite for years. Through a relentless crusade, Dr. Ziegler got the Navy to eventually compromise and put a dual-power system of chemical batteries and solar cells on Vanguard. As predicted, the chemical batteries failed after a week and the solar cells kept Vanguard operating for years.

Despite solar cells' success in powering satellites in the 1950s and early 1960s, many at NASA doubted the technology's ability to power its more ambitious space ventures. The agency perceived solar cells as no more than a stopgap solution until nuclear-power systems became available. In fact, nuclear power is to this day the only viable solution for missions far from the Sun due to the very low density of sunlight. (Radioisotope thermoelectric generators (RTGs) have powered all missions to the outer planets: Jupiter, Saturn, Neptune, and Uranus. The rapid decay of Plutonium-238 generates heat that the RTG converts directly into electricity by thermocouples without any moving parts.) In the 1980s, NASA's Jet Propulsion Laboratory in collaboration with the Department of Energy had a relatively vigorous research effort, SP-100, to develop a viable nuclear power system for missions where solar power is not viable. The more austere times of the mid-1990s resulted in aborting the effort despite good technical progress.

NASA launched the Orbiting Astronomical Observatory into space powered by a one-kilowatt photoelectric array in 1966. Space applications placed the emphasis on weight, volume, and durability. Thus, efficiency was a very important factor. Back on Earth, the most important factor is the cost of producing a kilowatt-hour. In the early 1970s, Dr. Elliott Berman, with financial support from Exxon Corporation, designed cheaper photoelectric systems using lower quality silicon and cheaper materials. His efforts reduced the cost of a 1-watt photoelectric array from hundreds of dollars to twenty dollars.

It was not until 1975 that the U.S. Government began a terrestrial photoelectric research and development project, which NASA assigned to its Jet Propulsion Laboratory. The Department of Energy formed the Solar Energy Research Institute (SERI) in 1977. NASA's Lewis Research Center (LeRC) became very active in building multi-kilowatt demonstration projects in 1979. JPL, LeRC, and SERI directed their efforts towards achieving cost effective large-scale photoelectric electrical production. Important applications were still limited to remote facilities where commercial power lines were far away or non-existent. Examples included offshore oilrigs, remote wells, buoys, railroad signals, microwave relay stations, and roadside call boxes. By 1983, the global photoelectric electrical production capability exceeded 21.3 megawatts.

The Department of Energy continues to fund research and development of photoelectric systems as a means of one day significantly augmenting or replacing fossil-fueled electric generating facilities. In 1991 SERI was renamed the National Renewable Energy Laboratory and in 1996 the Department of Energy established the National Center for Photoelectrics. Today, a plethora of products and applications employing solar cells as their source of electricity is available in the marketplace. However, there is still a long way to go before photoelectric systems provide a cost effective alternative to fossil-fueled electric generating facilities.

Again, there are some points of note regarding the development of solar cells. The observation of the phenomenon, the photoelectric effect, occurred long before Einstein developed the theory to explain it. A nearly century long arduous development effort transpired to go from the first operating photocell in the laboratory to commercially viable photoelectric systems. Laboratory research was essential to improving the solar cell — efficiency and cost. It has taken massive Government funding to push the development forward.

The intent of tracing the history of the development of the transistor, the laser, and the solar cell was to give some insight into the technology development cycle. In these three cases, the cycle began with experimentalists and theoreticians discovering something about nature. In the case of the transistor, it was the discovery of semi-conductive materials. For the laser, it was the study of molecular spectroscopy, which led to the maser, which eventually led to the laser. Finally, for the solar cell it was the discovery of photoelectric materials. In all cases, it took the theoreticians to explain the physics behind the observations. This portion of the technology development cycle is called the discovery phase of the cycle.

The second phase is one of building a device that makes use of the discovery of Phase One. In the case of the transistor, it was the building of both Brattain/Bardeen's transistor and Shockley's transistor. Shockley's transistor turned out to be the basis for commercialization. For the laser, it required the building of the lasers of Maiman, Gould, Hall, and Javan. The lasers of Gould, Hall, and Javan provide the basis of commercial applications. In the case of solar cells, it was the selenium cell of Charles Fritz. However, it was the cells developed by Pearson, Chapin, and Fuller, which provide the basis of today's photovoltaic systems. The second phase of the development cycle is called the device phase.

The third phase comprises building a prototype of a potentially useful assembly, subsystem, or product. A device rarely has any use without being a part of something larger. This is certainly true of the three examples discussed in this chapter: the transistor, laser, and solar cell. The transistor needed to be a part of an electronic circuit, and the first prototype was an amplifier. Bell Labs researchers demonstrated an amplifier circuit to prove that they had successfully achieved a transistor. The need to be part of something larger was amply evident in the case of the laser, where integrating everything together into a useful application proved elusive. A single solar cell produces a small amount of current at a very low voltage. It is only when they are arrayed and integrated with some control circuitry that they become useful. The third phase of technology development is called the prototype phase

The fourth and final phase of the cycle results in products that a manufacturer generally produces and sells in some quantity. It is true that some applications require the production of only a few units, and that these units can resemble a prototype as to their production, tweaking, and performance. Otherwise, in today's world, there has to be uniformity in the performance and functionality of the product, the product has to be acceptable, and production costs have to be reasonable so that it can be affordable in the marketplace. In some sense, this is the most challenging phase. In the case of the transistor, the first successful commercial applications were the hearing aid and the portable transistor radio. It was a long path from Bell Labs to these products. Regarding the laser, it took industrial giants the likes of IBM, Sony, and Phillips to bring to market the first highly successful laser applications. Hoffman electronics took the silicon solar cell of Bell Labs, improved its efficiency, and provided solar arrays for satellites. Terrestrial applications have been somewhat elusive due to the continued relatively high cost of solar arrays. Thus, research and development in all phases of the technology development cycle continues with the purpose of achieving photoelectric systems that are competitive with fossil-fueled electrical production and distribution. The fourth phase is called the product development phase or simply the product phase.

Thus, the technology development cycle is divided into four phases — discovery, device, prototype, and product. Recognizing that the technology development cycle comprises a number of distinct phases is not a new idea. NASA has divided the technology development cycle into nine technology readiness levels (TRL). TRL 1 is the lowest level of maturation and is the level where researchers observe and report basic principles. Level 2 involves the identification or formulation of practical applications. The application remains speculative. At TRL 3, researchers validate the critical function or characteristic by analytical and experimental means. A technology has achieved TRL 4 when researchers have validated a component or breadboard in the laboratory. At TRL 5, validation of the component or breadboard has occurred in a relevant environment. For TRL 6, component validation requires its incorporation into a subsystem or system prototype and its demonstration in a relevant environment. Demonstration of the system in a space environment is required to achieve TRL 7. A system is at TRL 8 when testing demonstrates that the system is "flight qualified." After a system has successfully completed an actual mission, it achieves a TRL 9 classification. Clearly, this division of the technology development cycle fits the needs of NASA's space mission. NASA's technology readiness scale has been highly successful in identifying the state of technology development. Subsequently, the Department of Defense (DOD) has tailored the TRL definitions to meet its needs and adopted them.

DOD divides its research, development, test, and evaluation budget into seven categories with each given a number. They are:

6.1 — Basic Research,

6.2 — Applied Research,

6.3 — Advanced Technology Development,

6.4 — Demonstration and Validation,

6.5 — Engineering and Manufacturing Development,

6.6 — Management Support, and

6.7 — Operational Systems Development.

Phase One, "Discovery," as defined in this book roughly corresponds to DOD's 6.1 — Basic Research. Phase Two, "Device," roughly corresponds to DOD's 6.2 and early 6.3 — Applied Research and Advanced Technology Development. Phase Three, "Prototype," similarly corresponds to DOD's late 6.3 and in some cases early 6.4 — Demonstration and Validation. Phase Four, "Product," corresponds in some degree to the remaining DOD categories of 6.5, 6.6, and 6.7.

Both the NASA and the DOD division of the technology development cycle divide Phase Four, "product," into several additional phases. This is necessary to some extent for the management of a technology/system development program since this last phase, which has simply been labeled the "product" phase, requires significant sums of money for its accomplishment. A number of other organizations divide the technology development cycle into three phases or categories: basic research, applied research, and product development. Various organizations that track funding levels employ this division as a means to achieve consistency in their data and/or as a matter of convenience.

A friend and colleague, Dr. William Spuck, has divided the technology development cycle into five distinct phases. He has developed a sound argument for using five phases to define the development cycle but has not published his work. The important point to observe is that the number of phases into which one divides the technology development cycle depends on one's needs. The observations and arguments made in this book appear to require more than three phases but do not need anywhere near the seven phases of DOD or the nine technology readiness levels of NASA. Four phases appear to be the minimum number required to support adequately the arguments contained herein. Additionally, its intrinsic simplicity makes differentiating among the phases relatively easy. The first two phases comprise what is often referred to as research and the last two phases comprise development. Together, research and development (R&D) refers to the technology development cycle.

Providing some structure to the technology development cycle is crucial to the discussions and arguments presented in this book. This structure provides a basis for understanding how technology becomes part of everyday products, how technology development is funded and who and what organizations actually do the research and development.

In closing, we note that each phase is iterative (may be repeated) and that subcycles are prevalent in the bringing of products and services to market.

FIGURE 1.1 THE FOUR STEPS OF TECHNOLOGY DEVELOPMENT

Observations or Questions

Phase One – Discovery
Ferdinand Braun discovers
rectifying action of crystals
(1874)

Discovery

Phase Two – Device
Bell Labs demonstrates first
transistor and first manufactured
transistor is made
(1947)

Device

Reprinted with permission of Alcatel-Lucent USA

Phase Three – Prototype
Texas Instruments develops
prototype of transistor radio
(1952)

Prototype

Smithsonian Institution SI Neg #NMAH2000-07520

Phase Four – Product
International Development
Engineering Associates –
Regency Division develops &
produces first transistor radio
(1954)

Products

Photo courtesy of Texas Instruments

Chapter 2. The Winnowing of Technologies through the Development Cycle

"Failure is the tuition you pay for success." — Walter Brunell

Few technologies ever make it into products. Nearly forty years ago and during the course of doing some advanced planning, Bernie Haber, who was a consultant to our company and a retired vice-president for engineering and research at North American Aviation, observed that less than a third of the technologies coming out of one phase ever make it through the next phase. This would say that approximately three in a hundred ideas in the discovery phase result in a technology that becomes part of a product. The precise numbers are subject to debate but the concept is not. It is a profound and extremely important concept regarding the technology development cycle.

A funnel in which scientific observations or questions enter at the top and products come out the bottom can represent the technology development cycle, as depicted in Figure 2-1. In the course of this chapter, we will investigate the nature of the winnowing process and explore the realm of making the process more efficient. This chapter begins with some examples of technologies that did not really make it.

One area involving numerous technology development efforts has been the quest for solid-state memories to replace the "hard disk" in computers. Before proceeding, let us consider for a moment some computer basics. Computers work with strings of 1s and 0s called binary strings. The computer performs all its operations including arithmetic on these binary strings. These strings can represent ordinary numbers, characters of the alphabet, punctuation, pixels of an image, instructions to the computer, et cetera. Collections of binary strings represent information and programs. Thus, to store information or programs it is only necessary to store binary strings of 1s and 0s. Hence, in theory, anything that has two states can be used to store binary strings and thus be used as a memory. One state can represent the 1 and the other state can represent the 0, or vice versa.

FIGURE 2.1 TECHNOLOGY DEVELOPMENT FUNNEL

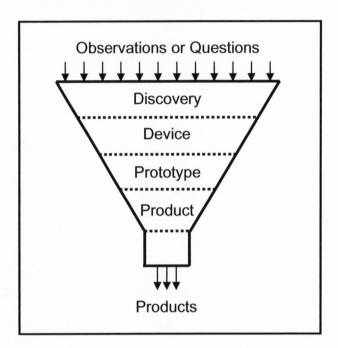

A punched card is a row of columns of locations. If the location is not removed, it represents a 0, and if it is punched out (removed), it represents a 1. It is an early means of representing a string of 1s and 0s where the two states are punched and not punched. Similarly, circles on a piece of paper or card represent a 0 or 1 depending on whether they are left blank or filled. Here the two states are blank and filled. Since magnets have polarity, the North Pole can represent a 0 and the South Pole a 1 or vice versa. The two states are north polarity and south polarity. Thus, if one has a flat sheet coated with fine magnetic particles, one could identify specific locations for storing a 1 or a 0, and, using an electromagnet, align the polarity of most of the magnetic particles at that location in one direction to represent a 1, and in its opposite direction to represent a 0. The two states are the opposite directions of the alignment of the magnetic particles. (This is the basic concept underlying magnet tapes and computer hard drives.) Similarly, the presence or absence of an electric charge can represent the binary 1s and 0s. Clearly, there are many ways to create memories. Good memories are those that can store an enormous quantity of binary strings in a very small space, those for which the binary strings can be stored or retrieved easily and quickly, those that can be reused numerous times, those that are inexpensive, and those that do not use much power. The following discussion highlights the quest for such memories.

Current hard disks used in home computers and notebooks have a number of drawbacks. They depend on a rapidly rotating platter and mechanically positioned read/write heads that are inherently prone to failure — ultimately they wear out. The hard disks are also relatively large and consume considerable power. This has quite naturally led to a quest for a solid-state memory that could be "written and read" millions of times without degradation, store a terabyte of data in a cubic centimeter, and consume almost no power.

This discussion of the quest for solid-state memories begins with so-called bubble memories. Bubble memories made it to market in products for a very short time but they never did achieve the dream held by the visionaries of the time. Bubble memories are attributed to being the brainchild of a single person, Andrew Bobeck. Now, Bobeck worked on two magnetic related projects in the 1960s. One was the development of magnetic core memories driven by a transistor-based controller. These memories were a forerunner of the semiconductor memories used today. The other was the development of the Twistor memory based on magnetostriction, which is an effect that can move magnetic fields. A simple example is placing a pattern on a magnetic tape and passing a current through the tape. The patterns will move down the tape without changing. By placing a detector at some point over the tape, the patterns will pass under the detector without any physical motion. AT&T pursued Twistor technology for a number of applications in the 1960s.

As fate would have it, Bobeck joined AT&T's Bell Laboratories in 1967 and started work on improving Twistor. (Twistor used a wire, which is a linear or one-dimensional device, and thereby afforded limited storage capacity and throughput.) Bobeck reasoned that if he could find a material with a preference for the direction in which the magnetic fields would move, then they would naturally form "tracks" and a two-dimensional memory would be possible. This would allow the introduction of magnetic patterns at one edge of the material, "movement" along the track to store the pattern in the material and later recovery at the other edge to effect readout of the stored pattern. While studying different materials and their properties he noticed an interesting effect: applying an external field to a magnetized patch of the material would cause the magnetized area to contract into a tiny circle, which he called a bubble. These bubbles were much smaller than the domains on magnetic tape. This suggested that data storage densities could be much higher than for normal magnetic storage media.

After studying numerous materials, Bobeck finally discovered that garnet had the desired properties. Bubbles would easily form in the material and they could be pushed along it relatively easily. The next problem was to make them move in only one direction along tracks. The solution was to imprint tiny magnetic bars along the surface of the garnet. By applying magnetic fields of one polarization and then another the bubbles could be passed from one bar to the next in a track. Placing tiny electromagnets at one side to form the magnetic patterns that become bubbles and detectors on the opposite side to read out the patterns forms a memory.

Bubbles were non-volatile. That is, the bubbles remained after removing the power just the same as the magnetic patterns remain on the surface of a disk drive or magnetic tape. Better yet bubble memory required no moving parts. In addition, a very enticing property is that in theory the data storage in bubble memories could be much denser than for disk drives. The one negative was that the memory was inherently slow because a track in a bubble memory was no different in performance from a magnetic tape. That is, accessing a particular portion of the data in a track required reading and rewriting back into the memory all the data preceding it. This proved to be its Achilles heel.

It was not long after discovering garnet had the essential properties for a bubble memory that Bobeck and his team successfully built a one-centimeter memory that stored 4096 bits. This was the same density as that of the then standard core memories. This sparked considerable enthusiasm in the industry. Bubble memories appeared to be the new technology to replace not only core memories but also tapes and disks as well. It appeared that bubble memories would be the only form of memory used except for those cases requiring high speed.

Every major electronics company including IBM, Intel, and Texas Instruments had teams working on bubble memories and their applications by the mid-1970s. By the end of the decade several products incorporating bubble memories made it to market and Intel released it own 1-Megabit version of a bubble memory. Within a few years, the "bubble" on bubble memories burst and all work ceased. Improvements in silicon memories and hard disk memories left no room in the marketplace for bubble memories, as they were not able to maintain any real advantages over the competition. This is an example, of a technology getting essentially to the end of the funnel only to fail as a viable product in the marketplace.

There seems to be no shortage of ideas for computer memories. None has gotten so far as bubble memory technology before failing. The Jet Propulsion Laboratory (JPL) worked on a solid-state memory concept for approximately five years in the 1990s under Government funding before the customers decided to cease pursuit of the memory and back other more promising concepts. The concept used bubble technology for inserting and retrieving data in a primary loop. Domain walls between the magnetic domains, which constitute the minor loops, serve as the storage medium. The presence or absence of micro-magnetic structures in bit cells defines bits. The researchers called it Vertical Bloch Line memory (VBL). If successful, terabits (a thousand gigabits or a million megabits) of data could be stored in a cubic centimeter and performance would rival that of disk drives. Thus, VBL memories would overcome the deficiencies of speed and storage densities inherent in a pure bubble memory. JPL was not alone in pursuit of this once promising technology. Others also conducted research and development in the United States, Japan, and France including Hitachi, NEC, and Sony.

Returning to JPL's development of VBL memories, Floyd Humphrey of Boston University performed the theoretical work. JPL performed the design work and the testing and evaluation of specific chips. Honeywell made the test wafers. The team had demonstrated that chips could be manufactured which appeared to have the essential memory properties. That is, researchers had successfully read and retrieved magnetic patterns at some locations. Just as a functioning memory seemed to be within grasp, customer funding for the project ceased. The lure of better and easier to achieve technologies without the problems that confronted existing concepts lured the customers away — the same sort of attraction that brought the initial funding to JPL for the VBL memory concept in the first place. Optimism always reigns supreme at the beginning of the effort to capitalize on a new phenomenon and make a useful device. Technical challenges and their associated complications in the design eliminate at some point most of the technology innovations from successfully completing the technology development cycle. Funding and timing are also critical factors on whether or not a technology ever comes to fruition — that is, emerges from the funnel as a successful commercial product.

In the case of JPL's Vertical Bloch Line memory development, the funding levels were inadequate to achieve the demonstration of a working memory chip within the approximately "five year window of opportunity" before the sponsors' attention moved on to "newer and better opportunities". Therefore, in a certain sense, one might observe that the "race horse" — the Vertical Bloch Line memory technology — feeding or funding was sufficient for it to show promise as a future winner but insufficient for it to ever become a good competitor. Actually, it was destined to be a loser from the beginning due to its level of feeding (or funding).

Today, researchers and funding organizations are pursuing a variety of new technologies for the next generation of memories. Of course, there are those researchers that are trying to break through the limitations in existing systems. Current approaches to existing systems include reducing the fundamental dimension of the components and moving to "stacked packaging" to achieve three-dimensional arrays. Immediate goals are to increase memory capacities by a factor of 25.

One of the "new technologies" that is being touted as the wave of the future is using holography as a memory system. Optical holography utilizes lasers to store data in three dimensions in a crystal. This differs from current optical disks such as DVDs and CDs in that the writing of light patterns is into the medium (crystal) rather than just on the surface. In theory, a five-inch diameter disk could hold roughly 200 DVDs worth of data. In addition, megabits of data could be stored and retrieved simultaneously rather than one bit at a time, as is the case with current magnetic storage systems. Researchers are pursuing several different approaches to achieve holographic storage including angle-multiplexed, wavelength-multiplexed, spectral, and phase-conjugate holography. The important thing for us to recognize is that even within a single concept, the research may span a multitude of technologies. It is worth noting that Joe Goodman explained the theory of holographic storage in his 1960s book, *Introduction to Fourier Optics*.

Another promising new technology is the solid-state molecular memory, which uses crossbar architecture. In this case, two layers of patterned electrodes blanket the memory layer. A chemical change of state, some physical change, or a charge migration within the material itself can serve as the basis for a memory. These memories offer the hope of much greater memory densities, much longer life, and lower costs than for current flash memory cards or hard disks.

The Air Force has made significant investments in chalcogenide memory technology. Chalcogenide memory gets its name from the materials employed, alloys that contain at least one of the elements of the Group VI elements of the periodic table. Data is stored as a change in a nanoscale portion of the material from crystalline (conductive) to amorphous (resistive) phases. As with so many, this technology promises extremely large non-volatile storage densities (bits per cubic centimeter) and to be extremely fast. It offers an additional benefit to space applications in that it is intrinsically radiation hard (i.e., survive the radiation environment of space). It just might displace the hard drives in today's computers.

Today, some researchers are working on ferroelectric memories, where information is stored as the direction of the electric field inside certain atoms. Others are working on magneto resistive type memories where data is stored as the direction of the alignment (polarity) of the magnetic field and sensing a resistance change provides knowledge of the polarity change. Still others are working on programmable metallization cells, which use controlled electrochemical buildup of ions inside a solid electrolyte to store data.

In an article in CNET News.com it was pointed out that the "demand for memory is huge and growing at exponential rates — beyond the capabilities of even the best-engineered conventional memory systems." Also noted was that "in 1981, Bill Gates thought that 64KB would be 'enough memory for anyone' on the desktop." Today, PDAs, MP3 players, and memory sticks with 16 GB of memory are commonplace. 64GB flash memory drives are available to replace disk drives in applications where weight and power consumption are primary concerns. Two terabyte (2000 gigabyte) memory sticks are likely to be on the market by the publishing date of this book.

The article went on to say, "We cannot say which of these new memory technologies will emerge as practical solutions, but we are confident that not all will." Additionally, "There is a major difference between success in the lab and simulations and success in the marketplace." Of the several tens of memory technologies currently under development, only a few will survive to be viable in the marketplace.

Electron Tunneling is the phenomenon that occurs in semiconductors when a "tunneling" tip and an electrode are within approximately 10 angstroms (10-billionths of a meter) of each other and a bias voltage is applied to the electrode. Electrons "tunnel" between the tip and the electrode under these conditions. A one-angstrom change in the distance between the tunneling tip and the electrode causes an order of magnitude change in the electric current when typical bias voltages are applied. Gerd Binnig and Heinrich Rohrer at the IBM research laboratories in Switzerland discovered this phenomenon. They won the 1986 Nobel Prize in physics for their work in scanning tunneling microscopy.

JPL has long sought more accurate and smaller sensors in its mission to explore the universe. Realizing that many sensors depend on measuring the change in the spatial distance between two masses or the motion of a plate or diaphragm, researchers at JPL began pursuing sensors employing electron tunneling in the late 1980s. They have been extremely successful in making a wide variety of sensors, which were a fraction of the size of their standard counterparts, were far more sensitive, and enjoyed a much lower internal noise figure. Some of their accomplishments included an accelerometer on a chip; a hydrophone that was the size of a quarter and was as good as what the Navy used that were bigger than a basketball; and a seismometer with electronics the size of a pack of cigarettes. JPL has custom built "ones and twos" of several of these type of sensors for its space missions. However, there has been no rush to take these devices to the commercial market. This is not to say that one of the electron tunneling based sensors may not be a commercial success in the future but it currently appears that most will never get beyond the Laboratory and the specialized applications, which provided the rationale for their pursuit.

Many might say that the dawn of the information age has made things different from the industrial age. The information technologies comprise either hardware or software or some blend of the two. In the case of memory technologies, which are examples of hardware portion of information technologies, there is a very strong winnowing process in effect.

So let us consider software. Software technologies are the underlying tools, processes, algorithms (procedures to achieve a goal), and techniques that permit the creation of applications. Examples of software technologies include compiler technology, search algorithms, data coding algorithms, data storage and retrieval algorithms, optimization algorithms, and graphics rendering technologies. Many of the information technologies rely heavily on mathematics. Again, no one algorithm or technology is right for every application. Furthermore, researchers are making new discoveries in mathematics and developing new algorithms continuously. Yet, there is no great proliferation of brand new "got to have" applications coming to market. Certainly, improving existing applications makes use of some new algorithm developments. Hence, most of the software technology innovations never really make it into the marketplace.

Computers are built with a very limited set of instructions (e.g., add or multiply) and syntax to form what is called a machine language. Writing programs or software (e.g., word processor programs or Internet browser programs) in machine language is very tedious, abstract, slow, and prone to errors. It is also difficult to get all the "bugs" out. Consequently, practically from the beginning of computers, software developers have written programs to translate one software language to another. The goal has been to provide languages that facilitate writing applications and reduces programming errors.

From the very beginning, a hierarchy of languages has evolved. Generally, a higher-level language's vocabulary–instructions or operators — are like macros in that they imply a sequence of operations in the lower level language. Assembly language is a step up from machine language. Its vocabulary or instruction set includes various logic operators, string operators, and mathematical operators that are common to all applications. The translator, called an assembler, translates the assembly program into machine language.

A compiler is a "translator" of a language for writing applications into assembly language or machine language. Compiler technology provides another good example of the winnowing effect in technology development. In the late 1960s, IBM invented the PL-1 programming language. At the time, FORTRAN was the primary language used to write scientific and engineering applications and COBOL was the principal language used for management applications. IBM's goal was to replace them with PL-1. It was highly touted and IBM even wrote some of its applications in it. A basic subset of the PL-1 language was used to write the full PL-1 compiler. But the bottom line is that PL-1 never made it in the marketplace.

In the 1980s, the Department of Defense (DOD) spent millions of dollars developing a programming language called Ada that would meet the Department's needs for decades to come. DOD even required its application developers to use Ada. DOD aficionados had dreams of Ada becoming the programming language of choice in the commercial software industry as well. It was a total bust, and the Department of Defense abandoned the effort in the 1990s when it realized that the commercial software industry ruled the marketplace and not DOD, as had been the case in the infancy of the information age. These are just two of the bigger examples of programs that had the goal of introducing a new compiler technology into the marketplace.

The story is quite the same for operating systems — the basic software that manages all the activities and functions that the computer and its peripherals are performing. (Microsoft's Windows is an operating system.) IBM made two unsuccessful attempts at the personal computer with unique operating systems before succeeding with the PC and Microsoft's Disk Operating System (DOS). Microsoft did not succeed with Windows until its third attempt. Prior to that, there was literally a plethora of "Windows-like" add-ons developed in an attempt to be the one to achieve market dominance. IBM even had its Windows competitor. In fact, there were a number of different approaches to the user interface prior to the success of the Apple Macintosh. At one time, the experts in ergonomics were espousing the limitation of menu lists and the number of options available to the user at any one time to no more than six. Professional and scientific journals published papers on the subject. The marketplace certainly proved these notions wrong.

In some areas of software technology, it appears that the marketplace will only sustain one or two products. This has been particularly true for the applications themselves. In the early days of the PC, there were more than half a dozen word processor programs, graphics/presentation programs, spreadsheet programs, and database management programs. Who remembers when Lotus 1-2-3 was the preferred spreadsheet? Alternatively, who remembers VisiCalc, the original electronic spreadsheet software for the PC that Dan Bricklin invented? Even though many are willing to try, most are certain to fail at some point in their development cycle. The winnowing process is just as much present in the software development process as it is in hardware.

There should be no doubt that a tremendous winnowing process dominates the technology development cycle. There are those who believe that the technology development process could be much more efficient. To them, it is just a case of improving management oversight and using the proper decision tools. This is a far too simplistic perspective of the technology development process.

Chapter 1 demonstrated how the technology development process could be broken into several distinct phases. It also pointed out the innovative nature and the search and discovery aspects of completing each phase of the development cycle. It provided examples where many materials have been tested and tried in the quest for the right one. What if the right material was never found? Forecasting such a negative result is essentially impossible. How does one know when to stop? Will the next trial be the successful one? Recall that Edison went through many trials and failures before discovering that a carbon wire with the right properties including length and diameter would provide adequate lighting and last long enough to be practical. What would have happened if he had been dependent on government funding or belonged to a corporate research and development organization and a manager seeing the inefficiency of his effort terminated it before he had come up with the practical incandescent light bulb? If Edison had been denied success, then when would the incandescent light bulb have been invented? Alternatively, maybe it would have been lost in Edison's laboratory manual as an interesting but impractical phenomenon, like so many other technologies.

Major research laboratories pursued solid-state lasers for years. Most likely, none of the early researchers ever dreamed of the BIG commercial application — CDs and DVDs. Certainly, CD/DVD applications were not the basis of justifications for research and development efforts involving the development, the characterization, and the control of the solid-state crystalline laser. In fact, the organizations that developed the solid-state laser were not the great beneficiaries of their research. The beneficiaries were the likes of Sony, Panasonic, and Phillips. What if the managers responsible for solid-state laser research and development efforts prematurely ended them for the sake of efficiency? In his book on managing disruptive technologies, Clayton M. Christensen points out that frequently, the company that develops a new technology fails to be the one that capitalizes on it. In fact, Christensen identified numerous situations where a company's own invention put them out of business.

Should there be only one or two approaches to computer memory technology pursued today? Which should they be? What would researchers and research organizations do that had an approach that differed from the anointed one or two? What would have been the memory situation if JPL had been funded another year or two at an adequate funding level to continue research on Vertical Bloch Line memories? The result might have been the replacement of the hard disk drive in laptops with a cubic centimeter chip having the storage capacity of greater than 40 gigabytes by now. The bottom line of this brief discussion on the management of the research and development process is that it requires different management tools and techniques than the rest of business. Specifically, progress within each of the first three phases of the technology development cycle is not linear, is not subject to forecasts of success, and is not predictable. The only certainty is that results will surprise the researcher, progress will be slower than expected, and unforeseen challenges will arise.

Experience has shown how short term research grants of one to three years duration stifles research by inhibiting risk taking through the encouragement of proposals with easily achievable milestones and objectives. The tendency to terminate research efforts that fall behind schedule, overrun budgets, and/or fail to achieve objectives and goals further inhibits risk taking. In this environment, the researcher's objectives become winning the next grant and keeping it, rather than achieving revolutionary results. This certainly is not an effective way to develop truly paradigm-changing technologies.

Pursuing this line of reasoning a bit farther, the truly revolutionary technology developments lead to the creation of whole industries around them. Past examples include the light bulb, the telephone, the transistor, and the cell phone. From a national perspective, Americans should want to be the developers of the revolutionary technologies. However, only one out of what has to be many hundreds of technologies, which make it through the development cycle, is truly revolutionary in this sense. In other words, the most desirable technology development successes are extremely rare events. Treating the success/failure of a technology to pass through the development process as a random event, then the probability of any one technology entering the development process being a revolutionary technology is much less than one in ten thousand. Opposite this is that the payoff can be beyond imagination (i.e., trillions of dollars added to the gross domestic product over decades, many thousands of new jobs, improved standard of living for all). There is no means of knowing the outcome beforehand and the expected return on investment makes no sense for these cases.

The expected return on investment in these cases involves multiplying a very small number, the probability (e.g., smaller than 0.0001), by a very large number, the payoff (e.g., greater than 1,000,000,000,000), to get a very large number, the expected return (e.g., 100,000,000), which is then divided by a very large number, the R&D costs (e.g., within an order of magnitude of 10,000,000). The uncertainties in the values of the numbers used in these calculations are generally more than a factor of ten. One can obtain almost any desired result by making slight changes in the assumed values. Worse yet, the revolutionary technologies are not the ones for which the integration into existing products is evident. Maximizing the efficiency of the development cycle may well eliminate the revolutionary technologies from ever being developed.

The foregoing presents one of the foremost management dilemmas. Would the technology underlying Google be developed under effective management? After all, the Google search engine is said to be the result of the research of two computer graduate students, Larry Page and Sergey Brin, in their quest for doctorates.

This is not to say that there is not a role for good management. Here are some personal observations regarding effective management of technology development. One can identify at the outset of a research effort rules and conditions for stopping the effort. Technical reviews can determine when these rules or conditions apply. A skilled research manager can also identify when the research team is hopelessly lost in the jungle of unsolved problems with no clear approaches for solution. This gives a hint of how one can effectively manage technology development efforts. After all, a complete treatment of technology development management encompasses more than enough scope for an entire book.

Lastly, one might argue that if management techniques will not effectively turn the technology development funnel into a straight pipe then betting on researchers with a proven record of accomplishment is the appropriate way to achieve a more efficient technology development process. This certainly has proven to be an effective method for increasing the return on investment for those venture capitalists that invest in companies that are dependent on a successful technology development effort to bring a product to the marketplace. However, one might legitimately ask, "When do researchers make their biggest impacts?" Moreover, "When does a researcher have a proven track record?"

Let us consider just one case, that of Albert Einstein. He failed his college entrance exam. Furthermore, when he did get into college he did so poorly that after graduation he was fortunate to obtain a patent examiner's position rather than a sought after teaching position. Einstein wrote four papers in 1905 while a patent examiner. One might argue that three of these papers provided the basis for his life's work. The Nobel Foundation awarded him the 1921 Nobel Prize for one of the 1905 papers, which became the theoretical basis for the solar cell and the laser a half century later. A 1919 eclipse of the sun verified some of the predictions in his general theory of relativity; it was only after that that he was seen to have an established record of accomplishment. Many would argue that he had already completed his greatest works by then. Einstein is not the only example whose landmark works were written before he had an established record of accomplishment. The same applies to research teams as well.

Today, one might seriously ponder whether a highly regarded U.S. university would ever admit a young Einstein. Further, would today's young Einstein find a job that would permit or promote his research? Where are the funds going to come from to support the unproven young Einsteins? If only those with a proven record of accomplishment receive research dollars in today's world of high cost research, then the time will come when there will be no one with a proven record of accomplishment to conduct research.

The first part of this chapter established that historically a strong winnowing effect exists throughout the technology development cycle. The latter part of the chapter was devoted to showing that there is no permanent means to eliminate the winnowing effect. Given more than a century of history and the material presented in this chapter, it is most unlikely that the development process will become the model of efficiency. Therefore, one will just have to accept the winnowing effect as inherently part of the technology development process.

CHAPTER 3. THE PACE OF TECHNOLOGY DEVELOPMENT

"There is no greater impediment to progress in the sciences than the desire to see it take place too quickly." — Georg C. Lichtenberg

Chapter 1 presented a review of the history of some examples of technologies that had a significant impact on America during the twentieth century. Nearly a hundred years transpired between the discovery of the underlying principle of semiconductors and the demonstration of the first transistor. It took essentially ten years from Bell Labs initiation of a concerted effort to develop the transistor until the first commercial products employing the transistor made it to the marketplace. This was after two decades of research on semiconductors in search of a solid-state amplifier.

Albert Einstein identified the principle underlying lasers in a paper in 1905. It was not until 1960 that Theodore Maiman demonstrated the first laser and it was not until 1969 that Xerox demonstrated the first product (a laser printer) using lasers. It took another ten years before IBM introduced the first commercial laser printer. The story is similar for the solar cell. Edmund Becquerel discovered the photovoltaic effect in 1839, Charles Fritts demonstrated the first solar cell in 1877, Einstein established the theoretical basis in 1905, Bell Labs' researchers demonstrated the first solar battery in 1954, and NASA launched the first satellite employing solar cells in 1958.

The examples presented in Chapter 1 suggest that the technology development cycle frequently takes decades to complete. On the other hand, the clarions of the news media point to the ever-quickening pace of technology development. The captains of the technology sector of industry tout the rapidity with which technology is moving. Moreover, everyone has experienced the obsolescence of their high-tech products — cell phones, home or office computer, software, et cetera. The temptation is to believe that the pace of technology development is no longer of decadal duration but rather one of a year or so.

There seems to be two conflicting perspectives of the technology development cycle. Is this possible? First, a little closer look at the observations related to the rapid pace of technology development is needed. R&D personnel at Pittsburgh Mineral and Environmental Technology, Inc. articulated their achievements in completing the technology development cycle from "concept through commercialization" very well in their paper, "Technology Development: From Concept through Commercialization". Interestingly, they acknowledged, "Technology development, from concept through commercialization, is all too often a troublesome process. Under the best of circumstances, technology development is difficult; under the worst of circumstances, it is inefficient or downright dysfunctional. Technology continues to languish in universities, research institutes, and corporate laboratories." However, the technology development cycle they identified and addressed starts with a concept for a product. This corresponds to starting in Phase Three of the technology development cycle. They based their new products and processes on existing materials and processes. Their accomplishments certainly were not trivial, easy, or straightforward.

However, there is a significant difference between Pittsburgh Mineral and Environmental Technology, Inc.'s technology development and that, which is the focus of this book. The technology development cycle as defined in this book starts with scientific discovery. Next, the conception and demonstration of a device occurs. The conception and prototyping of products employing the device follows. New manufacturing tools and processes are frequently developed. At this point, the two development cycles converge in the development of the product or service. Clearly, there is much more to the technology development process of concern in this book than that presented in Pittsburgh Mineral and Environmental Technology's paper. Many observers and those involved in R&D within industry are likely to entertain a technology development cycle similar to that of Pittsburgh Mineral and Environmental Technology, Inc.

A whole industry has sprung up that focuses on the study and management of the R&D process. At least a dozen journals publish articles on understanding, managing, and improving the R&D process. Certainly, "best practice" should be the goal of every organization. Furthermore, issues abound regarding R&D: funding, staffing, educational, organizational, managing, intellectual capital, et cetera. The focus though remains on Phases Three and Four: prototyping and product development. This can be expected since Phases Three and Four are the most costly. Moreover, as measures such as expected return on investment, risk, resources involved, and confidence in cost and schedules dominate the selection of R&D projects then the results will tend to lead to product improvements rather than to what Clayton M. Christensen calls disruptive technologies. Fortunately, there continue to be those individuals, who are involved in R&D and do create entirely new products and services. We will find that it takes decades to proceed through the entire four phases of the technology development cycle. Let us look at the situation more closely through the examples of our most familiar high-tech products.

Let us begin with the cell phone. A number of technologies coalesced to bring about the cell phone. The major ones were integrated circuits, fast inexpensive digital processing, spread spectrum technology, effective coding/decoding techniques for digital communications, digital coding of speech, battery, and low cost/low power displays. Thirty years ago a "cell phone" would have filled a room with equipment and consumed kilowatts of power.

The transistor enabled the integrated circuit, which Texas Instruments and Fairchild Semiconductors developed during the 1950s. Both companies produced the first commercial integrated circuit in 1961. The integrated circuit is at the heart of making the cell phone the compact low powered device everyone knows and loves. The evolution of the integrated circuit into those containing multi-millions of transistors makes for fast inexpensive digital processing. This permitted the move from the single central tower approach for mobile communications to the cellular approach of the cell phone system. It takes lots of computational capability to keep track of a user's cell phone as it is moved from one cell tower coverage (cell) to another, to code and decode the signals, to handle all the calls in a cell simultaneously, and to handle the speech digitization.

Spread spectrum technology development began during World War II. The military developed spread spectrum technology to prevent the enemy from detecting, intercepting, and jamming their radio communication links. Its value in cellular phones is that it provides privacy and allows many users in a cell to use the same portion of the radio frequency spectrum simultaneously. (Spread spectrum technology provides the basis for all the new wireless communications capabilities including wireless computer networks.) There are multiple ways of using the frequency spectrum, and not all cell phone systems use the same method.

In the early days of the space program, NASA needed to provide reliable communications with distant satellites using very little power. Thus, NASA's and the military's space programs are responsible for developing many of the digital coding techniques used by the cell phone industry. The impact on cell phones is clear, reliable communications.

Digital coding of speech together with compression algorithms permits many more simultaneous users in a cell and provides the basis for privacy. DARPA spent millions of dollars in the 1970s developing the technology of digitally encoding of speech. The first applications were the encryption of telephone conversations. For this, the participants needed to be able to recognize each other's voices. By the mid-1980s, the government was widely using encrypted digital voice systems.

Battery technology has come a long way from the disposable carbon batteries of the mid 1900s. Today's batteries last a lot longer before running out of power because of their higher energy density. In addition, they need replacement only after hundreds or even thousands of recharges. Man's venture into space provided much of the impetus for creating today's battery technology. Without this more powerful battery technology, the cell phone would be of limited use and a caller would likely be carrying around a "pocket full of batteries" in addition to a heavier and more bulky cell phone.

Finally, users are highly dependent on the display of their cell phone. It provides a plethora of services beyond those for basic cell phone use including text messaging, photos, and video. Liquid crystal displays (LCD) provide this capability at low cost and low power consumption. Friedrich Reinitzer discovered liquid crystals in 1888 and researchers developed the LCD during most of the 1960s with the first use being in a calculator in 1970.

What can one conclude about the rapid obsolescence of cell phones? The foregoing discussion suggests that the technologies supporting the latest digital capabilities have been around for a while. It would appear that the cell phone did not need to pass through the analog technology and one or more coding techniques to get to today's cell phone. One thing that appears clear is that the cell phone industry is very capable of doing the final phases of technology development — namely, bringing to market commercial products incorporating proven technology. It is also appropriate to conclude that establishing the technology base for the cell phone has been a multidecadal affair. It is also possible to credit industry with the ability to rapidly refine or incrementally improve the cell phone.

Another high-tech product that has permeated the work place and many homes, the personal computer, provides another example of what appears to be a counter example to the thesis that the technology development cycle is decadal in length. Industry produces ever-faster machines that follow Moore's Law. Precisely, Moore's Law says that the number of transistors in the central processor chip of the personal computer doubles about every 24-months. In 1965 and just 4 years after the building of the first integrated circuit, Gordon Moore observed that the density of transistors in an integrated circuit doubled approximately every 12 months. Caltech professor, Carver Mead, coined the term "Moore's Law" around 1970. As the pace slowed slightly, Moore gradually changed it to reflect more accurately reality until in 1975 he gave the doubling time its current incarnation of 24-months. By 2000, manufacturers packed in excess of 40,000,000 transistors into the central processor chip. As previously noted, industry believes that it can see the way to continuing on the path of Moore's Law for at least the next decade. This again gives rise to the perception that the pace of technology is quickening.

Considering just the central processor in the personal computer, one finds that in reality little has changed. Silicon is still its basis. The basic manufacturing process for integrated circuits has changed little in the past three decades. The machines have gotten better, the quality and quantity have improved, and in some cases, the improvement has been spectacular. The process of manufacturing an integrated circuit of a central processor starts with making a silicon wafer — a thin slice of a single silicon crystal. After repeatedly applying a layer of one of several possible materials on the wafer and then etching away unwanted portions, using a photographic technique, a finished wafer containing many chips emerges. A diamond saw cuts the wafer into individual chips and a specialized machine attaches wire leads finer than a human hair. After packaging, the familiar integrated circuits or computer chips emerge.

One must not lose sight of the tremendous improvements that industry has achieved in the underlying technology. Most certainly, the machinery that is used becomes obsolete almost as fast as the products that they produce. Nevertheless, the basics have not changed. Some have predicted the end of the silicon "era" for some time. Yet, improvements in the manufacturing systems have continually forestalled that eventuality. On the horizon lies the promise of single electron computing. Beyond that, the photon will replace the function of the electron altogether in what will be optical computing. In addition, there are those that are investigating using quantum theory as a basis for a radically different kind of computer. As revolutionary as these concepts are, the technology base for them has already been developing for decades.

The story does not change for the rest of the hardware comprising a personal computer. The CRT was the standard desktop display until very recently and it was an application of the CRT used in televisions. Again, the development of the CRT has been a decadal process. The LCD has always been the standard for notebook PCs and since 2000 has come on strong to replace the CRT on the desktop. The previous discussion of the cell phone already pointed out the decadal nature of the development of the LCD. Plasma displays may come into vogue for computer displays as they have in TVs. Again this is a technology that has been decades in the development cycle.

One might be tempted to claim that the printer is the one part of the PC where technology has exploded in the last decade. Laser, inkjet, dye sublimation, thermal, and impact printers are in use today. Most people are familiar with the laser and ink-jet printers. Major manufacturers come out with new models about every six months. Again, the appearance is deceiving. One manufacturer, HP, has used four teams to develop a line of printers.

HP staggered the start of the four team's development cycles by six months to allow for a 24-month long development cycle while producing a new model every 6-months. Again, this is the final phase in the technology life cycle. HP separated the individual technology development efforts from the product development cycle. Technology developments followed their own developmental paths. The product development teams integrated new technologies into the products, when the technologies became available. If there were problems in incorporating a given technology into one team's product then the team slipped it to the next team so that the product development teams could maintain their delivery schedules. Hence, HP has achieved a nearly continuous stream of "new" printers with new or improved capabilities entering the marketplace. All this belies the fact that the life cycle for the technology base is one of decades in length. This demonstrates the efficiency at which industry can introduce innovation into the marketplace.

Similar considerations would lead to the same conclusion regarding the decadal nature of the data storage technology. This is true for solid-state memories, magnetic based hard disks or the optical based disk systems of the CD and the DVD. Solid-state memories are made of integrated circuits (IC's) and that story is already familiar. Clayton M. Christensen chronicled the development of the magnetic hard disks for PCs in his book, *The Innovator's Dilemma*. The laser enabled the CD and DVD once the technology base existed for ICs with millions of transistors, precision motors, and the remainder of the components for the computer hard disk. Again, Chapter 1 provided a discussion of the long development life cycle of the laser.

Before leaving the PC let us, consider the realm of software that turns the hardware into a useful tool. After all, users really do have a relationship, good or cursed, with the software. Programmers developed the basic elements of today's software backbone in the 1960s and 1970s. IBM introduced the first rudimentary word processor in 1964. Ray Tomlinson of Bolt Beranek and Newman sent the first email over the ARPANET in 1971. Xerox's Palo Alto Research Park introduced the first system with mouse, windows, and Icons user interface (graphical user interface) in 1972. This was the forerunner of the Macintosh and Windows user interface.

Gary Kildall of Digital Research developed the CP/M operating system in the 1960s and had sold over 600,000 copies prior to the advent of IBM's PC. (As an aside, IBM tried to engage Kildall to develop the operating system for the PC, but Kildall's wife rebuffed IBM's representatives. This was most fortunate for Bill Gates, whom IBM then engaged; he made the most of this fortunate twist.) Through what some would say was a little chicanery, Gates' disk operating system possessed considerable commonality with Kildall's CP/M. Actually, at IBM's insistence, Gates purchased the kernel for the PCs DOS operating system, QDOS (Quick and Dirty Operating System), from Tim Paterson for $75,000. Kildall and others claimed that Paterson had stolen it from CP/M to develop QDOS. Paterson unsuccessfully sued, claiming defamation of character.

DARPA developed the ARPANET in this same period with the first network established in 1969. This was the precursor to today's web. IBM introduced the first relational database management software in 1974 based on a 1970 paper by E.F. Codd. Richard Mattessich pioneered computer-based financial spreadsheet analysis. He worked at first on paper and later on a computerized form. In 1969, Rene Pardo and Remy Landau co-invented "LANPAR" (LANguage for Programming Arrays at Random), which was a spreadsheet type of program that ran on mainframes. In 1979, Dan Bricklin and Bob Frankson introduced the first spreadsheet program, VisiCalc, which ran on a personal computer and had the look and feel that users associate with spreadsheet programs today.

As with hardware, the development of software often takes decades. In fact, users of early software products had to be hardy souls with stout spirits. Results were never entirely predictable and systems at times turned one's work into trash or worse yet, lost it. This has given rise to such phrases as "bit bucket," "my system trashed it," and "gone to bit heaven." It also gave rise to the euphemism of "feature" for "limitation" or "undesired result." In conclusion, the development and evolution of the personal computer has built on decades of technology development and has not been linear. It took IBM three attempts at the PC before achieving a commercially successful product. Microsoft made three attempts at the Windows operating environment before the user community accepted Windows 3.1.

The television and the microwave oven permeate the lives of almost every American. The stories of their invention are both interesting and further the argument that the technology life cycle is one of decades in duration. The vacuum tube was critical to the invention of both the television and the microwave oven. It is hard to believe that the story began in 1875 when an American, G. R. Carey, invented the phototube. This is a vacuum tube with a cathode in it that, when hit with photons, makes electrons flow through the attached wire and out through the pin (typically at the base of the tube). An Englishman, Sir William Crookes, invented an early prototype of the cathode-ray tube in 1878. Users watched TV on the face of a cathode-ray tube up until very recently with the advent of liquid crystal and plasma display TVs.

It was not until 1904 when John Ambrose Fleming invented the first practical electron tube and called it the "Fleming Valve." Lee DeForest improved the Fleming

Valve by adding a third element to the tube, called a "grid." Known as the "triode," it became the mainstay of electronics until displaced by the transistor.

One last invention of note is that of the magnetron in 1921 by the American Albert Hull. A magnetron in the microwave ovens generates the microwave energy that heats the food.

RCA began the first commercial production of electron tubes in 1920. This was nearly 50 years after the demonstration of the first primitive laboratory vacuum tubes. In addition, the conception of the television itself was an equally time-consuming process. In 1884, Paul Nipkow developed a mechanical rotating-disc scanning system for transmitting pictures over wire. British and American inventors pursued this approach up through the 1920s but abandoned it in favor of the all-electronic scanning systems.

Vladimir Kosma Zworykin laid the foundation of television when he invented the iconoscope in 1923, an early television camera, and the kinescope in 1929, a tube essential for television transmission. Zworykin also filed a patent disclosure for an all-electronic color television system in 1925. Ironically, Zworykin was an employee of the Westinghouse Corporation at the time and his bosses wanted him to work on things that his bosses staunchly believed would be more useful. A thirteen-year-old farm boy in Utah, far from the research centers of the Eastern United States and Europe, conceived the basic operating principles of electronic television. Philo T. Farnsworth, educated at nearby Brigham Young University, developed the first all-electronic television in 1927 at the age of 21. He gave a public demonstration a year later. Farnsworth had trouble obtaining adequate financing for his fledgling company. His shareholders forced him to present his "television system" to RCA in 1929.

Meanwhile, David Sarnoff became General Manager of RCA in 1921. Sarnoff had the vision and RCA's financial resources to develop the television industry. After all, RCA was born at the behest of then President Theodore Roosevelt so that the United States would have its own radio industry. The Marconi Company sold its United States interests to RCA. Financing was not a problem for RCA. (Sarnoff spent the hefty sum of thirteen million dollars during the Great Depression on television research.) Sarnoff recruited Zworykin to head RCA's television research in 1929. Zworykin immediately demonstrated his all-electronic television system. Thus, RCA had little need for the Farnsworth system. Sarnoff attempted to buy Farnsworth's company but Farnsworth wanted a share of the profits. However, elements of Farnsworth's "Image Dissector" television camera were essential to making Zworykin's iconoscope practical. This led to the patent "wars" of the 1930s between Farnsworth and RCA that dragged on until 1939 when they reached a cross-licensing agreement.

Continuing the story of television technology development, consider the question; who invented color television and when? Not surprising, the notion of a color television parallels the conception and development of black and white television. The answer to the question depends on how one interprets it. A Polish inventor, Jan Szczepanik, obtained the first patent for a color television concept in 1897. His concept was infeasible. If one is literal and adheres strictly to the dictionary definition of television, the answer is the Scotsman, John Logie Baird. He demonstrated an electro-mechanical device in 1925. Using the strictest interpretation of what constitutes a color television, the answer is Guillermo Camarena of Mexico in 1934. If one insists that the invention resemble a color television set with a color image on a screen then the answer is Peter Goldmark of CBS in 1940. However, it was not until 1946 that Goldmark demonstrated his first color television system. His television set also employed an electromechanical approach with a spinning color wheel in front of the CRT and was incompatible with a standard black and white television. CBS established a limited network broadcasting color television in 1950 and went into production of color TVs in early 1951. The National Television System Committee (NTSC), representing the various companies of the television industry, began developing a color television that would be compatible with black and white television in 1950. RCA demonstrated its color television system in the summer of 1951, and that became the basis of the NTSC standard for color television. By the end of 1951, CBS ceased color television broadcasting, ceased production of its color televisions, and bought back those they had sold. Therefore, if one interprets the question to mean a color television that finally made it all the way through the development cycle into the marketplace, the answer is Sarnoff's engineers at RCA.

Let us turn now to the commercialization and broadcast portion of the story of television. Bell Labs and the United States Commerce Department demonstrated the first long distance use of television between New York and Washington, D.C. in 1927. The Federal Communications Commission issued the first television license in 1928. CBS began television development in 1937. BBC began "high-definition" television broadcasts in London in 1937. There were only approximately 200 televisions globally at this time. A number of demonstrations of television occurred in 1939 including those at the New York World's Fair and the San Francisco Golden Gate International Exposition. The Federal Communications Commission released the NTSC standard for black and white television in 1941. The Second World War brought the commercialization of television to a stop. By 1948 and greater than 20 years after the first demonstrations of television systems, only a million homes in the United States had television sets. In 1950, the Federal Communications Commission issued the first color television standard. The NTSC obtained FCC approval of its proposed standard in 1953 that superseded the 1950 standard. On January 1, 1954 the first coast-to-coast colorcast of the Tournament of Roses Parade occurred. A number of manufacturers offered color televisions for sale to the general public beginning in 1954 but the public essentially ignored them. By 1959, RCA was the sole remaining manufacturer that offered a color television for sale. It was not until 1962, again more than 20 years after the invention of color television, when the television industry produced its one-millionth-color television.

There is a great deal more to the history of television than has been presented in this brief discussion. A number of companies were responsible for significant inventions, which enhanced television greatly, and introduced them into the marketplace. However, the objective is not to present a comprehensive history. Rather, it is to demonstrate that it took more than half a century from the identification of the first principles of the technological underpinnings of television until it was a commercial product. Again, the development of television passed through all four phases of the technology development cycle — discovery, device, prototype, and product.

We pick up the story of the development of the microwave oven with the invention of the magnetron in 1921. The magnetron is a particular type of electronic tube used in radars. The term radar was coined in 1941 and is an acronym for Radio Detection and Ranging. A radar is simply an object detection system that uses "radio" waves to determine the location and velocity of objects. Development of the radar was essential to the development of the microwave oven. Contrary to the case of the television, the Second World War accelerated the development of the radar. It was important to know about attacking aircraft long before the aircraft arrived over their targets. Sounding of air raid sirens could warn of the pending attack; thereby allowing populations to take cover. Air defenses could prepare to counter the attack. Radar was important to providing this early warning. Hence, radar technology matured significantly during the War.

Percy LeBaron Spencer was a self-taught scientist/engineer and worked for the Raytheon Company performing experiments on advanced radar equipment in the mid 40s. Spencer had a "sweet tooth" and happened to be carrying a candy bar in his pocket one day and when he went to eat it, he discovered that it had melted. The only cause Spencer could imagine was that the radiation from the testing of radar equipment had melted it. Spencer then placed some popcorn kernels near the equipment and powered it up. As most children today would expect, the kernels popped. The next day he invited a colleague to join him when he placed an uncooked egg near the equipment. Now, as fate would have it, just as his colleague bent over to see what was happening to the egg, it exploded — leaving egg on his face. (The temperature in the egg increased so rapidly that it created an extreme internal pressure, which caused the egg to explode.) Thus, the discovery of the basis for the microwave oven was purely accidental.

LeBaron experimented with "flooding" the inside of a metal box with microwaves through a hole in the box. He learned that microwaves heated some foods much more rapidly than a conventional stove. The Raytheon Company filed for a patent in 1946. They produced the first microwave oven for use in restaurants in 1947. It is important to recognize that the systems to produce microwaves with significant power already existed in 1945. Thus, in 1945–46, when LeBaron discovered this phenomenon, the first three phases of technology development had already occurred. Only the product development phase needed to be completed. Now this "Radarange" as Raytheon called it was nearly six feet tall, weighed 750 pounds and cost approximately $5000.

At first, customer acceptance was low. Many had concerns for the safety of eating food heated in the microwave oven. Food preparers had concerns for their safety when being exposed to the microwave energy while heating food. Imagine what the Radarange could do to a live person given what it did to the food that it cooked. Moreover, these early Radaranges did leak a lot of energy. By 1967 Raytheon introduced the first countertop Radarange into the marketplace at a price of approximately $500. Amazingly, by 1975 there were more microwave ovens sold than gas ranges. A span of forty-five years from 1921 to 1967 elapsed while all the research and development was performed that led to a viable product.

By now, one should be convinced at this point of the decadal nature of technology development. One might wonder what in the process of technology development that makes it inherently decadal. The discussion of the technology development cycle in Chapter 1 points to it being strictly order dependent. There are four distinct phases in the cycle — discovery, device, prototype, and product. The undertaking of anyone of these phases requires the completion of the prior phases.

It is impossible to imagine building a device that exploits some physical phenomenon or principle without first discovering, understanding, and digesting the phenomenon. Building the first transistor depended on gaining considerable insight into the behavior of semiconductors. This has been true for all of the examples presented so far. Further, discovery of a phenomenon rarely provides a clear motivation for building a particular device. Again, using the transistor as an example, it took the development of amplifiers using vacuum tubes and the employment of transoceanic telephone cables to motivate AT&T's Bell Laboratories to look for a smaller more reliable solid-state replacement for the vacuum tube. The process of building a device is one of trial and error. There is no "blueprint" or "roadmap" for making a device based on the phenomenon. Here, little has changed from Edison and Bell's time. History forgets all the failures, many of which are noble attempts. Nevertheless, just as with Edison and the light bulb the failures build an understanding or intuition that eventually leads to success. Further complicating the challenge of realizing a laboratory device is that it frequently involves exploiting more than one phenomenon. For example, the ability to synthesize crystalline materials while controlling the impurities is required to make a transistor. One might even argue that inventing new devices is harder today because inventors have already exploited the easy to pick "low hanging fruit." It is not hard to imagine how years lapse into decades before someone invents a device exploiting a particular phenomenon.

Similarly, conceiving an assembly that utilizes a newly demonstrated device is also one of great learning through trial and error. It is one thing to build a device that demonstrates a phenomenon. It is another to be able to "manufacture" devices that behave in a predictable and consistent manner. However, that is required to conceive, design, and build a prototype assembly that does something useful. Recall that Brattain and Bardeen's transistor failed to be practical for use in amplifiers. It was Shockley's transistor design that ended up being the one that became the basis of the transistor revolution. Moreover, it took two more years before Phil Foy, a technician in Shockley's laboratory, built a working model of the Shockley transistor. Undoubtedly, after enhancing the initial device, someone has to characterize the behavior of the device under various conditions. A company will not have the design manual for integrating the device in products written until the device enters into production. This may be years after the device's invention. Moreover, in the case where a new part is replacing an old one, engineers have to relearn design rules. This is often more difficult than when everything is completely new. This was certainly the case in the design of circuits with transistors in them rather than with vacuum tubes. Add to the "fog" of invention the fact that the first prototype rarely serves as the basis for the most significant exploitations of a new device. Again, the real exploitation of transistors was not to be in communications amplifiers for undersea cables but rather in the digital circuits that permeate everyone's lives. It seems reasonable to assume that the pace of the prototype phase will remain slow and arduous.

It is a long way from a prototype working in the laboratory and having a product in the marketplace. The prototype could be hand crafted and carefully tuned to function properly. The marketable product must be manufacturable and function properly given the variations of production and conditions of use. In addition, the product must be reliable, given today's competitive marketplace. For example, Motorola pioneered the concept called "Six Sigma," a business management strategy for reducing the rate of defects. The result is that customers return less than one in a million of Motorola's consumer products due to defects. Today most manufacturers have adopted and practice six-sigma and the consumer expects defect free products.

A manufacturer needs to invest in the requisite infrastructure to produce and test the product employing the new device. Validating the quality of the product is an essential part of bringing a product into the marketplace. Finally, the product has to have a "form factor" and pricing structure so that there will be sufficient demand to warrant the infrastructure investment. Gorillas weighing 750-pounds and costing $5000 called Radaranges do not make it in the household market. In addition, the public did not see the value in a color television priced nearly as much as a new car when a black and white one cost a small fraction of that. "Living color" certainly had a strong price demand curve. It is a long way from the prototype in the laboratory to a product on the retailer's shelf. In addition, once the first edition of a new product is out there, its rapid evolution and enhancement is evident, as was noted in HP's desktop printers.

There are no short cuts in the technology development life cycle. The challenges will remain each step of the way. It is the nature of the beast. One might as well accept it and accommodate it. Decades will continue to transpire between theory and having products based on the theory.

Chapter 4. The Technology Players

"Accident is the name of the greatest of all inventors." — Mark Twain

In this chapter, we explore the people and the organizations that perform the different phases of the technology development life cycle. By now, one can anticipate the basic conclusion of this chapter that different people and organizations perform each phase in technology development. As will be seen, this is because each phase requires different talents, training, and facilities.

Let us start at the beginning: Phase One — discovery. This is the world of Sir Isaac Newton and Albert Einstein. Alternatively, in the case of the development of the transistor it is the world of German physicist, Ferdinand Braun. People who engage in Phase One research are those who find answers to paradoxes. They develop theories for what might be, or they validate theory through experiments, measurements, and observations.

Consider Albert Einstein as an example of a discoverer. As a secondary student in Aarau, he wrote in an essay, "If I were to have the good fortune to pass my examinations, I would go to Zurich. I would stay there for four years in order to study mathematics and physics. I imagine myself becoming a teacher in those branches of the natural sciences, choosing the theoretical part of them. Here are the reasons, which lead me to this plan. Above all, it is my disposition for abstract and mathematical thought, and my lack of imagination and practical ability." Einstein succeeded and graduated in 1900 as a teacher of mathematics and physics.

Looking back, it is hard to imagine that Einstein had trouble finding a teaching position after graduation. Three of his fellow students obtained positions as assistants at Eidgenossische Technische Hochschule in Zurich — a position Einstein wanted very much. It was not until mid-1901 that Einstein found a temporary job as a teacher at the Technical High School in Winterthur and had given up getting a teaching position at a university. After another temporary teaching position at a private school, his dad helped him get a job as a technical expert third class at the patent office in Bern. He worked at the patent office until 1909 and meanwhile obtained his doctorate from the University of Zurich in 1905. Such were the humble beginnings of the man who arguably was the greatest theoretical scientist of the twentieth century.

As pointed out in Chapter 1, Einstein provided the theoretical basis for the laser in his 1905 paper explaining Planck's quantum hypothesis of electromagnetic radiation. Einstein continued to develop quantum theory in the years following 1905. He also wrote two other landmark papers in 1905 on his special theory of relativity and statistical mechanics. He obtained his first university position in 1908 as a lecturer at the University of Bern. In just three years, he achieved a full professorship at the Karl-Ferdinand University in Prague. He spent the rest of his life at the prestigious research centers and universities of the time, including: the Prussian Academy of Sciences, Kaiser Wilhelm Institute of Physics in Berlin, California Institute of Technology, and Princeton University. He published his general theory of relativity in 1915. He made his last major scientific discovery in 1924 on the association of waves with matter.

The popular press touted Einstein's works on relativity. He received numerous awards and prizes including the Nobel Prize in 1921. Oddly, the prize was for his 1905 work on the photoelectric effect and not for relativity. The Israeli Government offered him the position as their second president in 1952. In Einstein, one finds a person driven to explain nature. He thrived in an academic atmosphere. His friends and associates were other leading theoreticians.

In Chapter 1, it was noted that Karl Ferdinand Braun was the first to observe the unusual electrical behavior of semiconductors. Braun was born in 1850 in Fulda, Germany. He studied at the Universities of Marburg and Berlin and graduated in 1872. He started out as an assistant to a professor at Wurzburg University. Just four years after university graduation he was appointed Extraordinary Professor of Theoretical Physics at the University of Marburg. Thereafter he held professorships at Strasbourg University, Technische Hochschule in Karlsruhe, and University of Tubingen.

Braun first worked on the oscillations of strings and elastic rods. His most important work was in the area of electricity. Papers included those on deviations from Ohm's law and on the calculations of the electromotive force of reversible galvanic elements from thermal sources. In 1898, he turned his attention to wireless telegraphy. He was one of the first researchers to send electric waves in definite directions. Braun published his papers on wireless telegraphy through water and air in 1901. Summoned to New York as a witness in a breach of patent lawsuit, Braun traveled to New York shortly after the start of World War I. Afterwards, illness and absence from his laboratory kept him from further work. He received the 1909 Nobel Prize in Physics. In contrast to Einstein, Braun was an experimentalist. However, like Einstein, the need to understand the workings of nature drove him and the academic environment of the university and its research institutes nurtured and supported him.

Next, let us consider the life of John Bardeen, who was a key person in the development of the transistor. Bardeen earned his BS and MS in Electrical Engineering at the University of Wisconsin. He earned a Ph.D. in mathematical physics at Princeton

University, where Professor E.P. Wigner introduced him to solid-state theory. He began his career as a fellow and assistant professor.

He worked at the Naval Ordnance Laboratory in Washington D.C. during WW II. Bell Laboratories recruited him in the fall of 1945 to join their newly formed solid-state research group. It was here with Brattain that he discovered the transistor effect. He left Bell Labs in 1951 to become a Professor at the University of Illinois, where he continued theoretical investigations in the electrical conduction in semiconductors and metals, surface properties of semiconductors, and the diffusion of atoms in solids. He received the Nobel Prize in physics with Brattain and Shockley for the "discovery of the transistor effect" in 1957 and with Cooper and Schrieffer for the "theory of superconductivity" in 1972. While at the University of Illinois, he served as a consultant to Xerox Corporation and General Electric Corporation. He also served on the Board of Directors of Xerox Corporation. Bardeen was someone who was greatly devoted to finding and explaining the fundamental truths about his sphere of expertise. Even though Bardeen ventured into the research laboratories of government and industry, he was most comfortable in the academic community of the university. It was at Bell Labs that the coupling of Bardeen's theoretical skills with those of the device builders led to the invention of the transistor.

In summary, the discoverer of Phase One has a passion to understand and to explain the workings of nature, the order of the universe. The fruits of their labor are their published writings. The university and research institutes are where they congregate, feel most comfortable, and prosper.

Since this investigation emphasizes American technological innovation of the late nineteenth and the entire twentieth centuries, it is worth looking at the early inventors of this period. Essentially all of the significant early inventors had their own private or independent laboratory. This included Alexander Graham Bell, Thomas Edison, and Wilbur and Orville Wright. When one looks closely at these early inventors, one can detect patterns that become more predominant by the close of the twentieth century. To do this the mystique surrounding these early inventors needs penetration. The following discussion provides a closer look at a few examples.

Certainly, Thomas Edison obtained recognition for being a proficient inventor with more than a thousand patents credited to his name. This was the direct result of him excelling at selecting the problems he chose to solve. He began as a telegraph operator and built upon his experience base. Edison was a methodical experimenter. In modern terms, he did an excellent job of his experimental design, made pertinent measurements and observations, and kept good laboratory notebooks. He really did employ the scientific method in his experiments. However, he did not attempt to explain phenomenon with theory and validate it through experimentation. It appears that he was aware of theory but frequently was beyond theory in his inventions. Only, later did the physicists and chemists explain what made his inventions work with appropriate theories and then validate their theories through experimentation.

This is an exception to the general linearity of the technology development cycle. However, Edison is an early contributor to the evolution of today's technology development cycle. Before Edison's time, there was no real technology development process. Today, the devices emerging from laboratories require a firm theoretical basis.

When results do not match theory, device development comes to a halt until the researchers develop an update to the underlying theory to reflect their results. Today's device developers thoroughly understand the theoretical basis of their work.

Returning to Edison and his inventions, he was not a one-person show. He had a significant supporting cast. A staff of physicists, chemists, technicians, model builders, and machinists supported him. His laboratory was equipped with the finest machine tools and stocked with everything that he could imagine needing for his work. He also had a library containing the pertinent books and journals to his work. This included patent reports from all over the world. He sought isolation and hence freedom from the influence of industry. He had a limited involvement in the starting of the companies built upon his inventions, but he was not involved in the day-to-day operations. He also left to these companies the job of taking his laboratory prototypes and turning them into manufacturable, useable, and reliable products. The entrepreneurs and businessmen of the day were the ones who supplied the capital, built the infrastructure, and operated the resultant companies. Edison financed his laboratories with the income derived from these businesses and his inventions. He was essentially a full time inventor during his prolific years.

Alexander Graham Bell was a part-time inventor. His regular job was that of a professor of speech and vocal physiology at Boston University. He had worked on improving the telegraph and had financial support from his father-in-law. However, his education and his wife's deafness probably led him to try to solve the problem of reproducing human speech electro-mechanically. This led to the invention of the telephone. He also had a laboratory and a support staff. Being a part-time inventor, he did not employ on his staff the model builders and machinists that Edison did. He rather made use of them as needed. At this time, there were entrepreneurs who built their businesses on serving the independent inventors with the expert craftsmen and the best machine tools that they could obtain. Bell was also an experimenter with great laboratory skills. His was the epitome of scholarship and invention. Like Edison, he left the building of an empire around his invention to the entrepreneurs and businessmen.

Orville and Wilbur Wright caught the fantasy of human flight as youngsters playing with a rubber-band powered model helicopter. It is no secret that they were "hobbyist" inventors. A combination of enthusiasm and the possibility of fame probably were strong motivators in their invention of the airplane. However, they were no mere tinkerers. They got in touch with the Smithsonian Institute to obtain the important literature on flight. They developed a long lasting relationship with an adviser in the form of Octave Chanute. They carefully analyzed the work of others to ascertain explanations for their failures. To them the main problem was maintaining equilibrium. Their friend and adviser, Chanute, described them as improvers rather than inventors. Nevertheless, their improvements proved to be the inventions that turned the impractical into the practical. They considered the money that they spent on their aeronautical experiments "was a dead loss in a financial sense." On the other hand, Chanute encouraged them to obtain the patents that provided them a tremendous financial reward. Again, it was a long way from Kitty Hawk to a commercially successful aircraft.

There are many independent inventors who represent the late nineteenth century through the early twentieth century and provide the necessary observations for this discussion. One person, though, seems to stand out. Elmer A. Sperry is the father of modern feedback controls and was, for many, the first to venture into cybernetics and automation. With more than 400 patents including those on the gyrocompass, he established himself as one of the great inventors of the early twentieth century. He maintained an independent laboratory which he modeled after Edison's laboratory. He, too, had great appreciation for the modelers and machinists. His inventions led to the formation of companies, but he did not get involved in their operations until he was in his fifties. Then he became intimately involved in his Sperry Gyroscope Company. Although he headed the research staff, he continued with his own independent research leaving to the staff the realm of "product improvement." Sperry was an avid follower of the work of other inventors. As the number of inventions in an area of interest crested, he jumped into the fray. Here he looked for the toughest problems, which others eschewed. He made a career of solving these problems, which led to his landmark patents. His approach to invention and his pioneering work in automation is what epitomizes the technology development of the twentieth century.

Let us now turn to the device builders of the mid-twentieth century. In the case of the transistor, Walter Brattain was the one who actually fabricated the first working transistor. Brattain attended Whitman College in Walla Walla, Washington, got his Masters from the University of Oregon and his Doctorate from the University of Minnesota. Brattain went to work at Bell Labs immediately after receiving his Ph.D. He spent the 1930s working on copper-oxide rectifiers and photo-effects on semiconductor surfaces for Joseph Becker. They thought they could build an amplifier by putting a small metal grid in the middle of the rectifier, similar to what de Forest did in a vacuum tube. It never worked. At one point, William Shockley came by with a similar idea that failed to work, as well.

Brattain spent the war years trying to detect submarines at a Government laboratory. He returned to Bell Labs as Kelly was reorganizing the Lab and starting his "Manhattan Project" to develop a solid-state amplifier. It was Brattain in collaboration with his theoretical colleague John Bardeen and no doubt a number of assistants that built one device after another until on Tuesday, December 16, 1947 they had their first transistor. Brattain had the ability to transform theory into the physical reality of devices. After the invention of the transistor, he remained until his retirement at Bell Labs where he worked to understand the surface properties of semiconductors. Obviously, he was very comfortable at Bell Labs, which provided the essential laboratory support for his life's work.

Theodore Maiman built the first working laser while he worked at Hughes Research Laboratories from 1955 to 1962. In 1962, he formed his own company devoted to the research, development, and manufacture of lasers. Afterwards, he worked for TRW from 1976 until his retirement. Before inventing the laser, he made a number of innovations in Towne's MASER. Again, Maiman was an individual who was able to take theory and turn it into a device. He spent his career in the corporate research laboratory. Some would say that his greatest contributions were done while at Hughes Research Laboratories.

Robert Hall, inventor of the semiconductor injection laser, spent his career, other than during World War II, at General Electric Research Laboratories. Hall's other inventions include the large area PIN rectifier and a process for making extremely pure germanium. Hall's very nature was to turn theory into practical devices and he spent his career in a corporate research laboratory.

Common among these mid-twentieth century device builders or Phase Two researchers is that they worked in a research laboratory at the time of their invention. This leads us to look closer at some of the innovations that have come from some of the great research laboratories of this country. Bell Laboratories provides a starting point since it represents such a prominent part in America's technology development.

Bell Labs' illustrious achievements actually began prior to its establishment in 1925. H. Nyquist began trying to send pictures over telephone circuits in 1918 and achieved the first facsimile transmission in 1924. In the early twenties AT&T engineers invented the technology that added sound to movies. They also pioneered the technologies that led to the first two-way conversation across the Atlantic.

Bell Labs contributions relative to the transistor, solar cell, and the laser have already been highlighted. One of the earliest Bell Labs' inventions was the artificial larynx. Today's products rely heavily on Bell Lab's research in this area. The stereo phonograph resulted from the work of two researchers' efforts to reduce distortion in phonograph records. Another researcher's efforts led to the radio telescope. Bell Labs created the world's first electronic speech synthesizer. Claude Shannon developed a theory of communications that bears his name. Bell Labs researchers developed technologies that led to the communications satellite. Later, researchers developed the technology of cellular switching which is the basis of the cell phone.

Bell Labs researchers invented the UNIX operating system and the C programming language. A combination of work in speech recognition and speech synthesis forms the basis of a real-time language translator. Bell Labs introduced the concept of fault tolerant software. Other inventions led to providing phone access to Internet web page content and interactions. Today, Bell Lab researchers are making important contributions to quantum computing. Clearly, Bell Labs has had a broad and almost overwhelming impact on the creation of new products by turning theory into devises.

Let us turn to another of the great industry owned research laboratories, the IBM Research Laboratories and the famous Watson Scientific Computing Laboratory. Researchers at the IBM Research Laboratories have made many hallmark inventions and the brief discussion here can only scratch the surface. Today's hard drives are derived from IBM's invention of magnetic storage systems in the early 1950s. In the late 1980s, IBM researchers discovered the Giant Magnetoresistive effect (GMR), wherein multilayer materials of various metallic elements exhibit greatly increased inherent magnetoresistance. Subsequently, IBM researchers invented processes to harness the power of GMR economically that someday will result in disk drives with the capacity to store up to 40 Gigabits per square inch.

IBM researchers Gerd Binnig and Heinrich Rohrer have won the Nobel Prize in physics for the invention of the scanning tunneling microscope and for the discovery of high-temperature superconductivity. John Backus of IBM invented the FORTRAN programming language, which became the most widely used programming language for technical work. Bob Dennard invented the one-transistor dynamic RAM (DRAM) in 1966. DRAM chips are still a dominant form of computer memory. Then in 1988, President Ronald Reagan presented Dennard with the National Medal of Technology. Benoit B. Mandelbrot introduced the world to fractals. Fractal geometry has brought new insights to areas as diverse as mathematics, earth sciences, economics, and the arts. Ted Codd invented relational databases in 1970. Today, this concept serves as the basis for most large database structures. A whole sub-industry of database-management software companies led by Oracle has evolved based on the relational database concept. IBM achieved its first operational application of speech recognition with a vocabulary of 5000 words in 1971. Many of today's speech recognition systems employ IBM technology.

An IBM researcher, John Cooke, invented the Reduced Instruction Set Computer (RISC) in the early 1970s. Today, RISC architecture is the basis of most workstations. IBM researchers invented Trellis-coded modulation (TCM) that is widely used for achieving faster and more reliable data communications. In 1989, IBM researchers invented the silicon germanium transistor, which will lower the cost of chips while significantly improving their operating frequency, current, noise, and power capabilities. Clearly, IBM researchers have made significant contributions to Phases Two and Three technology developments that go far beyond benefiting their employer, IBM.

Xerox's Palo Alto Research Center (PARC) is another industry owned research laboratory of some special interest in this discussion. In 1970, Xerox gathered a team of world-class researchers in Palo Alto and gave them the mission to create "the architecture of information." Notably, PARC does not have the long history and tradition of Bell Labs or the IBM Research Laboratories. However, PARC researchers have had a tremendous impact. They began by inventing the laser computer printer. Interestingly, HP and Canon have been the companies to really capitalize on it and one would almost think that Xerox was an "also ran."

In 1973, PARC researchers conceived the client/server architecture and personal distributed computing that underlies the distributed computational schemes of today. A patent memo describing a new networking system used the term "Ethernet" for the first time. This protocol has become the global standard for interconnecting computers on local-area networks.

PARC researchers invented the technology that enables quick manipulation of the pixels of an image. This technology is the basis for overlapping screen windows and pop-up menus. PARC researchers gave the world "what-you-see-is-what-you-get" (WYSIWYG pronounced wis-ee-wig) cut and paste editors, which are the standard of today's document processing programs such as in Microsoft Office. Back in 1973, they invented the graphical user interface (GUI), which is the user interface to personal computers. Apple drew heavily on PARC's inventions and PARC's first personal computer (Alto) for its Macs. PARC researchers also invented the page description language (PDL) construct, which is the basis of Interpress and Postscript. PARC researchers created the first object oriented programming language, Smalltalk-80, in 1980. PARC researchers have been leaders in developing workstations and programming languages for artificial intelligence applications.

PARC researchers invented the distributed feedback (solid state) laser using gallium arsenide. PARC researchers obtained in excess of a hundred patents resulting from their research in gallium arsenide lasers. *Lasers and Applications Magazine* selected one of their lasers as the outstanding product of the year in 1984. PARC researchers have developed amorphous silicon thin film transistors and sensors, which are the basis of computer displays that are becoming as easy to read as paper.

PARC is a research facility that has made tremendous contributions to Phases Two and Three technology development. Additionally, PARC was not involved in the development of the most important products that exploited their inventions. Furthermore, PARC's parent, Xerox, has not been the prime beneficiary of a vast majority of this research. One might say companies such as Apple and Microsoft owe much of their success to the research performed at PARC.

Any one of a number of other industry-owned research laboratories including GE, Hughes, and Kodak, to name a few, could be used to support the discussion points of this chapter. Recanting the achievements of these laboratories is certainly interesting and engaging but that is not the objective. The objective has already been achieved by establishing the role that the corporate owned research laboratories have played in the second and third phase of the technology development cycle. A discussion of the Government-owned research laboratories completes the consideration of the players in Phases Two and Three research. Again, a few examples make the case.

The Jet Propulsion Laboratory (JPL) has had its notable achievements. Among its "firsts" is the invention of the jet assisted take-off rocket during World War II; the first U.S. guided ballistic missile, the first U.S. satellite, the first craft to land on the moon, the first vehicle to land on Mars, and numerous first satellite images of planets, moons and other objects of the solar system.

JPL has been a pioneer in image processing technology. The medical industry has exploited the imaging techniques used on JPL's Mariner for CAT scans, diagnostic radiography, brain and cardiac angiography, and ultrasounds. JPL developed 3-D animation techniques, which Hollywood has refined for its use, and JPL has produced a number of synthetic flight videos for IMAX.

JPL scientists adapted the imaging technology used in spacecraft to create the Charters of Freedom Monitoring System. This system is at the Library of Congress and monitors the state of aging of the Declaration of Independence and the Constitution. The system scans the documents periodically and then compares the differences between the images, thus detecting changes in contrast, shape, and other features.

Other JPL developed image processing technologies have resulted in locating War of 1812 warships sunk in Lake Ontario. The U.S. Forest Service has used a forest fire mapping system that exploited JPL's digital image processing capabilities, which JPL uses to enhance images of planets taken by spacecraft.

JPL developed error correction codes to support communications with its satellites at and beyond Mars. These codes are fundamental to cellular phones and to digital communications.

JPL was an early developer of technology that "clean rooms" employ. Hospital operating rooms and electronic chip manufacturing facilities are disparate examples of clean rooms. JPL was an early pioneer in the development and use of solar arrays for space applications. In 1975, JPL introduced the hybrid automobile to the world. JPL developed infrared sensor technology, which enabled the ear thermometer. Senator John Glenn, riding aboard the Space Shuttle, helped test the Electronic Nose, a device developed at JPL that measures trace vapors in closed environments.

Innovations in Global Positioning Satellite (GPS) technology allowed the Topex/Poseidon satellite to measure sea surface height to within two centimeters, leading to better predictions of El Nino and other ocean/climate phenomena. JPL's GPS software has received NASA's Space Technology Hall of Fame recognition. In addition, JPL's work in high precision GPS receivers produced some of the basic technology underlying today's consumer products employing GPS receivers.

JPL researchers have contributed numerous innovations to radar data processing technology. Interferometry techniques led to the Shuttle Radar Topography Mission (SRTM) that provided the first global (+/- 60-degree latitude) topographic map with postings every 30 meters at an absolute accuracy of less than 10 meters.

JPL researchers have invented numerous micro-electronic devices. Focal planes comprise one area of research. NASA's Space Technology Hall of Fame has honored JPL's Quantum Well Infrared Photodetectors (QWIP). A focal plane technology called the Active Pixel Sensor (processing electronics for each pixel is embedded in the focal plane) is finding wide-ranging applications. The automotive industry is considering it for night vision enhancement. The medical industry is using the sensor for dental and skeletal x-rays employing ten percent or less x-ray energy than conventional film x-ray systems. It is also the basis for the camera function in cell phones and video cameras where low power is essential. The Active Pixel Sensor has also received NASA's Space Technology Hall of Fame recognition.

JPL has developed advanced gratings, which enable very small and extremely accurate hyperspectral-imaging spectrometers. A variety of satellites and aircraft systems has or will exploit this technology. JPL's work in semiconductor lasers led to the development of the Eximer Laser Angioplasty System, which also received NASA's Space Technology Hall of Fame recognition. The foregoing discussion represents only a small portion of the laboratory's contributions to the Phases Two and Three technology developments.

Let us now turn our considerations to one of the Defense Department Laboratories. Each of the services has a research laboratory devoted to research and development in support of that service's needs. The unique beginning of the Naval Research Laboratory (NRL) provides the rationale for highlighting it. A 1915 article in the New York Times quoted Thomas Edison: "The Government should maintain a great research laboratory.... In this could be developed ... all the technique of military and naval progression without any vast expense." Then Secretary of the Navy, Josephus Daniels, solicited Edison's support and participation, since Edison headed the new Naval Consulting Board of civilian experts with the charter to advise the Navy on science and technology. This Board was responsible for the creation of a modern research facility, which was completed in 1920. Thus NRL was born.

Initial work was devoted to radio and sound. Among its achievements in radio were the development of quartz crystal frequency control, high-powered transmitters, and receivers that became the basis of Naval and commercial long-range communications for a half-century or so. NRL established numerous firsts in long-range communications. A most interesting one is that NRL maintained regular communications with the Antarctic base and support ships of Commander R.E. Byrd's expedition to the South Pole in 1929.

In the 1950s, NRL pioneered bouncing radio waves off the moon and actually developed the technology for effective communications using the reflections off the moon. NRL was the first to transmit and return human voice through outer space and the first to demonstrate transcontinental satellite communications. They established the first operational satellite communications system.

NRL scientists discovered the radar principle in 1922. They followed this with the invention and development of the first U.S. radar. NRL pioneered pulsed radars and developed the duplexer, which allowed the use of a single antenna for both transmission and reception. In 1943, NRL developed the monopulse radar, which is the basis for all modern tracking radars.

NRL has a long and productive history in rocketry, which began with experiments using the German V-2 rockets after World War II. They accomplished a number of scientific firsts. These initial experiments led to the development of the Viking sounding rocket and culminated in the first American satellite program called Vanguard. NRL has been a pioneer in developing one or first of a kind of satellites. Consequently, they have developed numerous instrument payloads for the satellites. One of the most famous is the Clementine mission that took 1.8 million images of the moon. Advocates heralded it as a "faster, better, cheaper" approach to space missions. It received numerous awards for technological innovation.

NRL researchers have been leaders in numerous areas including astronomy, meteorology, oceanography, and materials science. They made the first positive identification of discrete sources of stellar x-rays. In the late 1940s, NRL pioneered the development of instruments and techniques for measuring atmospheric parameters such as temperature, pressure, and humidity. They have developed many of the capabilities used for weather forecasting.

NRL provided the technology for the development of the widely used aqueous film-forming foam, which rapidly extinguishes aviation fuel fires as well as all other liquid fuel fires. They also developed a non-toxic thin surface film for the control of mosquitoes. Finally, NRL holds all the fundamental patents for permanent magnets made from rare earth-iron-boron alloys. These magnets provide almost twice the magnetic energy density of the best materials previously available. NRL with a decidedly military bent has been a significant contributor to Phase Two of the technology development cycle. A similar observation applies to the other Department of Defense Laboratories — Army Research Laboratory and Air Force Research Laboratory.

The Department of Energy Laboratories have equally interesting histories and contributions. The Lawrence Livermore National Laboratory (LLNL) was a Government response to the Soviet Union detonating their first nuclear bomb in 1949. The initial staff set out to be a "new ideas" laboratory and pursued innovative solutions in the areas of nuclear weapons science and technology. Initially, four areas of research were undertaken: diagnostics for weapons experiments, weapons design, magnetic fusion, and basic physics.

LLNL physicists achieved their goals in weapons design as exemplified by the success of the Polaris system in 1962, the Army nuclear artillery shells, and the nuclear tipped anti-aircraft missiles. They provided needed instrumentation of tests and pioneered underground nuclear weapons testing. These efforts led directly into today's effective nuclear weapons monitoring capabilities. They also provided a basis for technical support of arms negotiations. In addition, LLNL has contributed significant technologies including those related to the testing and storage of nuclear waste.

Weapons testing moratoriums gave rise to non-nuclear testing and verification. This has in turn led to the need for improved technologies in particle accelerators for which LLNL scientists have provided numerous innovations and received many patents. LLNL scientists have also become leaders in large-scale computer modeling and simulation. One of their computer simulations predicts the plume from toxic releases that the National Atmospheric Release Advisory Center uses. The Center has used it for more than 160 global alerts and incidents including the Chernobyl nuclear power plant meltdown, the eruption of Mount Pinatubo, an industrial cesium-137 release in Spain, and a large tire fire in California. Advanced climate modeling efforts are using LLNL developed computer modeling and simulation technologies. LLNL mechanical engineers developed the three-dimensional structures analysis computer code, DYNA3D. Industry has used this code for making everything from safer planes, trains, and automobiles to better drink containers.

The demands of making nuclear weapons led to the development of the world's most accurate lathe. It is 1000 times more accurate than conventional machine tools and is capable of machining a surface to 1-millionth of an inch. Applications include machining the optical mirrors for the Keck Observatory and NASA's next generation of telescopes. A LLNL researcher, Jim Bryan, made an improvement on a British invention for testing machine tool performance. Today, one can find his invention used globally. *Forbes Magazine* named Jim Bryan as one of the "Heroes of U.S. Manufacturing" in 2000 for this invention and other contributions to manufacturing technology.

From its inception, fusion energy research has been a major activity at LLNL. First, researchers worked on magnetic containment, which led to building the world's largest superconducting magnets in the Mirror Fusion Test Facility. Subsequently the research thrust has been towards the use of very high-powered lasers. LLNL has constructed laser facilities with the ability to put out for a brief 1-billionth of a second twenty-five times more power than the total U.S. electrical output. LLNL is constructing a laser fusion facility with the goal of producing 10 times more energy from nuclear fusion than the lasers used to drive the implosion required for fusion to occur.

No summary can provide a complete and comprehensive review of the technologies that the laboratories discussed in this chapter have developed. Since 1963, *R & D Magazine* has annually recognized the most technologically significant new products and processes with the R &D 100 Awards. LLNL has won in excess of 90 of these coveted awards. This speaks volumes regarding the contributions that LLNL researchers have made in Phases Two and Three of the technology development cycle. Again others than LLNL have developed the countless commercial applications of LLNL's inventions.

Clearly, the foregoing discussion establishes the fact that, for the most part, small teams led by an "inventor" in a laboratory — private, industrial, or government — perform Phase Two of the technology development cycle that results in the building of devices. Further, the coupling between Phases One of discovery and Two of device building has grown over time. In addition, the challenges of building devices have become far more difficult.

The foregoing discussion also establishes the laboratory as a place where significant Phase Three development of the "laboratory" prototype occurs. In the latter half of the twentieth century, these prototypes are associated more with the laboratory than with individual inventors. The need to use a number of teams to produce a single prototype has resulted in this loss of personal identity. The building of a prototype has evolved from the handiwork of a modest number of model builders and machinists to the employment oftentimes of several highly specialized machines and facilities costing many tens of millions of dollars. As a result, Phase Two research teams tend to stay within the device-building realm even though they may use some of the machines and tools of Phase Three or prototype development.

The only thing that remains is to identify the "who and where" of Phase Four, product development, of the technology development life cycle. As one might expect, this is almost entirely the realm of industry. American industry excels at developing and bringing to market new or improved products in its product development centers. Entrepreneurs are constantly forming new companies to capitalize on a new product idea. The reading of any high-tech corporation's annual report provides evidence of the prowess of the company in improving on current products and developing new products.

Intel's *2007 Annual Report* serves as an excellent example. The following excerpts, which could have come from literally hundreds of American companies, are cited:

> "Intel continues to challenge the status quo with ground-breaking products, cutting-edge process technologies, and world-class manufacturing capabilities."

> "Our goal is to be the preeminent provider of semiconductor chips and platforms for the worldwide digital economy."

> "We are committed to investing in world-class technology development, particularly in the area of the design and manufacture of integrated circuits."

> "We are focusing our R&D efforts on advanced computing, communications, and wireless technologies as well as energy efficiency by developing new microarchitectures, advancing our silicon manufacturing process technology, delivering the next generation of microprocessors and chipsets, improving our platform initiatives, and developing software solutions and tools to support our technologies."

> "As part of our R&D efforts, we plan to introduce a new microarchitecture for our mobile, desktop, and Intel Xeon processors approximately every two years and ramp the next generation of silicon process technology in the intervening years. We refer to this as our 'tick-tock' technology

development cadence. Our leadership in silicon technology has enabled us to make 'Moore's Law' a reality."

Hewlett-Packard's (HP) *2007 Annual Report* provides the following insight regarding the emphasis of their R&D:

> "We remain committed to innovation as a key element of HP's culture. Our development efforts are focused on designing and developing products, services and solutions that anticipate customers changing needs and desires and emerging technological trends. Our efforts also are focused on identifying the areas where we believe we can make a unique contribution..."

IBM provides the following statement on their R&D strategy in their *2008 IBM Annual Report*:

> "IBM's research and development (R&D) operations differentiate the company from its competitors. IBM annually spends approximately $6 billion for R&D, focusing its investments on high-growth, high-value opportunities. As a result of innovations in these and other areas, IBM was once again awarded more U.S. patents in 2008 than any other company, the first company to achieve over 4,000 patents in a year."

These three examples clearly illustrate industry's ability and commitment to the development and improvement of their products.

Chapter 5. The Finances of Technology

"Follow the money." — Bob Woodward and Carl Bernstein

Figure 5.1. Total U.S. Expenditures in R&D (Constant 2000 $)

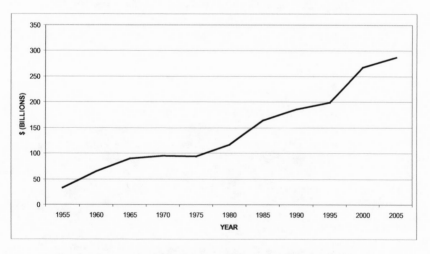

Based on data extracted from Science and Engineering Indicators 2008.

Just as it is important to know how technology is developed and who develops it in order to gain an understanding of the decline in U.S. technology, it is important to know something about the finances of technology development. This chapter provides some basic information on the historic levels of research and development (R&D) funding in the United States, where that funding has come from and where it has gone. As it is with so many other cases, one can gain significant insights into what is really happening relative to technology development by following the money.

First, the overall funding of R&D in the U.S. is depicted in Figure 5.1. R&D funding has risen continually from 1953 (starting time of the figure) to present times with only relatively short periods where it has tended to be relatively flat. This alone would indicate a robust R&D effort in the U.S. As one might expect, there is much more to the technology story than the total expenditures on R&D.

The fraction of the gross domestic product (GDP) spent on R&D more accurately reflects what has really occurred relative to the nation's R&D efforts. This ratio indicates whether the R&D investment is keeping pace or falling behind the economy. A decline in the ratio would result in a proportionate future decline in new products and services flowing into the economy. Understanding which organizations fund R&D in the United States is also an important part of following the money. Figure 5.2 depicts these items. The top line shows the total amount of R&D funding as a fraction of the GDP. We see that it has been essentially flat at approximately 2.5% of GDP since the late 1950s. The middle two lines depict R&D funding by the Federal Government and industry. The bottom line shows the rest of R&D funding provided by other sources including private foundations, colleges, and universities. While funding by other sources represents an increasing fraction of the total it still represents less than 7% of the total investment in R&D and thus provides marginal utility in following the money.

FIGURE 5.2 — R&D EXPENDITURES AS A PERCENT OF GDP

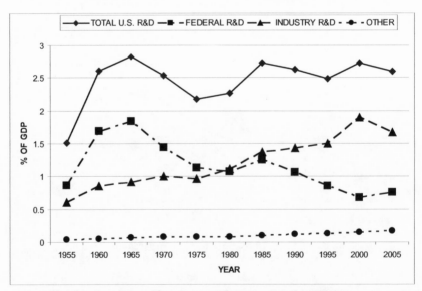

Based on data extracted from Science and Engineering Indicators 2008.

There are several observations of note regarding the federal and industrial funding of R&D. First, federal funding peeked at approximately 1.9% in the 1960s at the height of the Cold War. At that point, it declined to a little more than 1.0% of GDP where it remained until the fall of the Berlin Wall (1989). Since then it has declined to approximately 0.7% of GDP and remained relatively constant for the past decade. More importantly, there has been a steady and dramatic rise in industry's share of R&D expenditures since 1953. Industry's R&D funding exceeded that of the Federal Government for the first time in 1982. Industry R&D funding has exceeded 1.75% of the GDP for the past decade peaking in 2000. Industry funding of R&D has been essentially double that of the Federal Government during this period. Therefore, there should be no surprise regarding who has the greatest influence over R&D directions and what new innovative products make it into the marketplace.

Let us turn now to uncovering which organizations perform the nation's R&D. Figure 5.3 depicts this (note that the y-axis uses a log scale). This figure allows us to draw several interesting observations. Industry has consistently performed approximately 70% of the R&D over the fifty years depicted in Figure 5.3. It not only performs most of the R&D that it funds; it performs much of the federally funded R&D as well. The federal laboratories have gone from performing nearly 16% of the R&D to approximately 7%. This decline began in the 1970s. An important conclusion is that the federal laboratories are less than half as important as they once were relative to those performing the nation's R&D. The FFRDCs include the Department of Energy (DOE) laboratories, Lincoln Laboratories, and the Jet Propulsion Laboratory. FFRDC research peaked in the 1980s at approximately 5.5% and declined since then to a level of approximately 3% of the total.

FIGURE 5.3 — PERCENT OF R&D PERFORMED BY VARIOUS TYPES OF ORGANIZATIONS

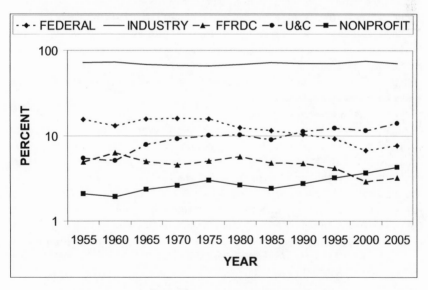

Based on data extracted from Science and Engineering Indicators 2008.

The universities' and colleges' share of the R&D funding pie steadily increased during this time from approximately 5% to 14%. The nonprofit organizations have doubled their portion of the R&D activity over the half-century depicted. In summary, the nonprofit research organizations, universities, and colleges have made significant gains in their research levels, whereas federal laboratories and FFRDCs portion has declined proportionately. Finally, industry's portion of the R&D total has remained essentially constant, independent of the mix of funding sources.

It would be convenient and make the discussion easier if economic data relevant to R&D were more complete, more precise, and covered more years. Unfortunately, this does not seem to be the case. Other than for the DOD, there are no formal reporting requirements for identifying and categorizing R&D expenditures.

The American Association for the Advancement of Science (AAAS) has provided definitions of three categories of funding that are widely used by others including Congress. They are as follows:

1) In *basic research*, the objective is to gain knowledge or understanding of phenomena without specific applications in mind.

2) In *applied research*, the objective is to gain knowledge or understanding necessary for meeting a specific need.

3) *Development* is the systematic use of the knowledge or understanding gained from research directed toward the production of materials; devices; systems; or methods, including design, development, and improvement of prototypes and new processes. It excludes quality control, routine product testing, and production.

Comparing these definitions with those of the four technology development phases used in this book yields the following correlations:

Phase One — discovery — corresponds quite well with basic research.

Phase Two — device — pretty much corresponds to applied research. Phase Two can include some of the very early development efforts of the AAAS categories in the development of devices.

Phases Three and Four — prototype and product — correspond to the bulk of AAAS's development category.

While AAAS's categories do not precisely match up with the four phases of the technology development cycle, they do provide a means to glean some insights into the funding structure as it relates to them. Subdividing the development category similar to that of the Department of Defense (DOD) would provide much greater utility. Undoubtedly, the three categories reflect the availability of data. Certainly, the assignment of technology development activities to one of AAAS's categories is subject to some interpretation and latitude. As a result, some ambiguity exists relative to the purity of the numbers. Relative values, trends, and relationships that are evident in the data are certainly valid so long as one does not try to glean the slightest nuance.

Figure 5.4 depicts the decomposition of the total R&D expenditures into the three categories of basic research, applied research, and development. (This is a stacked chart.) Again, percentages of the GDP provide the appropriate measure for assessing trends. Funding for basic research and applied research has been a relatively constant fraction of the GDP since 1965. Basic research has received nearly 15% of the total R&D funding over this period. Applied research funding has constituted approximately 23% of the total R&D funding. Development has received a relatively constant 1.5% of GDP or 62% of the total R&D funding.

FIGURE 5.4 — THE DECOMPOSITION OF R&D INTO CATEGORIES

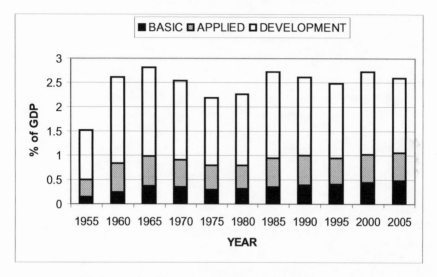

Based on data extracted from Science and Engineering Indicators 2008.

The relative funding levels for the three categories of funding are consistent with the fact that the cost of completing one phase of a cycle is significantly more than the previous phase. A rule of thumb that some use, is that the cost increases by an order of magnitude from one phase to the next. The relative funding level for each phase cannot follow this rule due to the tremendous winnowing effect, which was explored in Chapter 2. The observation that the total funding for all three categories of R&D has remained relatively constant at approximately 2.5% of GDP for greater than fifty years is significant.

The next three figures depict the funding levels for the three categories of R&D provided by the two primary sources, the Federal Government and Industry. Figure 5.5 depicts basic research funding. The Federal Government's portion of basic research funding has varied between 60% and 80% of the total while industry provides the remainder. This ratio has changed slightly in the favor of the Federal Government in recent years.

Figure 5.6 depicts the relative levels of the funding of applied research. The roles of the Federal Government and industry reversed in the late 1970s, with industry providing nearly 60% of the funding for applied research in 2000. In recent years, the two sources of funding have tended towards becoming equal.

As might be expected, industry dominates the development category of research funding at this time. This has not always been the case when in the 1960s the Federal Government dominated development funding. The Government and industry roles reversed around 1975 as depicted in Figure 5.7. Federal funding has eroded as a fraction of GDP since about 1985 to where today it represents less than 20% of develop-ment funding. The development of weapon systems is a major factor in the Federal component. This may explain the decline in federal funding since 1985. Interestingly, the totality of development funding has stayed relatively stable at around 1.6% of GDP since 1960.

FIGURE 5.5 — DECOMPOSITION OF BASIC RESEARCH FUNDING BY SOURCES

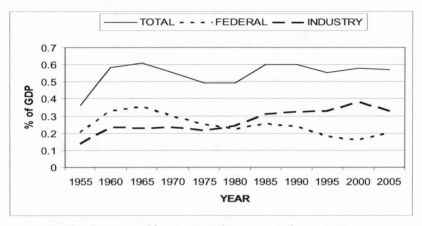

Based on data extracted from Science and Engineering Indicators 2008.

FIGURE 5.6 — DECOMPOSITION OF APPLIED RESEARCH FUNDING BY SOURCES

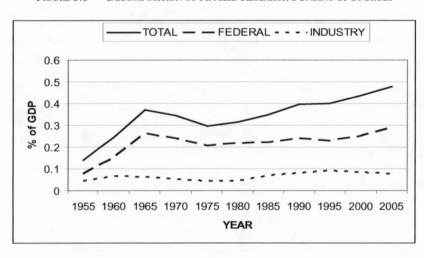

Based on data extracted from Science and Engineering Indicators 2008.

FIGURE 5.7 — DECOMPOSITION OF DEVELOPMENT FUNDING BY SOURCES

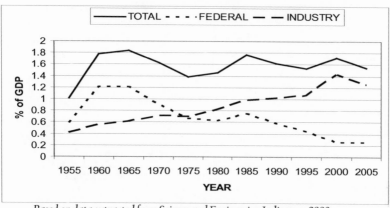

Based on data extracted from Science and Engineering Indicators 2008.

The Federal Government initiated a five-year program to double NIH funding in FY'99. Figure 5.8 depicts the impact of this program where the share of GDP accorded to NIH R&D nearly doubles in the five years from 1998 to 2003. The figure also shows the federal funding of all the life sciences' R&D. Very little Federal Government funding of R&D goes to the life sciences other than NIH. Federal funding of NIH R&D has declined by approximately 20% from the peak in FY 2003. Approximately half of NIH funding goes towards basic research. This surge in NIH R&D has been at the expense of R&D in the physical sciences and engineering since total Government R&D expenditures have decreased as a fraction of GDP during this time (see Figure 5.2).

FIGURE 5.8 –R&D FUNDING BY NIH & TOTAL R&D FUNDING IN LIFE SCIENCES

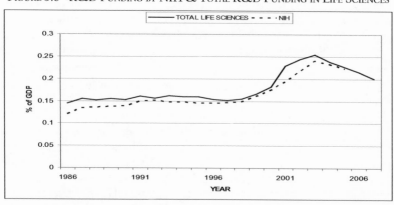

Based on data extracted from R&D Budget and Policy Program: Guide to R&D Funding Data-Historical Data.

FIGURE 5.9 — R&D FUNDING BY THE TOP FIVE FEDERAL AGENCIES

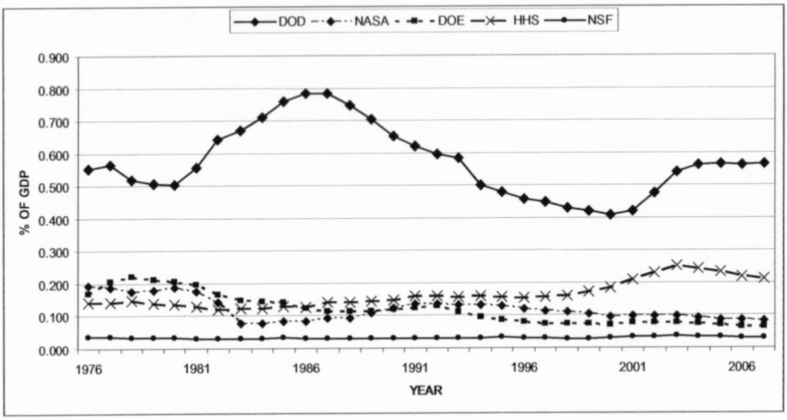

Based on data extracted from R&D Budget and Policy Program: Guide to R&D Funding Data-Historical Data.

Figure 5.9 depicts the composition of the funding of R&D by the Federal Government for the five major agencies. NIH's budget is part of Health and Human Services (HHS) and represents the preponderance of HHS's R&D funding. The other agency acronyms are the Department of Defense (DOD), National Aeronautical and Space Agency (NASA), Department of Energy (DOE), and the National Science Foundation (NSF). DOD represents by far the greatest source of R&D funds within the Federal Government. In fact, DOD's R&D funds tend to represent approximately 50% of the total Federal Government's R&D funding during the fifty years represented by Figure 5.9, fluctuating between 0.4% and 0.8% of GDP. DOD funding in current year dollars peaked in 1989, the year of the fall of the Berlin Wall and the end of the Cold War. The peak in terms of the fraction of GDP occurred two years earlier. DOD R&D funding increased somewhat after the "nine-eleven" terrorist attack on the U.S. One item of note is that NSF's R&D funds represent a distant fifth relative to the other agencies. NSF funds go mostly to basic research at universities. One last observation is that NIH (HHS) funding has been increasing (although slightly) relative to the GDP since 1982.

Before leaving the world of R&D finance, it is worth considering how the U.S. compares with some other nations. Both Government organizations such as the NSF and private associations such as the AAAS have recently given this greater attention and publicized it more extensively. Table 5.1 provides basic information on the funding of R&D by some of the industrialized nations relative to their GDP. Looked at in this way, the United States is literally in the middle of the pack. Sweden, Finland, Japan, and South Korea spend a significantly larger proportion of their GDP on R&D. Japan (the second largest economy globally) spends approximately 20% more of its GDP on R&D than the United States does. Clearly, the United States is not alone and the competition is keen. Various organizations have chronicled the consequences of not keeping up with the rest of the world.

TABLE 5.1 — SELECTED NATIONS R&D FUNDING

	% of GDP = Total R&D	% of GDP = Gov R&D	% of GDP = Ind R&D	% of GDP = Other
Sweden	3.7%	0.89%	2.37%	0.44%
Finland	3.5%	0.84%	2.38%	0.28%
Japan	3.4%	0.54%	2.65%	0.21%
South Korea	3.2%	0.80%	2.37%	0.03%
United States	2.6%	0.77%	1.70%	0.13%
Germany	2.5%	0.70%	1.40%	0.40%
France	2.1%	0.80%	1.07%	0.21%
Canada	1.9%	0.95%	0.59%	0.36%
United Kingdom	1.8%	0.52%	0.85%	0.43%
European Union	1.8%	0.61%	0.99%	0.20%
China	1.4%	0.35%	0.98%	0.07%
Spain	1.2%	0.52%	0.56%	0.12%
Russia	1.1%	0.69%	0.32%	0.09%

Based on data extracted from Main Science and Technology Indicators (MSTI): 2009/1 edition.

The foregoing provides a basic background of the financing of R&D in the United States. This background is important to the chapters on the rise, the Golden Age, and the beginning of the decline of technology in America. Just one note of caution, the numbers do not tell the whole story. Together with an understanding of the structure of the technology development cycle, they provide a useful backdrop for the remainder of our discussions.

Chapter 6. The Rise of Technology in America

"Americans usually believe that nothing is impossible." —Lawrence S. Eagleburger

Figure 6.1 — Annual Patents Issued by the United States Patent Office

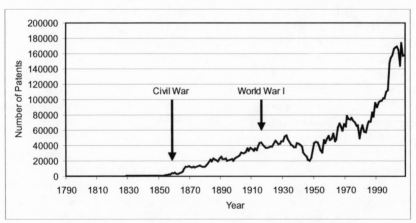

Based on data extracted from U.S. Patent Activity Calendar Years 1790 to the Present.

The rise of technology in America occurred during a most dynamic period in the history of the United States. Certainly, innovators such as Ben Franklin with his many inventions including bifocals, the lightening rod, the Franklin stove, and an odometer sowed the initial seeds of America's technology prowess prior to the Revolutionary War and afterwards. Other examples include James Fitch's invention of the steamboat in 1787 and Eli Whitney's invention of the cotton gin in 1793. Technology development expanded dramatically after the Civil War as indicated by the number of patents granted (Figure 6.1). The number of patents awarded by the U.S. Patent Office increased from approximately 3,000 annually before the Civil War to approximately 40,000 annually at the close of World War I. During this same period, the United States admitted twelve states to the Union. This brought the contiguous United States to 48. In addition, the United States completed two very significant construction projects; namely, the transcontinental railway in 1869 and the Panama Canal in 1920. (Actually, the canal was completed and opened in 1914 only to have a slide close it in 1915 and it remained closed until the end of World War I. It had its grand opening in 1920.) The country expanded with the purchase of Alaska from Russia and the annexation of Hawaii. The population more than tripled to just over 100 million and those living in urban areas increased from 20% to approximately 50% of the population. The gross domestic product grew to more than twice its Civil War size to propel the U.S. economy into the largest on the globe. It was the time of the Industrial Revolution. By every measure, this period was one of great expansion for the United States and it was one of great confidence for the people.

What has been the hallmark of the American spirit, "rugged individualism," began and propelled the rise of technology. It was the inventions of individuals during this period that gave us the light bulb (Edison), the telephone (Bell), the "Brownie" camera (Eastman) and the airplane (Wright brothers). Other notables included Elihu Thomson (arc-light), Nikola Tesla (alternating current power systems), William Stanley (alternating current power systems including the induction coil), Elmer Sperry (control systems including the gyrocompass), Lee de Forest (vacuum tube used in radios, televisions, etc.), and Edwin Armstrong (frequency modulation including FM radio). The inventors and their inventions of this period have been the subject of numerous periodical articles and books. At one time, they were as much America's heroes as George Washington, Davy Crockett, and Babe Ruth. Every child learned about them in school. In-class projects included making battery operated Morse code keys, electric motors and rubber band powered airplanes.

During this period, the modern laboratory came into being, in which researchers turn science into products (i.e., inventions). The inventors and researcher of the rise developed the formal methods for conducting research in these laboratories, which gave way to the Golden Age of technology in the U.S. after World War I. It is in these private laboratories that one finds the nexus for the story of the rise of technology in America. It is here that many misconceptions regarding the methods of Americans' hero inventors are revealed. One might describe the stereotypical inventor of this era in the following manner: he worked alone or with an assistant or partner, was an amateur inventor, lived in poverty or near it, was a social outcast, was a tinkerer, hoped for a "Eureka!" moment, relied on trial and error, and had one big idea during his lifetime.

It is true that you can find examples of inventors with one or more of these characteristics but most do not even come close to this caricature. Bell is an example of an amateur inventor whom Boston University employed as a professor of speech and vocal physiology. He did focus on a single invention, the telephone, including everything necessary for a global telephone system. His inventions made him extremely wealthy. Another example of amateur inventors is the Wright brothers who had their successful bicycle shop for income. They, too, focused solely on a single invention, the airplane. It also brought them fame and fortune. Yet another example is Eastman who worked as an office boy and at the age of twenty became fascinated with photography, went on to invent the role film and then invented the camera to use it. His photographic inventions supplied him with great wealth.

The professionals included Edison with 1093 patents; Thomson with 700 patents, Sperry with 400 patents, De Forest with 300 patents, Tesla with 272 patents, Stanley with 129 patents and Armstrong with 42 patents. Invention was a way of life for these professionals and they turned out inventions the way an author spins a story or a composer creates new compositions. Most had an entrepreneurial bent as they created businesses, whose purposes were to commercialize their inventions, or they obtained financial backing from the business tycoons of the era to pay for their efforts, including staff and facilities. Edison and Sperry are examples of those that created businesses and Tesla is an example of one who sold his patents (e.g., to Westinghouse) and obtained sponsorship of his inventive work (e.g., J.P. Morgan). Most died wealthy. Armstrong, the inventor of FM radio, was a tragic counterexample. He spent the last five years of his life in litigation with RCA and others over patent infringements and plunged to his death from his tenth story apartment — beaten, exhausted and near financial ruin. His widow obtained complete vindication through court judgments in excess of $10M.

Edison embodied the rise of technology in America as much as any single person could. In a sense, one might say that some of his most important work was inventing the methods of technology development. He pioneered as much as anyone the means of taking an idea — an invention — and turning it into a marketable product. He accomplished so much more than demonstrating an incandescent light bulb (or any of his thousand plus inventions) in his laboratory. The requirements on a practical light bulb included lasting for many hours of use, sellable for a reasonable cost at a profit, and easy manufacturability. However, a light bulb alone was nothing. With the invention of the light bulb came the need to invent and implement a whole system of electrical power generation and distribution so that the light bulb could be of use. Edison understood this and contributed mightily to its realization.

Edison worked long and persistently on developing a practical light bulb. A key element was finding a proper filament, which was a materials problem. It had to have sufficient resistance in order to heat to white hot, be structurally sound at that temperature, and survive many thermal transitions between being off and on. Amazingly, Edison did this at a time when material science was virtually unknown. After all, no one ever wanted to know the resistance properties, tensile strength at extreme temperatures, et cetera that bear on the selection of a filament until the pursuit of a practical electric light bulb. Thus, he did not have at his disposal the scientific basis on which to select candidate filaments. It is true that Edison tried many filaments in his quest. Critics would later denigrate Edison as a hunt-and-try experimenter. True, technology development would become more scientific and methodical as the technology development process evolved and became more rigorous. However, Edison's quest was not random hunting for a needle in a haystack. His intuitions were driven by conclusions and inferences from the experience gained in building and testing different materials and configurations. For this, he engaged craftsmen to fabricate the various components required to find the proper components and configurations for the light bulb. He relied heavily on experimentation and for him no experiment was a waste as failures were important in his discovery process. He was a single individual who proceeded through all the phases of technology development supported by a laboratory and craftsmen employing the best tools available. Additionally, he was creating the technology development process as he went along, as were his contemporaries. This was truly the beginning of the structured technology development process and at the time, its name was invention.

Edison was involved in all aspects of bringing lighting into the homes and businesses of America. This included the research, development and manufacture of the various components and subsystems of the lighting system which included the generation, distribution and control of electricity to power the lights. It also included the ownership, installation, and operation of these electrical generation and distribution networks known as the electrical utility. Moreover, he raised capital for these enterprises from the tycoons of what would become Wall Street.

As time went on and he gained experience, his research and development laboratories evolved along with the process of inventing (i.e., technology development). He established his first "laboratory" in the model-building shop of Charles Williams, after quitting his job as a Western Union operator in 1869 to devote himself to invention. Here he focused on improving telegraphic components. In 1870, he rented a large building in Newark, New Jersey, equipped it with the best machines available, and hired the best machinists possible. In 1871, he began keeping a journal to keep a record of his concepts, the setup of his almost daily experiments, and their results. Western Union Telegraph Company and New York tycoons provided the financial support and bought the patented devices he manufactured.

FIGURE 6.2 EDISON'S MENLO PARK LABORATORY, REMOVED TO GREENFIELD VILLAGE IN DEARBORN, MICHIGAN.

Photo copyright by Author

By 1876, his personal wealth was sufficient for him to establish his second laboratory at Menlo Park. Edison equipped his Menlo Park laboratory so well that it rivaled or exceeded any university laboratory in the U.S. or Europe. Figure 6.2 shows Edison's laboratory as one sees it today but it does portray the workspace and conditions, which supported Edison's inventing. This laboratory had a small office for Edison, a library, a drafting room and the essential machine shop. It also had its own electrical power plant. Here, Edison with the aid of a staff of approximately twenty machinists and model builders set a goal of "a minor invention every ten days and a big thing every six months or so." It was here in 1879 that Edison invented the incandescent light bulb. (Many of us were given in grade school the caricature of Edison working in some make do closet cobbling his inventions together.) In 1881, he had to leave Menlo Park to move back to New York to oversee the building of the first central electrical generation facility and the manufacture and sale of electrical lighting components. He continued to invent and experiment in a friend's facility. As an aside, one might note that the electrification of America sowed the first seeds of American consumerism. Contrary to much of Europe, where electric lighting was initially for the gentry, electrification in America was from the beginning for everyone. Of course, the urban population saw it first but special Government programs pushed electrification into the countryside and its sparsely populated farmlands.

Edison built and moved to his last laboratory facility at West Orange in 1886. This was a great expansion of scope and scale on Menlo Park. Edison insisted on having everything he needed on hand and therefore had the storerooms extremely well stocked. Edison claimed that an inventor could not foretell what he might need until he needed it. Here at West Orange, an entire building was devoted to chemistry and several chemists with German doctorates were hired. Edison reserved a bench for his exclusive use. As always, Edison had his private room for his experiments. He provided for the library in the same manner as the storerooms in that one could find the latest books and journals on science and technology and the all-important volumes on patents. The machine shops and workrooms for the machinists and model builders dominated the facility.

Edison's laboratories became the models for other inventors. Edward Weston patterned his laboratory after Edison's Menlo Park facility. Tesla's laboratory in Colorado followed the pattern of Edison but on a much grander scale. The inventors certainly fed off each other through their shared interests. The *Patents Office Gazette*, which was a must read for the inventor, provided abstracts of all patents and served as a means of staying abreast of what the inventors were doing. Edison, Thomson, Sperry, De Forest, Tesla, Stanley, Armstrong, and many others of this period invented the process of technology development as they gained experience and sophistication in their inventing activities.

It is during this period that the corporate research and development laboratories came into being. The number grew from essentially none at the end of the Civil War to more than 100 at the start of World War I. Among these are the laboratories of AT&T, General Electric, DuPont, General Motors, and Standard Oil of New Jersey.

Probably the most significant driver for the establishment of these laboratories was the expiration of patents. Since 1790, U.S. patent law has given individuals exclusive use of their intellectual property for a limited time. It is worth noting that the Sherman Act of 1890 and the Clayton Act of 1914 (antitrust laws) prohibited certain monopolistic practices. However, they did not prohibit an entity having a dominant position based on inherent capability. Attorneys and judges in antitrust cases have often quoted Senator George Hoar, one of the authors of the act, who argued during debate on the act that one "who merely by superior skill and intelligence . . . got the whole business because nobody could do it as well as he could was not a monopolist." This guiding principle persists to this day. Thus, use of patents has been and continues to be a legitimate method to protect one's monopoly.

Bell's patents provided AT&T with its initial monopoly in telephone communications. The acquisition of additional patents enhanced AT&T's monopoly. AT&T provided long distance telephone service for its parent American Bell Telephone Company, which provided more than half of the telephones in the United States by the early 1900s. Most competitors did not offer long distance service. The corporation vigorously defended these patents with a team of lawyers. However, as happens with all patents, Bell's basic patents expired in 1894. At this time, the purchase of patents from independent inventors was uncertain. A competitor could possibly gain a foothold or worse yet a commanding advantage by acquiring key new breakthrough patents.

A patent interference case involving an independent inventor's patent and that of a researcher within AT&T made this point most poignantly. Both patents were for similar devices (a loading coil), but AT&T lost the suit. As a defensive measure, AT&T had acquired the license to the outside inventor's patent prior to the culmination of the suit. Two things were clear because of this experience: first, independent researchers would continue to be a source of patents of value to the company and second, both researchers relied heavily on an in depth knowledge of fundamental physics. This made it clear to AT&T management that science and scientists were essential to dominating long distance communications.

AT&T's efforts to establish transcontinental telephone service clarified the importance of formally trained scientists and engineers. AT&T acquired the rights to de Forest's patent of the three-element vacuum tube (triode) as a key element in this effort. De Forest was similar to many of the independent inventors, who were not university educated in the sciences or engineering. Twenty-five university educated researchers and their assistants were required to develop the triode into an amplifier over a three-year period. Notably, Bell spoke from New York to his assistant Watson in San Francisco on January 25, 1915. Needless to say, AT&T's internal research and development capabilities and staff grew significantly after Bell's historic transcontinental telephone call.

General Electric (GE) found itself in a similar plight to that of AT&T with the expiration of Edison's basic lamp patents in 1894. Worse yet, scientists in Europe, especially Germany, were patenting incandescent lamp filaments that would threaten GE's near monopoly in the United States. GE responded by hiring Willis Whitney, a University of Leipzig Ph.D., as its first director of GE's laboratory in 1900. Prior to this, GE, like AT&T, had depended on purchasing patents from independent inventors. Further threatening GE's commanding position in the incandescent lamp market was Westinghouse's acquisition of the rights to a metallic filament, invented in Germany. GE was clearly in a losing position with its inefficient carbon filaments. GE's highly qualified research staff responded in 1909 with the tungsten filament — still in use today. The value of a science based research and development laboratory was clearly established.

As one might imagine, these laboratories tended to focus exclusively on developing the products along with the machines and processes for their manufacture in support of their parent companies. Parent companies required the justification of research budgets and therefore research became more structured and disciplined. As previously discussed, threats to the laboratories' parents were serious and immediate. This gave precedence to greater professionalism among the researchers. Companies relied on researchers with university degrees in physics, chemistry, and engineering. Many laboratories recruited doctorates (PhDs) from German universities due to the reputation and success of the Germans in the chemical and electrical fields. Graduates of American Universities and some of their professors flocked to the corporate research and development laboratories. Physicists employed in corporate research laboratories made up a quarter of the membership of the American Physical Society by 1920. The growth and maturation of the corporate research laboratory led to a better understanding of the technology development process and its continuous improvement.

Two innovations, which would have tremendous impact on how business performed its various functions, including research and development, were scientific management as conceived and expounded by Frederick Winslow Taylor and the assembly line of Henry Ford. They were the forerunners of today's highly evolved program management, systems engineering, systems analysis, process engineering, and operations research disciplines. (The decomposition of the research and development process into a sequence of phases and the analysis of them as presented in this book are relatively simple examples of process engineering and systems analysis.)

Taylor looked at the entirety of a "production system" including both the human and machine components in his scientific management system. His goal was to organize these components in as efficient a way as possible. He and his people went into a plant or operation that they were evaluating and with stopwatches in hand timed all the various component activities in a production system. He approached the human components as though they were machines, thereby ignoring the psychological and emotional aspects of the human. The concept that efficiency of production would benefit everyone was his driving force. (Economists continue to measure the health of an economy by the growth in the value of goods and services per hour of labor — the productivity index.) He recognized that design of the work place, sequencing as well as scheduling of work, and the design of tools all contributed to the efficiency of the system and its total output. He decomposed the whole into its component parts and rearranged them for greater efficiency — seeking the most efficient organization. He would set the work schedule on the amount of work the best performers could do. He espoused paying employees on the amount of work performed — this enhanced the efficiency of the individual. The world over admired and adopted Taylor's scientific management and it was simply referred to as Taylorism.

Henry Ford took a systems approach to the assembly of an automobile. He decomposed the production into a sequence of steps, laid them in a line, and moved the assembly of the automobile down the line. In so doing, he recognized many factors leading to improved efficiency in the assembly of the automobile. He brought the work to the workers rather than the workers to the work. The workers stayed at a workstation and various means, primarily machine driven conveyors, brought everything to the workstation including the car assembly and all the parts the workers at a particular workstation installed. Further, the worker repetitively performed a relatively easily learned task on each vehicle. The workers and the tools they used were specialized to a particular task. This meant Ford and others employing the assembly line method of production could hire untrained workers and quickly train them to work on the assembly line. This significantly reduced the number of highly skilled workers as well as the number of work hours required to produce an automobile. Ford's production line approach and Taylor's scientific management forever changed how the work place is conceived, whether it is the factory or the office. (Its impact on the execution of research and development was explored in previous chapters.) One of Ford's driving objectives was to achieve a relationship between the pay of workers and the price of his product — the automobile — such that the workers could afford to own the product. This was a second great step in the evolution of the American consumerist society. (The first was in the electrification of America.)

Thus, the period between the Civil War and the First World War saw improvements in the standard of living based on technology based products and services, a revolution in the way work is performed (a science or technology based approach), the invention of the technology development cycle with its research and development laboratories, and the birth of the American consumerism. This clearly was the period of the rise of technology in America. In the process, the United States became an admired world leader for its science, technology, industry, and economy. Interestingly, both fascist and socialist leaders would embrace America's scientific and technological ways.

Chapter 7. Inventions of the Rise

"If I have seen farther than others, it is because I was standing on the shoulders of giants." — Sir Isaac Newton

We explored how technology development evolved from the single inventor with a number of assistants into the corporate laboratory staffed by university-trained scientists and engineers in the previous chapter. In the process, some insights were provided on how a few products came to be during this period in which America rose to economic and technological dominance. This chapter provides a discussion of some additional inventions that occurred during this period, to illustrate how they came to be and to provide the backdrop for America's Golden Age in technology development. It goes without mention that inventors in other countries made significant contributions. After all, Europe was the preeminent science and technology center prior to America's rise. Before that, Asia and the Middle East were leaders in innovation. However, what emerged was a development cycle that was purely American and overwhelmed the rest of the world in the diversity and superiority of its products in the marketplace.

1879 — Electric Light Bulb

See Chapter 6.

1886 — Dishwasher

It took a woman to invent a practical dishwasher. Unhappy that her servants were chipping her fine china, Josephine Cochrane invented the first practical dishwasher in 1886. Now Josephine was not the first inventor in her family for she was the granddaughter of John Fitch, the inventor of the steamboat. Nor was she the first to patent a dishwasher. Joel Houghton was the first to patent a device for washing dishes in 1850. Joel's device did little more than splash some water on the dishes.

L.A. Alexander patented his dishwasher in 1865 but it was not really any better than Joel's was. Josephine unveiled her hand-operated (before electrification) mechanical dishwasher at the 1893 World's Fair with considerable fanfare. She expected the public to embrace her invention but only hotels and large restaurants bought them. She founded a company to build them that later became KitchenAid. It was not until the 1950s that dishwashers became commonplace in the home.

1900 — Brownie Camera

George Eastman, the inventor of the Brownie Camera, defined his company for generations to come with the slogan for his first camera: "You press the button, we do the rest." Eastman recognized right off when he became involved in amateur photography that there were two kinds of amateurs: those willing to devote the time to acquire the knowledge and skills comparable to those of a professional and those who merely wanted to take pictures of their everyday lives, families, and travels as personal keepsakes. He observed that the second kind outnumbered the first by at least ten to one. George Eastman was an inventor unlike Thomas Edison, Alexander Graham Bell or any other inventor of the Rise in American Technology that was discussed in the previous chapter.

George's dad died when he was but a boy. Finally, when family finances became most desperate, he quit school at the age of fourteen and went to work for an insurance company as an errand boy. His meager earnings of $3 per week were insufficient to right the family's financial condition. After taking a position as an office boy for a second insurance company, he took the initiative to learn to file policies and even write policies. His reward was a two-dollar increase in pay. With the family still needing more income, George studied accounting on his own at night. After five years working in the insurance business, a local bank hired him as a junior clerk at more than triple his prior salary.

Planning to take a trip with his mother, a friend talked him into buying a photography kit for the occasion. Although he did not take the trip, George became an avid amateur photographer. He studied all aspects of photography — chemistry, physics, and optics. Unsatisfied with the wet plates of the time and knowing that British technologists were experimenting with gelatin plates, he began his own experiments, which resulted in him developing his own gelatin dry plates. He then invented and patented a dry plate-coating machine. Recognizing the commercial potential of his dry plates, he opened the Eastman Dry Plate Company in 1891 with financial partner, Henry Strong, and left his career in banking. George continued to pursue his passion to simplify photography by inventing roll film. He then teamed with William Walker to develop the Eastman-Walker roll-holder to hold the film in the proper position in the focal plane of the camera. He followed this with his invention of his first camera in 1888 that he designed to use roll film. Looking for a name for his camera that could be distinct in all languages and would start and end with his favorite letter, "k", he came up with the name Kodak. Eastman targeted the camera at the second kind of amateur photographer. He sold the camera for $25 and it came loaded with a hundred-exposure roll of film. After exposing all the film, the photographer mailed the camera back to Kodak for processing and printing. The Eastman Dry Plate and Film Company, the then current name of Eastman's company, returned the photographs from the previous roll of film along with the camera loaded with another hundred-exposure roll of film for an additional ten dollars. Hence, anyone could take photographs with just the press of the button and leave the rest to Kodak. Eastman advertised the Kodak in the mass media of the time rather than photography journals. By the mid-1890s, Eastman had sold more than one hundred thousand Kodak cameras with half of them sold in Europe. In 1896, Eastman gave the final name to his company, Eastman Kodak Company.

Having popularized photography, he turned his attention to the children's market in 1900. He directed Frank Brownell to design a simple camera that could be manufactured inexpensively and still take good photographs. A camera that was made of jute board and wood, employed two simple glass lenses, used a simple rotary shutter, and took a six-exposure roll of film was the result. The camera cost a dollar and film was fifteen cents. The Eastman Kodak Company developed, printed, and mounted the six photographs for forty cents more. The first five thousand cameras sold instantly. The Kodak Company organized Brownie camera clubs and held competitions specifically for young photographers. The Brownie camera went through many makeovers and incorporated many innovations in its seventy-year history. Among its firsts were the first mass-market camera to come with a flash attachment using flash bulbs, the first camera to be made of molded plastic, and the first camera to use cartridge film. The fact that Kodak's competitors quickly imitated each new rendition attests to the Brownie's success. Throughout the Brownie's long life, Kodak held steadfast to its slogan of "You press the button, we do the rest."

George Eastman created one of the great corporate laboratories, which kept the Eastman Kodak Company ahead of the competition for much of the twentieth century in photographic papers, chemicals, and film. As a final note, Edison and his assistant William Dickson invented the movie camera and movie viewer in 1892 using flexible 35mm film supplied by George Eastman.

1903 — Airplane

See Chapter 3.

1904 — Alkaline Storage Battery

It is somewhat amazing that the alkaline storage battery that has become such a part of modern life traces its origins back to the one invented in 1904 by none other than Thomas Edison. He began working on a battery in 1900 to power electric vehicles. At the time, the electric vehicle's main advantage over those powered by an internal combustion engine was that it did not need cranking. Lead acid batteries similar to those used in today's cars powered the electric vehicles of Edison's time. Lead acid batteries required containers other than metal and were extremely heavy. Edison reasoned that an alkaline battery could be much lighter and could use metal containers. He quickly settled on potassium hydroxide as the electrolyte. However, identifying the electrodes was more difficult and the process resembled his efforts to find an appropriate filament for the light bulb. He eventually settled on iron and nickelic oxide. He brought his batteries to market in 1904, only to learn that they suffered from a number of defects. He stopped selling them in 1905 and offered to buy back all the batteries he had sold at full price. (Maybe this was the first-ever product recall). He continued to work on the battery and overcame its failings by 1910, but he was too late. By that time, Ford was producing his affordable Model T; and in 1911, Charles Kettering invented the electric starter, which the auto manufacturers installed on their gasoline-powered cars by 1915. Electric cars quickly faded from the market. Edison's battery continues to power electric vehicles where exhausts from gasoline engines are unacceptable. Examples include forklifts in factories and passenger transport vehicles in airports. Edison's alkaline battery has also proven to be a highly reliable standby emergency power source.

1904 — Vacuum tube

How many people could answer the trivia question: Who made the fundamental discovery leading up to the vacuum tube? Hint: It was not some physics professor in a European university, or an American university for that matter. It was none other than Mr. Electric Light Bulb himself, Thomas Alva Edison. Back in 1884, Edison was trying to discover why the inner glass surface of light bulbs blackened. He had a bulb made with a metal plate near the filament with an electrical wire coming out of the bulb. Edison discovered that electricity would flow from the positive side of the filament to the plate, but not from the negative side to the plate. Edison never suggested an explanation for what he observed. Nonetheless, people simply referred to it as the Edison effect. Unknowingly Edison had invented what became known as a vacuum tube diode. Electricity would flow in only one direction.

A bit later Edison hired an English university professor, Sir John Fleming, as a consultant to his Edison Electric Light Company. While working for Edison, Fleming became familiar with the Edison Effect. Now Fleming also consulted for the Marconi Wireless Telegraph Company from time to time. Early radio signal detectors, which made the signal audible, were nothing more than diodes. Fleming took Edison's light bulb with a plate and made a radio signal detector. He applied for a patent in 1904.

Lee de Forest refined Fleming's invention by adding a third element, a zigzag piece of wire between the filament and the plate. Later a screen, called a grid, replaced the zigzag wire. The grid allowed a small voltage to control a larger voltage between the filament and the plate. It was the first complete vacuum tube and because of its three elements received the name of "triode." This was the first device ever constructed capable of amplifying a signal. De Forest patented his tube in 1907 and called it an "audion." The U.S. Navy conducted a goodwill tour around the world in 1907–1908 and carried radios with de Forest's audion in them.

1906 — Gyrocompass

As noted, Elmer Sperry was one of the great individual inventors of the Rise of Technology in the United States. Few inventors obtained more patents and even fewer obtained patents in such a diversity of fields. He grew up on a farm in rural New York and received only a grade school education. Working with farm equipment stimulated an interest in machinery and technology, which he learned on his own. He attended a local teachers college or normal school and gained the determination to become an inventor. At the tender age of twenty, he formed the first of eight companies he founded during his lifetime, The Sperry Electric Company, which made dynamos and arc lamps. Other companies he founded made mining machinery, fuse wire with machines he invented, electric brakes for automobiles and streetcars, and electric cars.

The gyrocompass was by far Sperry's most famous invention and brought him the recognition as the "father of modern navigation technology." As the light bulb is to Edison, so is the gyrocompass to Sperry. He opened a new laboratory in 1900 in Washington, D.C. and continued work that he had begun on the gyrocompass in 1896. Now, G.M. Hopkins had invented the first electrical gyroscope in 1890, just as Sperry was graduating from normal school. A German scientist, Hermann Anschutz-Kaempfe, who had the goal of taking a submarine to the North Pole, actually invented the first gyrocompass in 1906. Elmer was aware of the invention. Elmer's contribution was to combine the knowledge of the gyroscope and Anschutz-Kaempfe's gyrocompass with their principles of behavior to create an improved gyrocompass which overcame the deficiencies that he found in the prior inventions. This was a hallmark of his particular inventive style. He was not an originator but a master at improving another's invention. Because the gyrocompass depended only on its own rotations and was unaffected by the "magnetic environment" that plagued the magnetic compass, its utility onboard ships was obvious. And as more and more steel and heavy electrical machinery were added to the ships, the magnetic compass, which had been introduced into wooden ships, became less and less reliable.

Sperry patented his gyrocompass in 1908 and the Navy installed one on the battleship U.S. *Delaware* in 1911. Sperry sold his gyrocompass to the German navy in 1914. At this point, Anschutz-Kaempfe sued Sperry for patent infringement in a German court. Albert Einstein was appointed an expert witness and the court found in favor of Anschutz-Kaempfe based on Einstein's recommendation. Anschutz-Kaempfe also sued Sperry in the United States and Great Britain, but in these cases the courts upheld Sperry's patent and dismissed Anschutz-Kaempfe's infringement claim. Worth noting is that Sperry was intimately involved in the defense.

Sperry's gyrocompass was such an improvement over the magnetic compass that the U.S. Navy adopted it for all its warships. He also sold it to the British and Russians during World War I. It performed so well that the Navy continued to use it with little change throughout the Second World War. Eventually, torpedoes, submarines, airplanes, and spacecraft utilized Sperry's gyrocompass technology. Sperry later modified the concept and created the gyrostabilizer, which in time found applications in the stabilization of ships, aircraft, and spacecraft. The Sperry Gyroscope Company eventually became part of the Unisys Corporation.

1907 — Electric Washing Machine

Prior to the invention of the washing machine, washing clothes involved carrying tubs and clothes to the water or vice versa. The clothes were then hand scrubbed, rinsed, hand-wrung, hang dried and then ironed with heavy heated irons. In 1805, the U.S. Patent Office issued the first American patent for a hand-operated washing machine. By 1880, the Patent Office had granted more than 4000 patents for hand-operated washing machines. This was an indication that no machine or approach had been a real winner when it came to the drudgery of washing clothes. Greater use of cotton in clothes and the invention of the sewing machine, which made available inexpensive ready-to-wear clothes, exacerbated the problem.

Two hand-operated design types are of importance. One involved two concentric horizontal cylinders. The outer cylinder held the soapy water while the inner cylinder, which held the clothes, was made of perforated metal with paddles welded lengthwise inside the cylinder. Using a hand crank to rotate the inner cylinder resulted in the paddles raising the clothes up out of the water and allowing them to fall back into the water thereby forcing the water through the fabric and achieving the desired washing effect. James King was the first to patent a machine of this type in 1851. The second type used an underwater agitator that had four blades attached to a vertical shaft, which was turned by a hand-crank on the outside of the machine. The Patent Office granted the first patent for this type of clothes washer in 1869. This type was not very effective due to the clothes becoming wrapped around the agitator until Howard Snyder of the Maytag Company developed a washing machine with an agitator with alternating reversible motion to swish the clothes back and forth through the water in 1922. The Patent Office issued the first patent for a clothes wringer, a separate attachment to the washing machine, in 1861. The wringer consisted of two cylinders, which turned in opposite directions to force the clothes between them thereby squeezing out much of the water.

Simply adding an electric motor to turn the shaft, which the hand crank turned, achieved the earliest electric washers. In fact, the first electric ones preserved the virtue of being able to be hand-cranked if the power failed. Both O. B. Wilson and Alva J. Fisher claimed to be the first to patent an electric washing machine in 1907. By 1910, a number of companies introduced electric washing machines with attached electric wringers. It was not until 1937 with the introduction of automatic washing machines that an operator was no longer required to perform the various steps of washing, rinsing and wringing. The advent of the electric washing machine in the home reduced and then eliminated the need for a laundress and the use of commercial laundries. The electric washing machine is a case of gradual evolution in innovation rather than radical change.

1908 — Interchangeable Parts in Mass Production

The use of interchangeable parts was the enabling technology that made mass production possible. The concept of interchangeable parts began with Thomas Jefferson when he was ambassador to France and saw a demonstration of uniform parts for musket locks. A few years later, Eli Whitney tried to make muskets from uniform parts but was never able to produce the precision necessary for truly interchangeable parts. Some filing and fitting of parts was necessary to assemble the final product. Finally, workers at the Harpers Ferry Armory in Virginia achieved the necessary accuracy in machining in 1822. A few years later, the Springfield Armory in Massachusetts also achieved it.

Henry Martyn LeLand grew up working in factories. During the Civil War, he honed his skills as a machinist in the Springfield Armory. After the war, he learned how to machine parts to within one-thousandth of an inch and used this ability to make the first mechanical barber's clippers. He moved to Detroit in 1890 to open an automobile engine manufacturing company, which became the primary supplier of engines to the first major automobile manufacturer, the Olds Motor Works. In 1902, the principal owner of an automobile manufacturer asked LeLand to take it over after the founder and chief engineer, Henry Ford, quit in a dispute. The company had to change its name due to the fact it could no longer use Ford's name. The name chosen was in memory of the French explorer who had founded Detroit, Antoine de la Mothe Cadillac. Here LeLand was relentless in demanding that the manufacture of parts be sufficiently precise so that filing and fitting was never necessary.

Then in 1907, Frederick Bennett, the British agent for Cadillac automobiles, visited the company's Detroit factory. The manufacturing process with its lack of filing and fitting greatly impressed him. Upon his return to London, Bennett convinced the Royal Automobile Club to sponsor a test of the precision of automobile parts. The only competitor turned out to be Cadillac. After taking three Cadillacs from stock in London, drivers drove them around a racetrack ten times to demonstrate that they were fully operable. Then mechanics completely disassembled the cars and totally mixed up the parts in the process. As a further test of interchangeability of parts, eighty-nine randomly selected parts were exchanged for replacement parts from the parts warehouse. Mechanics used the intermixed set of parts to build three cars. Drivers then drove the reconstructed cars around the racetrack five hundred miles. The Club awarded Cadillac its Dewar Trophy, which at the time almost equaled a Nobel Prize. Mass production was permanently changed. As a result, Cadillac became the top-selling brand in America. Cadillac would be the first acquisition of William Durant in the creation of General Motors.

LeLand resigned from Cadillac during World War I over LeLand's desire to make airplane engines for the war. He formed his own firm named after his favorite president, Abraham Lincoln, and between 1917 and 1918, Lincoln Motor Company turned out approximately four thousand aircraft engines. After the War, LeLand returned to making automobiles that set the standard for precision in the industry. A recession in 1921 forced him to sell the firm at auction to no other than Henry Ford. LeLand retired at this point and his name was overshadowed by all those he taught the importance of precision. Ironically LeLand, who is relatively unknown yet was a true giant in the rise of American technology, began the two nameplates, Cadillac and Lincoln, that would head the marquee of the two giants, General Motors and Ford respectively.

1913 — Assembly Line

See Chapter 6.

1913 — Electric Refrigerator

Use of ice to keep food from spoiling dates back to before George Washington's time when he had a large icehouse at his Mount Vernon Estate. Iceboxes became rather commonplace in the American home after 1890. By 1914, Americans used 21 million tons of ice annually. In 1805, Oliver Evans conceived the idea of the continuous circulation of a refrigerant in a closed cycle. All modern refrigeration systems work this way. Jacob Perkins built and patented the first closed-cycle vapor compression refrigerator in 1834. A French monk, Marcel Audiffren, conceived the idea of an electric refrigerator for home use in 1910. Fred Wolf invented the first electric refrigerator in 1913. The basement housed the condenser. Alfred Mellowes built the first refrigerator to contain all of its components in 1915. General Motors acquired the rights to Mellowes' refrigerator in 1918 and began mass marketing of it under the brand name Frigidaire in 1919. Kelvinator came out with the first refrigerator with automatic controls in 1918. Despite these advances, only a few thousand homes had refrigerators at the close of the decade (1920).

General Electric bought the rights to the General Motors refrigerator, and one of its engineers, Christian Steenstrup, improved the design to include a hermetically sealed motor and reciprocating compressor that is standard today. GE produced the first units in 1927. Steenstrup went on to acquire more than 100 patents of which at least 39 were in refrigeration. In this vignette on the refrigerator, one sees that it went through an evolutionary development cycle with first General Motors and then General Electric laboratories being responsible for furthering its development.

1913 — Thermal Cracking Process

The oil industry in the United States had its beginnings in the production of kerosene for use in lighting. By the mid-1880s, the annual production of refined oil reached eighteen million barrels of which eighty percent was kerosene for use in lamps. Solvents and lubricating oils comprised the remainder. Standard Oil was by far the dominant oil refiner and supplier with a 90% market share and exploited its position in the market place. At this point, the perfect storm rocked the oil industry over the next few decades. Pennsylvania was the center for oil production and its oil fields were running out. Exploration resulted in finding new oil fields in Ohio and Indiana, but the oil contained high quantities of sulfur that gave the refined products an undesirable smell. Edison and his electric industry were replacing kerosene lamps in urban and suburban America with electric lighting. Demand for kerosene was shrinking. The passage of the Sherman Anti-Trust Act in 1890 and its application to Standard Oil brought the break up of Standard Oil into its thirty-three subsidiaries in 1911. Gasoline consumption by automobiles created a growing demand by 1900. However, when Ford began producing automobiles on his assembly line in 1913, the demand for gasoline exploded. Distilling petroleum yielded approximately 40% kerosene and 15% gasoline. This was clearly the wrong ratio to meet the changing demand for refined products.

Herman Frasch had been a contractor to Standard Oil from 1876 to 1885; he left Standard Oil to buy an oil field near London, Ontario. The oil from this field was also high in sulfur; but Frasch had found that reusable copper and lead oxides successfully removed the sulfur. Standard Oil hired Frasch back as chief chemist and the oil fields of Ohio and Indiana provided an assured oil supply through the application of Frasch's process.

William M. Burton earned the first American Ph.D. in chemistry at Johns Hopkins University in 1889. He then went to work for Standard Oil as Frasch's assistant. In a short time, he moved to the Whiting, Indiana refinery that soon became Standard Oil's largest refinery, processing one third of the oil produced in the United States. Burton did not feel sufficiently challenged by routine laboratory work so he entered into management. He became vice-president of Standard Oil of Indiana in

1903. When the need for more gasoline became critical, his attention returned to research. Working with Dr. Robert E. Humphreys, the head of the Whiting Refinery's laboratory, and Dr. F. M. Rogers, an assistant, they began searching for a process to extract more gasoline from a barrel of oil. They tried heat with lighter oils, using aluminum chloride as a catalyst, heat with steam, et cetera. When nothing really worked, they decided to use heat and pressure which was dangerous because of the risk of explosion. Finally, in 1913, they found the right combination of heat and pressure that doubled the yield of gasoline from a barrel of oil.

Burton's thermal cracking process became the basis for gasoline production for some time. This was a case where experimentation led to results, which the science of chemistry had yet to explain. The process presented new and difficult challenges to the steel fabrication industry. Namely, it had to devise methods of building the necessary large pressure vessels at a time prior to the invention of welding. It was not long before other oil companies patented variants of Burton's original process. Litigation ensued and in 1931, the oil companies agreed to share their processes. The revelation that a Russian engineer received a Russian Empire patent for thermal cracking oil in 1891 may have partially stimulated this agreement. Nevertheless, the thermal cracking of petroleum begun by Burton was the first step on a path of continually increasing and improving the products produced from a barrel of crude oil. This has played a significant role in generally keeping the supply of gasoline up with the demand. This example illustrates just how important the corporate research laboratories had become to the well being if not the survival of the corporation by the dawn of the golden age of technology in America.

1917 — Food Quick Freezing

Henry Benjamin of Britain obtained the first known patent for quick freezing fish by immersion in a mixture of ice and salt water in 1842. Commercial exploitation of the concept required the invention of mechanical refrigeration. Still, as previously discussed there frequently is much involved in demonstrating an application of the principle, in building a prototype, and in realizing a commercially viable product. Clarence Birdseye worked in Labrador as a fur trader. Seeking to keep his wife and new baby well fed, he began to experiment with preserving vegetables in the freezing winds of Labrador. He learned that placing the vegetables in salt water and then the freezing winds preserved the vegetables without losing their fresh taste. He went on to apply what he learned to fish and rabbits. By 1924, he borrowed money against his life insurance and found three willing partners to invest in his new General Seafoods Company, which was located in Gloucester, Massachusetts. Although few American homes had refrigerators and there was a general lack of processing and distribution facilities, Birdseye found small niches for his products. Frozen foods were generally not competitive in the market place with canned or fresh foods. Birdseye continued to refine his freezing methods and delivered lectures and promotional talks on frozen foods. Then World War II brought shortages of both canned and fresh foods and presented Birdseye with expanded opportunities. Birdseye developed quick food freezers, which were transportable to the field at harvest time. Thus, he was able to freeze, for example, green peas within minutes of being picked from the vine. The improved appearance and flavor of frozen foods eventually overtook America's preference for canned goods but it was not until after World War II. Sometime after its founding, Birdseye's partners organized General Seafoods into General Foods.

The foregoing vignettes further illustrate how the technology cycle evolved and how the corporate research laboratories came to dominate the product development cycle. These vignettes also illustrate just how important the research laboratories became to the overall well being of their corporate parents.

Chapter 8. Technology's Golden Age

"You will never know when you're living in a golden age." — Alexander Payne

After World War I and until the end of the Cold War, technology flourished in America. For most of this period, conditions were very conducive to technological innovation. Heroes included Ford, Edison, Bell, and Einstein. The general perception was that one could find a technological solution to almost any problem. Funding for technology development was ample. Companies prided themselves in their research laboratories. In addition, the Federal Government turned to research laboratories for all manners of things. Researchers enjoyed relatively good salaries and oftentimes the freedom to pursue their dreams. As a result, new products entered the market at almost torrential rates. American made products flooded the world. This was indeed the Golden Age of technology in America.

Defining the conditions under which technology flourishes is a somewhat daunting endeavor. Certainly adequate funding for research is essential. An ample supply of very capable and well-trained technology developers is required. This implies the need for outstanding educational institutions. There needs to be significant rewards to those successful in developing technology. This certainly includes monetary, personal satisfaction, esteem of peers and others, and a sense of contribution to society. These certainly abounded during technology's Golden Age. There also needs to be a significant return on investment for those investing in technology development, whether they are private investors, corporations, or government. This was certainly the case during the twentieth century. Examples abound. GE's investment in the lamp business including the development of the tungsten filament yielded a 30% return on investment during the 1920s. The entire electronics industry or computer software industries testify to the rich returns on investments in research and development. Government's returns have been equally great from the winning of wars (e.g., the atomic bomb to end World War II and the engagement of the Soviets in a technological investment competition that led to their economic collapse to end the Cold War) to the achievement of a national pride of accomplishment in the landing of men on the moon. Government's investment in technology has resulted in the electrification of rural America (e.g., the TVA), the eradication of numerous diseases (e.g., small pox, polio, measles, and tuberculosis), an improved environment, and safer homes, work places and transportation.

From just before the First World War through the Twenties, technologists and inventors were in some sense the darlings of society. Although the inventors tended to stay aloof of society, they had access to America's tycoons. Early investors in technology development included the head of W. R. Grace and Company, Charles R. Flint; the financier of the Niagara Falls hydroelectric project, Edward Dean Adams; John Jacob Astor; the mayor of Chicago and editor of the Tribune, Joseph Medill; the son of President Rutherford Hayes; the financier J. P. Morgan; railroad magnate, Cornelius Vanderbilt; banker August Belmont; the Carnegie Corporation; and the Rockefeller Foundation. Almost everyone with the funds to do so invested in the technologists of the early twentieth century.

The public revered Edison and Bell to the point of their becoming almost mythological. They along with some others were front-page news. Stories abounded and one can argue that eventually they became caricatures in our history textbooks. Nonetheless, scientists and innovators from Edison to Einstein were as much America's heroes as presidents, movie stars, and sports figures. Boy Scouts and schoolchildren built telegraph keys, even made simple telegraphs, and learned Morse code. Lessons about Bell and the telephone always followed those about Samuel Morse and the telegraph. School students learned about Edison and performed all manner of electrical "experiments." Einstein was a household name in the forties and fifties. Teachers taught science together with the history of its practitioners in all grades and included learning about its applications such as the light bulb, the telegraph, and the telephone. People felt great admiration for American inventors and had much pride in their exploits. A sense of awe and wonder overcame the American public.

Technology was news and sometimes was the star of television programs. When computers were brand new, everything from game shows to news programs portrayed them with their flashing lights. Walter Cronkite, a legendary television news reporter and anchor, was the first to use a computer to make a prediction in the 1952 presidential election. The computer was just as much a part of the news as was the election as depicted in Figure 8.1.

The story about the use of the computer to predict the election outcome is nothing short of astonishing. The election pitted Dwight Eisenhower against Adlai Stevenson. The polls had them in a dead heat. The driving issue was an epic global struggle between democracy and communism. The Korean War had begun two years earlier, Senator Joseph McCarthy's "Red Scare" was going strong, and several nations were testing nuclear bombs. In the summer of 1952, Remington Rand approached CBS news chief, Sig Mickelson, about using the sole Univac in existence to predict the election outcome based on past voting patterns. Mickelson and Cronkite thought it to be no more than a publicity stunt but thought it would enliven the election night broadcast.

FIGURE 8.1 WALTER CRONKITE (RIGHT) USES COMPUTER FOR

FIRST ELECTION PREDICTION

Photo Courtesy of Unisys Corporation

University of Pennsylvania statistician, Max Woodbury, developed the statistical algorithms for the prediction software. The 16,000-pound UNIVAC stayed in Pennsylvania and a fake computer was set up in CBS's television studio (Figure 8.1). By 8:30 PM ET on election night and before the polls closed on the west coast, the computer predicted Eisenhower would get 438 electoral votes to Stevenson's 93 based on only a few million votes (less than 7% of the votes cast) having been counted. CBS did not believe the results and refused to report the prediction. Under pressure from CBS, Woodbury reworked the algorithms and with new results, Cronkite reported that the Univac gave 8 to 7 odds, that Eisenhower would win the election. Woodbury found an error in the modified algorithm and after correcting it, he got results corresponding to the original prediction. Late that night as the results piled up, CBS realized its mistake and that the UNIVAC predictions had been correct. CBS confessed to millions of viewers that the UNIVAC had predicted the results hours earlier. In fact, the UNIVAC was in error by less than 1% on the electoral vote and 3% on the popular vote.

The UNIVAC captured the American imagination. Edward R. Murrow, another famous television commentator of the time, made the remark that would become famous through repetition: "The trouble with machines is people." Similarly the quest to put man on the moon captured the public's attention making the live TV broad-cast of Neil Armstrong's first step on the moon the most watched program up to that time and the most memorable of all times. A central player in the broadcast was Houston control with its myriad of workstations powered by computers. These ex-amples highlight the standing that technology had with the American people during the golden age of technology.

This admiration and pride brought with it great expectations, namely, the belief that any problem was subject to a technical solution. The development of weapons that would over power an enemy could eradicate war. In the case of the nuclear stand-off between the Soviet Union and the United States, it could even lead to mass de-struction. Finding the cause of a disease and developing an appropriate vaccine could lead to its eradication. Mass produced or even factory produced houses could provide necessary housing. Technical solutions to congestion seemed possible. The panacea to solving the rising crime problem in America's cities lay with systems analysis and engineering. Expectations included finding technical solutions for finding and eradi-cating illegal drug production. The list goes on and on seemingly without end.

As an example, a number of Federally Funded Research and Development Centers (FFRDCs), which were founded and operated under the auspices of various offices of the Department of Defense, began to assist other Government agencies with their expertise. Examples included the Department of Justice including the FBI, the Fed-eral Aviation Administration, Housing and Urban Development, the Social Security Administration, and the Department of Highways. (The Federal Government estab-lished FFRDCs to provide capabilities and services that were not available within the Government or from industry.) The Rand Corporation, which existed to assist the Air Force, gave up some traditional areas of work so that it could apply its remarkable systems skills to pressing urban problems. MITRE Corporation added new FFRDCs to serve the Federal Aviation Administration, the Internal Revenue Service, and the U.S. Department of Veterans Affairs. Aerospace Corporation provided systems engi-neering support to the Department of Justice and the Department of Transportation. The Jet Propulsion Laboratory, a NASA FFRDC, developed a hybrid vehicle and a smart highway system for the Department of Transportation and a real time weather reporting system for the Federal Aviation Administration.

Another example of the hold that science and technology had on America is that Taylor's scientific management concepts, which were discussed in the previous chap-ter, grew into the fields of operations research, systems analysis, and systems engi-neering. These latter areas now permeate everything from the mundane, such as a queue in a fast food restaurant, to the ultra complex, such as a major construction project or a manned mission to Mars. (Queue management is a simple application of operations research. The single queue/multi-server approach is the fairest to the customers in that it minimizes the median wait time for customers.)

Although discussion of the biological sciences and related technologies is very limited in this book, it is clear that the period starting with the First World War has been a Golden Age for them as well. One might say that the growth of the electronics industry made possible many developments in medical diagnostics and monitoring systems (e.g., MRI systems and intensive care monitoring systems). The U.S. pharmaceutical industry has grown from being quite modest in 1960 to one of the largest and most profitable industries in the United States. This industry has flourished by using patents for a competitive advantage. Thus, it maintains an aggressive research and development effort. As an aside, only a small percentage of the drugs that are developed make it to market — the winnowing effect is prevalent here as well. American technology has largely been the basis for mapping the human genome. Today, the word "DNA" is used in general conversation. Today, drug development and usage, criminal identification, and agriculture make use of an understanding of DNA.

Futurists, not anticipating the development of super strains of rice, predicted in the 1960s that mass starvation would occur in many parts of the world by the end of the twentieth century. Researchers have developed strains of rice tailored to specific growing environments. The impact has been that many nations have become self-sufficient with regard to food production.

Scientists have made considerable progress in the understanding of the biosphere. Ecology and environmental science are major growth areas. "Green" is good for business. Again, American research and development provided major underpinnings for all the foregoing.

Given this backdrop, funding for technology development was more than adequate and at times plentiful. Corporations could achieve extremely high returns on their investment in research and development. News organizations chronicled the exploits of their laboratories. Furthermore, these exploits were a source of corporate pride. Corporations competed to have the "best" laboratory in this environment. Patents afforded companies a legal means of having a competitive advantage. As pointed out in the previous chapter the intent of the anti-trust laws was not the preventing of companies from dominating the marketplace by offering superior products and services. Previous chapters have already highlighted the cases of AT&T and GE. (Moreover, by no means were they unique.) Later, AT&T operated as a regulated monopoly (i.e., utility) and a portion of its rates went to fund Bell Laboratories. Under this arrangement, Bell Laboratories continued to flourish until the breakup of AT&T. (The Government's case against AT&T was over the use of the regional Bells monopoly/utility position to subsidize the long distance business in a predatory manner in violation of the anti-trust laws.) Other corporations were able to maintain a vigorous research agenda while operating in many respects as a virtual monopoly and staying within the anti-trust laws. These include IBM and its Watson Laboratories and Xerox and its Xerox PARC. More recently, the list includes Intel Corporation and its research laboratories. Interestingly, the Government's case against Microsoft was not over its virtual monopoly relative to the Windows operating system for personal computers, but rather over the use of this position in a predatory manner to enhance its business in other areas of the software market (i.e., browsers).

As indicated, the Government also sought solutions by funding research. The beginning of Government funded research and development was during World War I. Edison and the Secretary of the Navy conceived the Naval Consulting Board, which Edison headed. As head, Edison recommended that the Navy establish a laboratory to develop all manner of naval equipment. The Secretary of the Navy established the Navy Research Laboratory based on this recommendation. The National Academy of Sciences persuaded President Wilson that it could bring science to bear on such problems as anti-submarine warfare. (The sinking of the *Sussex* by a German submarine brought this to the forefront.) As a result, the Academy established the National Research Council to support the Government in science and technology matters and it continues to do so out of facilities on M Street in Georgetown. Thus was born an essential alliance between Government and technology.

World War II provided the greatest boost to this alliance. Fear that the Germans would develop the atomic bomb led to the most significant and massive technology development effort ever. The Manhattan Project encompassed every conceivable resource in its quest to beat the Germans. The scale of the effort is almost unimaginable. New laboratory facilities were built in a matter of months. The number of technical problems, which required solution, was immense. In the end, the scale and approach of subsequent efforts (e.g., the development of the ICBM, the nuclear submarine program, and the space program including the Apollo program) would forever change the research and development process.

During much of the Cold War, the Department of Defense enjoyed adequate funding for its research and development programs conducted by the service laboratories and its Defense Advanced Research Projects Agency (DARPA). The service laboratories were numerous and included the Naval Research Laboratory, the Naval Electronics Laboratory, the Naval Undersea Research Laboratory, the Air Force Weapons Research Laboratory, the Air Force Aeronautics Research Laboratory, the Army Night Vision Laboratory, the Army Ballistics Research Laboratory, and the Army Research Laboratory. Every aspect of warfare had a research laboratory to support it with new technology based solutions.

The art of warfare was not the only Government alliance with technology. Congress established the National Institute of Standards and Technology (NIST), which began life as the National Bureau of Standards, in 1901. NIST's mission is to "promote U.S. innovation and industrial competitiveness by advancing measurement science, standards, and technology in ways that enhance economic security and improve our quality of life." Among its activities is the conduct of research that enhances the nation's technology infrastructure (e.g., devices and standards of measurement), promotes performance excellence, and leads to potentially revolutionary technologies. NIST is the technology arm of the Department of Commerce, which helps American companies have a competitive advantage in the global marketplace.

The National Oceanic and Atmospheric Agency (NOAA) history dates to 1807 with the formation of the U.S. Coast and Geodetic Survey, the Weather Service in 1870 and the Bureau of Commercial Fisheries in 1871. The U.S. Coast and Geodetic Survey was America's first Government agency dedicated to the physical sciences. NOAA's science and technology achievements include improved measurement and monitoring systems for both the atmosphere and the ocean, and weather modeling and forecasting capabilities.

From its inception, the National Aeronautics and Space Administration (NASA) has been a technology driven organization. It is a product of the Cold War that the Government launched in response to the Soviet Union's orbiting of the world's first satellite, Sputnik. Its first decade was dominated by the race for the moon with the

Soviet Union and culminated with astronaut Neil Armstrong's first step on the moon and his declaration heard on radios and televisions around the world: "That's one small step for [a] man, one giant leap for mankind." NASA has pushed many techno-logical boundaries with commercial applications including those in the areas of pho-tovoltaics, communications, sensors, image processing, and composite structures in addition to the obvious technologies related to its space mission. NASA has been and continues to be a significant force in stimulating interest in science and technology.

Again responding to a crisis, the energy crisis of the 1970s, the Government estab-lished the Department of Energy (DOE) in 1977. It unified in one department the vari-ous energy related functions and organizations within the Federal Government. Its roots go back to the Tennessee Valley Authority (TVA), which was one of the largest public-works projects, and the Manhattan Project, which was one of the country's most significant research and development projects. Today, DOE conducts one of the Government's most extensive and vigorous technology research and development programs at its 21 laboratories, and through collaborations with industry.

The National Institutes of Health (NIH) traces its history to 1887. It provides most of the financial support for basic research in the health sciences through its 27 Institutes and Centers. NIH funding for research and development has grown sig-nificantly since 1995 as was discussed in Chapter 5. Its goals include protecting and improving the public's health and preventing disease.

The National Science Foundation (NSF) is the only federal agency with a mission to support basic research in all the sciences and engineering with the exception of the medical sciences. Established in 1950 "to promote the progress of science; to advance the national health, prosperity, and welfare; to secure the national defense..." the NSF provides 20% of the federal funding for Phase One basic research at America's col-leges and universities. The NSF prides itself in the funding of "high risk, high payoff" endeavors that one day may turn science fiction into the ordinary.

The foregoing discussion illustrates the degree to which technology development permeates the Federal Government. In fact, practically all Government agencies have established research programs and facilities. Figure 5.2 depicts how Government funding of research and development soared during the golden age of technology to reach 1.8% of GDP in 1965 and finally settled into the 1% range. (Industry funding of R&D grew from about 0.5% in 1953 to nearly 2% of GDP during this same time period (Figure 5.2).) This alliance between Government and technology has resulted in the most effective military systems known to mankind, the landing of man on the moon, a vast array of satellite based services, numerous vaccines, air traffic control systems, aircraft safety systems, automobile safety systems, nuclear power plants, et cetera. This alliance has influenced almost everything in modern society.

The push for technological advantage, whether from industry or government, cre-ated a great demand for researchers. This coupled with the tremendous rewards of a successful research program led to very competitive salaries for researchers. For example, DuPont hired Wallace Carothers, the inventor of nylon, in 1926 at an an-nual salary of $6000. This salary more than doubled what Harvard University was paying him. Salaries paid to scientists and engineers by industry tended to be at least twice those of academia during technology's golden age. In fact, salaries of scientists and engineers tended to be on a par with attorneys and significantly higher than the average annual wage of all workers (Figure 8.2). This does not reflect the financial rewards of founding a company that many entrepreneurial technologists received (e.g., Robert Noyce and Gordon Moore of Intel, David W. Packard and Walter Hewlett of Hewlett-Packard, **Leonard Bosack** and his wife, Sandra Lerner, of Cisco Systems, Stephan Gary Wozniak of Apple). As would be expected, the glamour (i.e., respect) and rewards (e.g., money) attracted some of the best and brightest minds to the science and engineering professions. Their contributions further enhanced their professions and thereby benefited the entire research and development enterprise.

FIGURE 8.2 HISTORICAL COMPARISON OF WAGES FOR SELECTED PROFESSIONS

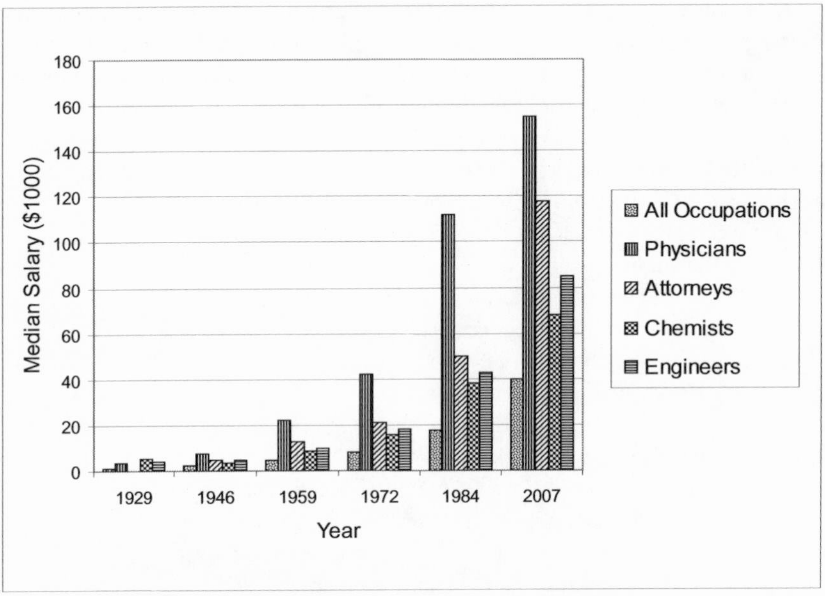

Based on data extracted from "AAES Reports the Engineering Salary Trends of 1994", "May 2007 National Occupational Employment and Wage Estimates", and Monthly Labor Reviews.

As was discussed in Chapter 6 on the rise of technology, the researcher evolved from a relatively untrained individual to one with a university education, often the recipient of a Ph.D. The demand for researchers that resulted from the establishment of corporate research laboratories and Government laboratories placed an unprecedented demand on the American universities. Edison's staffing and GE's initial staffing of their laboratories with foreign-trained researchers was a very impractical permanent solution for the country as a whole. Besides most of these immigrants were from Germany and World War I certainly interrupted the supply. Thus, it was mandatory that the American universities rise to the occasion. Government and industry also provided funding for the university faculty's research. Again, the glamour and prestige of America's evolving technology based society carried over to the universities. Funding and prestige for the universities resulted from having an outstanding research faculty, and graduating outstanding researchers. Indeed the American universities did rise to the occasion and became world renowned for their science and engineering curriculums. Today, American's universities attract the best and brightest from all over the world.

All of this resulted in a myriad of products and services. Essentially, every home appliance and power tool is a product of the golden age. All the electronic devices we have today came out of this period. Transportation systems changed greatly during this time. Technology revolutionized food production, processing, and preservation. Technology has brought a vast array of medical systems and medicines. There really is very little that technology did not affect during its golden age.

"Made in the U.S.A." became a hallmark of quality and value. At one time or another, the world-over has sought American goods. Americans have provided the world everything from clothes, to cars, to airplanes, to televisions and radios, to computers. Products that originated in America have found their way everywhere.

No matter how one looks at it, the period between World War I and the end of the Cold War has been technology's golden age.

CHAPTER 9. DISCOVERIES AND INVENTIONS OF THE GOLDEN AGE

"There are no great limits to growth because there are no limits of human intelligence, imagination, and wonder." — Ronald Reagan

The previous chapter described the conditions, which created the Golden Age, and indicated the scope and prowess of American researchers, developers, engineers, and innovators. This chapter elaborates on the scope of American innovations during the Golden Age by presenting a very limited number of examples, which had a profound impact on the American economy, its well-being, and the world. The scope and depth represented by these examples is truly astounding. A short vignette outlining the path of discovery and innovation presents each example, except those presented elsewhere in the book. These vignettes illustrate the technology development process at work. The conditions and the results support the claim that the period between the end of World War I and the end of the Cold War has been a Golden Age for American technology.

1923–1927 — Television

See Chapter 3.

1926 — First Liquid Propellant Rocket Flight

Although China had made and used solid propellant rockets since 1180 AD, the first successful launch of a liquid propellant rocket took place in a cabbage patch in 1926 in Auburn, Massachusetts. This is an example of a demonstration of a Phase Two device. Robert H. Goddard's lifelong interest in rockets and space travel led to this historical event, which opened the door to modern rocketry, satellites, and manned space flight. Goddard's pioneering work served as a basis for much of Herbert von Braun's work on Germany's V-2 weapons during World War II, and afterwards on the United States' space program.

The reading of such books as H.G. Wells' book, *The War of the Worlds*, spawned Goddard's interests in rocketry when he was seventeen. The ability to integrate concepts from diverse fields in a very practical manner served as a major contributor to Goddard's success. Goddard moved his research program to Roswell, New Mexico in 1930. These experimental efforts most closely resemble Phase Three prototype developments, though none of them led to a production version. This is of note because on July 8, 1947 the Roswell Army Airfield erroneously issued a press release about recovering a flying saucer. Retracted, forgotten, and ignored for thirty years until "eye witnesses" came forward claiming that the Government covered up the recovery of an alien spacecraft. Since then Roswell has hosted an annual UFO festival. Unfortunately, Goddard and his team's pioneering work in rocketry near Roswell is hardly more than a footnote to the extravaganza of the UFO festival. Goddard received more than two hundred patents, most of which his wife obtained for him posthumously.

1926 — Talking Movies

The movie industry of the 1920s wanted to have nothing to do with talking movies. After all, they were making a fortune and did not want to risk their sizable profit positions by introducing something as radical as talking films. Furthermore, the few attempts at talking films had been dismal failures. Harry Warner, who detested actors, commented after being presented the idea that actors could talk in movies as on stage: "Who the hell wants to hear actors talk?"

Therefore, it is no wonder that organizations outside the film industry developed the technology for talking movies. Bell Telephone wanted better long-distance telephone equipment and RCA wanted better radios. Consequently, both companies worked to improve sound recording and playback equipment. This is an example of Phase Four or product development. Neither Bell Telephone nor RCA could, or would enter filmmaking. Warner Bros. was prosperous although it was small with big ideas. The brothers secured needed financing from Goldman Sachs in 1924. They acquired a radio station as part of their expansion in order to advertise their films. They learned of the new technology the radio and telephone industries had developed to record sound and acquired the necessary equipment from Bell Telephone. The brothers developed a plan to record the most popular musical artists on film and offer these "shorts" as added attractions to theaters, which booked their feature films. They premiered their new technology that they dubbed, Vitaphone, in 1926. More than two decades had transpired from the time of the inventions of the vacuum tube and other essential elements, which enabled talking movies, until Warner Bros. released their first Vitaphone short. The package was a traditional silent film (*Don Juan*) with recorded musical accompaniments and several shorts. They premiered the first talking film, *The Jazz Singer*, a year later with sound only when Al Jolson sang. It was a success but critics questioned the staying power of talking films. They released their second talking film, *The Singing Fool*, a year later and broke all box office records of the time. An explosion occurred in Hollywood with more reporters stationed there than in any capital of the world by the 1930s.

1928 — Sliced Bread

Since innovation is the focus of this book and essentially everyone has heard and used a phrase similar to "This is the greatest invention since sliced bread," then it is most appropriate that this chapter includes a discussion of the invention of the bread-slicing machine. Otto Frederick Rohwedder, the unheralded inventor, grew up in Iowa and became a jeweler owning three jewelry stores in St. Joseph, Missouri. He began thinking about making a bread-slicing machine in 1912. In 1916 he sold all he had to fund his idea and began developing the concept and building a prototype. Disaster struck in 1917 when a fire burned down the factory, which was to begin production of his first bread-slicing machine and destroyed all the drawings and his prototype. Convinced of the future success of his invention, he set out to raise the necessary funds and worked as an investment and security agent. He began anew in 1927 on designing a new machine, which not only sliced the bread but also wrapped it. The following year he filed for a patent and formed a company to manufacture it. Bakers were skeptical and thought the sliced bread would quickly become stale and dry. He managed to convince Frank Benchbaker, a baker friend who owned Chillicothe Baking Company in Chillicothe, Missouri to use a machine. So on July 7, 1928, sixteen years after first thinking about it, the first sliced bread from the bakery was sold to the public off grocery store shelves. This is a very early example that convenience foods sell. Continental Bakeries capitalized on this in 1930 when they went national with Wonder Bread. The "wonder" in Wonder Bread was that it was sliced. The convenience of not having to slice the bread for toast or sandwiches made it an instant success. Adding a little controversy, Battle Creek, Michigan has claimed to be the home of sliced bread. Rohwedder sold his patents and his company and sadly, nothing remains of his original bread-slicing machine. Although few know of him, his invention is the standard by which all others are compared. Rohwedder's development of the bread-slicing machine provides a good example of the last two phases of the technology development cycle.

1930 — Freon

Prior to 1930 refrigeration units used a variety of gases for the coolant, including ammonia, sulfur dioxide and methyl chloride. These gases were either toxic or explosive. In fact, in the 1920s a refrigerator in a hospital in Cleveland leaked methyl chloride that resulted in an explosion. At the close of World War II, many homes still relied on iceboxes, and air conditioning was a novelty used to market movie theaters. Charles Kettering, director of research for General Motors, decided that they had to replace the sulfur dioxide which they used in their Frigidaires with a nontoxic and non-explosive refrigerant with good thermal properties. The task eventually fell on the shoulders of Thomas Midgley, Jr., Albert Hanne, and Robert McNary. They quickly identified difluoromethane (Freon) as having the right thermal properties and the right boiling point for use as a refrigerant. The only question was whether it was toxic. They prepared a few grams of Freon, put it into a closed chamber with a guinea pig, and were delighted to see that the animal seemed to suffer no ill effects. A setback occurred when the second batch killed the guinea pig. It turned out that an impurity in one of the ingredients produced a potent poison. A simple procedure completely removed the poison and the guinea pigs survived. Amazingly, it took a mere three days to complete this research project. However, this is nothing more than an example of product development or Phase Four of the technology development cycle. Refrigeration had been evolving for decades. The availability of a safe refrigerant had a profound impact on the United States. Not only did electric refrigerators become standard, so did air-conditioned homes, businesses, and cars. The Montreal Protocol on Substances that Deplete the Ozone Layer banned the production and consumption of freon in 1996.

1935 — Neoprene and Nylon

At the time of World War I, E. I. du Pont de Nemours and Company (DuPont) was an explosives manufacturer. Being concerned about its future and recognizing the need to diversify, Du Pont built a laboratory and hired a team of academic scientists to perform basic research in chemistry. A team headed by Wallace Carothers took on the study of polymers at the suggestion of the director of research, Charles Stine. At the time, chemists knew little about polymers and producing them was more alchemy than chemistry. Carothers proved that they were giant molecules with a repeated pattern. While studying short polymers of acetylene, a highly flammable gas, they literally stumbled onto neoprene, the first synthetic rubber. Being unaffected by oil, gasoline and temperature changes, it was ideal for belts, hoses and gaskets for automobile engines. Carothers' luck did not end there. Pursuing polyester molecules of unlimited size made from acids and alcohols, Carothers observed that the chemical reaction was producing water; the water was decomposing the polyester; and this decomposition was limiting the molecule's size. After successfully removing the water as the reaction produced it, Carothers found that he could stretch the polyester molecules to form very strong fibers. These were the first synthetic fibers. Luck had struck again. The low melting point of the polyester fibers made them unsuitable for textiles. Turning to another chemical group, Donald Coffman of the research team discovered the family of molecules that Du Pont coined nylon. Now the best nylon fiber the laboratory discovered was not the one that became a commercial success due to its being difficult to produce. Although the bristles of toothbrushes and ladies' stockings in which nylon replaced silk comprised the first uses of nylon, it found many applications during World War II because it was stronger than steel on a weight basis, almost nonflammable, nonabsorbent, and resisted abrasion. Nylon was the first commercially successful synthetic fiber. This example illustrates:

- Phase One, discovery, in the study of various molecular groups' properties.
- Phase Two, device, in the creation of neoprene and nylon.
- Phase Three, prototype, in the selection of the precise nylon molecule to be commercialized.
- Phase Four, product development, in the development of applications such as fan belts and tooth brushes.

1938 — Xerox

James Watt of steam engine fame was the first to develop and patent a letter-copying machine in 1780. It produced copies of documents by pressing a very thin piece of paper on the original, on which the author had used a special ink. By reading from the backside of the copy, one could read the writing normally. People used his letterpress to make copies throughout the nineteenth century. Even Edison invented a copier in 1877. A. B. Dick invented the mimeograph, which used a special stencil and a gelatin material to pick up the ink from the stencil and transfer it to the copy. One master stencil could make a hundred or more copies. Mimeographs were in common use, especially in schools, well into the 1970s. Developers created a variety of photographic methods in the early 1900s that included photostats and blueprints, which employed light sensitive paper in contact with the original. By coating paper with a heat sensitive material one can make copies using a technique called thermography. In 1944, Carl Miller developed a thermography-based system, the Thermofax, which Minnesota Mining and Manufacturing Company built and distributed.

Chester F. Carlson invented Xerography in 1938 when he successfully transferred the inscription "10-22-38 Astoria" onto waxed paper. He used electrostatic charges to image the document. Then, particles of a dry powdered ink that had a charge opposite to that of the image would adhere to the electrostatic image. He completed making the copy by using heat from a sun lamp to fuse the image created by the ink particles permanently onto the waxed paper. Commercial success was far from immediate.

Thank goodness, Chester came from a humble background and lived frugally. He used ten dollars a month from his meager earnings from his job at the P.R. Mallory Company to finance the development of his copier. It was not until 1946 that he finally interested the Haloid Corporation, a photographic company, into licensing his copier. It took another fourteen excruciating years of development involving Carlson, the Haloid Corporation's financial backing, and engineers and scientists at Battelle Memorial Institute before the first Xerox 914 entered the market in 1960. Twenty-two years had transpired since Carlson first demonstrated xerography. The Haloid Corporation changed its name to the Xerox Corporation and royalties from Xerox allowed Chester to donate $100 million to research organizations and charitable foundations before his death in 1968.

Chester's Xerox has become a synonym for the act of making a copy. Furthermore, all laser printers employ xerography in their printing mechanisms. Xerox's impact on communications is difficult to ponder. What if Chester had given up on his invention? How many people would devote eight years to something that seemed to be going nowhere? Furthermore, what if neither Haloid nor any other company had come forward to back the final development of the Xerox copier? Why did Haloid's management continue to support an extremely challenging development for fourteen years? If the effort had failed, it certainly would have been a good case study for the *Harvard Business Review.*

Chester's first demonstration of a Xerox prototype is a good example of Phase Three in the technology development cycle. He continued in prototype development until the Haloid Corporation became involved. The effort with Battelle is an example of Phase Four in the development cycle.

1943 — Silly Putty

Silly Putty was truly an invention looking for a problem to solve. James Wright, a researcher at General Electric, was trying to come up with a synthetic rubber when he combined boric acid and silicone oil. Although the resulting gooey blob was no replacement for rubber, it possessed some rather interesting elastic properties and when made into a ball it would bounce 25% higher than an ordinary rubber ball. However, James could not think of anything useful to do with the stuff. He sent samples to scientists around the world and they all came back with nothing. Two other inventors, Earl Warrick and Rob Roy McGregor, working for Dow Corning, claimed to have received their patent for the substance before Wright did. Evidently, they both invented the substance independently and simultaneously. However, Binney and Smith, the makers of Crayola crayons and the owner of the rights and distributor of Silly Putty, credit Wright as the inventor. In any case, it was James Wright who found that its most salient characteristic was that it was fun to play with. He would entertain guests at parties with the gooey stuff. Eventually, Peter Hodgson, an advertising consultant, became aware of it in 1949, gave it the name of Silly Putty and sold an ounce of it in a plastic colored egg for a dollar. It was a marketing miracle and became one of the top selling toys for a period. Sometimes, R&D failures find success in a most unexpected manner.

1943–1946 — Digital Computer

Computers, devices that perform mathematical calculations, have been around since the first century BC. Divers found a mechanism used to calculate astronomical locations that dated back to approximately 100 BC in a shipwreck off the coast of a Greek Isle. Numerous mechanical devices were invented prior to the electronic computer. Herman Hollerith devised a punched-card calculator to aid the Census Bureau in processing the 1890 data, thereby reducing the time to complete the census from seven years in 1880 to one year. The hanging chads of the 2000 election became an important turning point in presidential elections. Hollerith invented the punched card, the first cardpunch, and the first card reader and tabulator. In 1911, his company and three other companies combined to form what would later bear the moniker, IBM.

An English group of mathematicians and engineers working on machines for code breaking (cryptography) invented the first electronic digital computer, the Colossus, in 1943. The Colossus was a specialized machine designed just to break German encrypted messages. One of the inventors of the Colossus was Alan Turing. Now, Alan was the first person to document the concept of a general-purpose computer in a paper he wrote in 1936.

The American military required a reliable and quick means of producing mathematical tables used to aim artillery during World War II. John Eckert and John Mauchly spent three years at Pennsylvania's Moore School of Engineering devising a solution they coined the Electronic Numerical Integrator and Calculator (ENIAC). Completed in 1946, this was the world's first electronic general-purpose digital computer. It takes three qualifiers to make it a "first." The ENIAC contained more than 17,000 vacuum tubes, 70,000 resisters, and 10,000 capacitors. It took about five million hand-soldered joints to connect the parts together. Finally, it weighed in excess of 50,000 pounds, took up nearly 700 square feet of space, and consumed more than 150 kilowatts of electricity. Its size and complexity were truly overwhelming.

John von Neuman joined Eckert and Mauchly in designing ENIAC's successor, the Electronic Discrete Variable Automatic Computer (EDVAC). The EDVAC was the first computer that could accommodate a stored program as visualized by Turing. Frustrated over patent issues, Eckert and Mauchly left the Moore School of Engineering and formed the Electronic Control Company. Under contracts to the National Bureau of Standards and the Census Bureau, they began work on the Universal Automatic Computer (UNIVAC). As happens in high-tech development projects, they ran into overrun problems and the Government did not bail them out. They then took on several smaller projects in order to pay for the overrun. One was with Northrop Corporation for an airborne computer, which would be the first commercial sale of a stored-program computer. Bad business decisions and misfortune forced Eckert and Mauchly to sell their company to the Remington Rand Corporation. IBM had the chance to buy it but demurred. Eckert and Mauchly finished the UNIVAC using Remington Rand resources.

As noted earlier the UNIVAC ushered in the information age with its 1952-election prediction. Those first computers were more prototypes than they were early production units. The UNIVAC would eventually go into production more than a decade after the invention of Colossus in 1943. For a period, it did not matter what company made the computer, the public referred to them as a UNIVAC. This is no different than a facial tissue being referred to as a Kleenex or cellophane tape being referred to as Scotch tape.

1945 — Atomic Bomb

The effort to build the "bomb" began in earnest in 1942 under the management of the Manhattan Military District and was quickly dubbed the Manhattan Project. The research and development of the atomic bomb was incomprehensibly large and complex. Scientists developed the theory almost simultaneously with laboratory tests, which were nearly simultaneous with building the "bomb" itself. That is, the performance of the first three phases of technology development was nearly simultaneous. The Government considered the Project so important that researchers and developers were able to obtain anything they thought was required for the success of the project. The Manhattan Project had the three cities of Oak Ridge, Tennessee, Hanford, Washington, and Los Alamos, New Mexico built practically overnight to house significant portions of the development as a means of protecting the secrecy of the project. This did not count the myriad of other plants across the country that was involved in one aspect or another of the effort. The Project assembled a diverse team of two hundred of the best scientists the country had to offer at Los Alamos, New Mexico under the direction of J. Robert Oppenheimer to design and build the bombs. Numerous technicians and craftsmen supported their efforts.

General Leslie Groves, the project manager, selected Oppenheimer to be the technical director because of Oppenheimer's diverse technical skills and keen mind. His intellectual capabilities are legendary. Missing his first year at Harvard due to illness, he completed undergraduate work in three years by taking six courses at a time and graduated magna cum laude. He not only took math and science courses, he had great interest in Greek architecture, the classics, art and literature. His major was chemistry but Harvard admitted him as a graduate student in physics based on independent study without his ever taking a college course in physics. His scientific research was all over the map of theoretical physics. Consequently, Oppenheimer became known as a founding father of the American school of theoretical physics. His role on the Manhattan project brought him the distinction of "father of the atomic bomb." He never received the Nobel Prize in spite of his accomplishments.

The first successful detonation of an atomic bomb occurred on July 16, 1945, a mere three years after the start. Nothing before or after has been accomplished like that of the atomic bomb. The first test and the bombs used on Japan were truly prototypes. The Manhattan Project illustrates the first three phases of the technology development cycle with the emphasis on Phase Three of prototype development. The fourth phase of developing production units came after the end of World War II.

1945 — U.S.'s First Guided Rocket Test

Hungarian born, Theodore von Karman received his Ph.D. from the University of Gottingen in Germany in 1908. It was in 1908 that he saw an airplane for the first time and was hooked on flying machines. In 1930, he immigrated to the United States to become director of the Guggenheim Aeronautical Laboratory at the California Institute of Technology (Caltech). He and his student, Frank Malina, began experimenting with rockets in 1935. The U.S. Army Air Corps took note of von Karman's team and began to fund their research. This led to the establishment of the Jet Propulsion Laboratory and the invention of the jet assisted takeoff rocket. The team's rocket research, which was funded by the Army, led in 1944 to the first ever Government contract to develop a liquid guided rocket to become known as the Corporal. After numerous failures of which some were most spectacular, the Corporal made its first successful flight barely a year after initiating prototype development. (This was still a decade after von Karman's first rocketry experiments at Caltech.) In this example, von Karman performed Phase Two research that led directly into JPL's Phase Three development of the prototype Corporal. Firestone Tire and Rubber Company became the production contractor for the first 200 Corporal missiles. Again, decades transpired between the first experiments in rocketry and production of the Corporal.

1946 — Microwave Oven

See Chapter 3.

1948 — Transistor

See Chapter 1.

1948 — LP (Long Playing) Record

As with many corporate developments, several contenders have vied for the credit of inventing the LP depending on who was telling the story and what their position within the corporate structure was. First, RCA claimed to be the first company to introduce an LP record into the marketplace in 1932. Thus, their researchers claimed the title of LP inventor. However, the combination of player and record that RCA brought to market reproduced sound so poorly that it had to be withdrawn from the market a year later.

Columbia Broadcasting System (CBS) earned the recognition as the developer of the modern LP since it was their system which became the lasting standard in the marketplace. A prominent version of the story has Peter Goldmark as the inventor along with a team of engineers who worked for him at CBS. He was the director of research and engineering at CBS. As the story goes, Goldmark was at a party listening to a recording of Brahms' Second Piano Concerto played by Vladimir Horowitz. As he listened, the quality of the sound and the frequent interruptions to change records began to irritate him significantly. The concerto required six of the "78" records that were standard at the time. He immediately began work with a team of engineers on a new record format that could accommodate classical music such as the Brahms' Concerto. A number of innovations were required including vinyl disks rather than hard rubber, closer spacing of the grooves, slower speeds, quieter player mechanisms, and a lighter tone arm and cartridge. The first LP recording featured a secretary on piano, an engineer on violin, and Goldmark on cello.

In 1938, CBS acquired American Record Corporation (which controlled Columbia Records). It revived the Columbia Records label and installed Edward Wallerstein as president of the records division. Wallerstein related a very different version of the invention of the LP in an article published in *High Fidelity* magazine titled, "The Development of the LP." According to Wallerstein, work on the LP began before World War II and ceased during the war. Wallerstein restarted the effort in conjunction with CBS's president, William Paley, immediately after the war. Wallerstein claimed a very active role in the development of the LP including participating in bimonthly meetings with Paley and the development team on the progress of the LP effort. He said that he defined what constitutes a long-playing record by timing a great many classical performances. He stated, however, "The team of Liebler, Bachman, Savory, Hunter, and Kodman was responsible for it. If one man is to be singled out, it would have to be Bachman, whose work on the heated stylus, automatic variable pitch control, and most especially the variable reluctance pickup was a starting point for a great deal of what was to come." He went on to say, "Peter Goldmark was more or less the supervisor, although he didn't actually do any of the work."

Interestingly, Frank Stanton, who replaced Paley as president of CBS in 1946, provided a much different perspective in his "Reminiscences of Frank Stanton (1994)" as part of an oral history project done by Columbia University. He related the following account. "That's an interesting chapter in itself, because Wallerstein was a traditional, 78 rpm, shellac-record man. He had no use for vinyl, which was a development of the war years, and he had no interest in innovation. Goldmark was just the reverse, and I said to Wallerstein, who was then running that division of the company, if you don't want to fund this development work, I'll fund it out of corporate. But if it's a success, and you take it into your group, I'm going to charge you for all the expense that the corporation went to develop it. No problem. He just thought it was Goldmark's folly."

The reader will have to decide who, within CBS, invented the LP. In any event, the LP was not a big success until CBS released the original cast recording of *South Pacific*. LP sales grew eventually to constitute one third of CBS sales. Although the compact disk (CD) replaced the LP for mainstream recordings, the LP still has millions of aficionados who prefer records to CDs. The development of the LP, which constitutes Phase Four of the development cycle, provides an interesting insight into the world of corporate R&D. The decadal nature of the development cycle is evident with the realization that the LP built on its predecessor, the 78 record, required the World War II development of vinyl, and depended on improved electrical and mechanical components.

1948 — Polaroid Camera

A three-year-old girl asked her father why she could not see the picture he just took of her while on a family vacation. This led Edwin Land, a Harvard University dropout, to invent the first instant camera, the Land "Polaroid" Camera.

Land claimed that it took him only an hour to conceive of the basic idea for the camera. Working in secret, it took Land and a team of chemists and engineers just six months to develop the first instant camera. However, lest one draw the conclusion that the Polaroid camera is a great counter example to one of the precepts of this book that technology development is a decadal process, one needs to take cognizance of the fact that researchers had identified the basic chemistry of the camera nearly a hundred years earlier in the 1850s. Development of the Polaroid Camera consisted of a simple prototype development based on existing cameras followed by a more traditional product development. Although the original photographs were a warm-brown tone, the camera was an instant success. Land and his associates discovered how to make very good instant black and white photos within a year of the commercial roll-out of the original camera. Somewhat surprising, the Polaroid Camera has nothing to do with polarized light. Land had a passion pertaining to color perception. Seeking fame and fortune, he formed the Polaroid Company to develop and market products based on certain very small polarizing crystals. The invention of polarized glasses was essentially his only success prior to his invention of the Polaroid camera, which was indeed a great success until the advent of the digital camera. By 2009, Polaroid ceased making cameras and film. Land garnered over 500 patents in his lifetime.

1953 — DNA Structure Discovered

The quest to discover what was the genetic material and its structure began nearly a century before its accomplishment. A Swiss physician named Friedrich Miescher was the first to isolate nucleic acid, a component of DNA, in 1868. It was not until 1944 when American biologists Oswald Avery, Colin Macleod, and Maclyn McCarty isolated DNA. Their research suggested that it was indeed the long sought genetic material. Throughout the rest of the forties there remained considerable skepticism that something so simple could indeed contain the genetic code. By the 1950s there was a significant race as to who would be first to discover DNA's structure. Linus Pauling, who received the Nobel Prize in Chemistry in 1954, put forward a triple helix model and worked hard to prove it. Rosalind Franklin obtained X-ray diffraction images of DNA in 1952. American scientist James Watson and British scientist Francis

Crick used the data collected by Franklin and another researcher, Maurice Wilkins, to show the structure of DNA to be a double helix in 1953. Watson and Crick published their results in the April 1953 issue of *Nature* in which they made one of the most famous understatements ever: "This structure has novel features which are of considerable biological interest." This is a good example of Phase One, basic research.

1953 — Polio Vaccine

From the first reports of a polio epidemic in 1916 to the 1950s, polio had become a greatly feared disease. It developed into a great race among researchers to be first with a vaccine. Jonas Salk was the son of a New York garment worker and worked his way through New York University School of Medicine. Salk strongly believed in the safety of using a dead form of the virus for a vaccine. Albert Sabin emigrated with his family at the age of fifteen to the United States from Poland and received his medical degree from New York University School of Medicine. Sabin was convinced that a live virus had to be the basis of an effective and enduring vaccine. Salk won the race with a vaccine that he grew in monkey tissue culture and killed it with formaldehyde. It was shown to be 60-90% effective and incidents of polio were greatly reduced in the United States through its use. Meanwhile, Sabin developed mutant strains of the virus that would not cause paralysis in humans but was effective in causing the human body to produce the essential antibodies for immunization. The vaccine had the additional advantages that one could take it orally and Sabin never patented it, thereby reducing its cost. Misfortune struck the Salk vaccine when a pharmaceutical company produced a batch of the vaccine in which they had not completely killed the virus. The resultant cases of polio caused panic and a loss of public trust. In spite of the global impact of the polio vaccine, neither Salk nor Sabin received the Nobel Prize. Developing the vaccines was a melding of Phases Two and Three of the technology development cycle. The development of the production process by the pharmaceutical companies constituted Phase Four product development.

1954 — Transistor Radio

Development of the transistor progressed quite slowly at Bell Laboratories after its invention in 1948. Therefore, in 1951, Bell Laboratories' executives decided to license the technology to anyone interested for $25,000. Pat Haggerty, Texas Instruments' (TI) vice president, bet the company by buying a license. The germanium transistors, which Bell Laboratories made, did not work well at high temperatures or high frequencies. This limited their applicability.

TI's goal was to grow from a $20 million company to a $200 million one, and Pat saw the opportunity by replacing millions of vacuum tubes with transistors. Thus, he was eager to establish a high-volume, high-profile consumer market before anyone else did. The portable AM radio served his purposes perfectly. Therefore, even though TI was making progress with silicon transistors he decided to launch the development of the radio using germanium transistors. He believed that mass production would bring the cost of production down and that what ever they learned in the manufacture of germanium transistors would be applicable to silicon transistors.

Therefore, in late spring of 1954 Pat committed $2 million (when TI's total revenue was $20 million) to bring a transistor radio to market for Christmas of that year. He picked Paul Davis to head the effort. Pat was demanding and inspiring at the same time. Paul' response was a working prototype in four days. This exemplifies Phase Three, prototype development. Pat's goal was to sell it for $50. The design of the prototype was a straight forward one of replacing tubes with transistors. With eight transistors costing approximately $10 at the time, there was no way of meeting the $50 goal. Furthermore, Pat wanted the radio packaged in a case Emerson was using for a portable vacuum tube radio that measured 6-3/4 inches by 3 inches by 1-1/4 inches (see Figure 1.1).

TI's plan was to find a radio manufacturer with which to partner. None was interested and Pat finally found Industrial Development Engineering Associates (IDEA), an antenna booster manufacturer that was seeking to expand. After signing the agreement in June, IDEA assigned Richard Koch as their project manager. They had to reduce the size of practically every component and the number of transistors from eight to an acceptable level. They managed to cut the number of transistors in half and they miniaturized the electrolytic capacitors and the coils through highly innovative designs. IDEA placed an initial order for 100,000 sets of four transistors at a price of $10 a set, less than one quarter of the going rate for transistors. IDEA engaged the design house of Painter, Teague, and Petertil to design a plastic case that one could put into a shirt pocket. Their design was a classic one of simplicity, form, and function. This exemplifies Phase Four, product development (see Figure 1.1).

On October 18, 1954, they announced the first pocket transistor radio, Regency TR-1. IDEA and TI sold over 100,000 units over the ensuing year. Having been scooped, all the major radio manufacturers rushed to catch up and made announcements of their transistor radios during 1955. The Regency TR-1 was a technical and marketing success but it was a strategic failure. Neither IDEA nor TI made any money on the radios by selling them at $50 a piece. The marketplace would have just as readily paid $65 and with the additional funds both of the relatively small firms could have stayed in the market. Instead, a small-unknown Japanese electronics company eventually launched a superior product, the Sony radio, which it rode to become the world's consumer electronics behemoth. At TI's fiftieth anniversary celebration of the transistor radio, Pat Haggerty stated, "Had we each had the additional hundreds of thousands of dollars that the difference in pricing would have made available, and hence the funds to go on and develop additional products, we probably would have... stayed in the consumer business. I think the likelihood is very high that we would have been the Sony of consumer electronics."

1954 — Photovoltaic Solar Cell

See Chapter 1.

1960 — Laser

See Chapter 1.

1960 — Birth Control Pill

The development of the birth control pill, or simply the pill, required the understanding of a number of basic biological functions. Scientists discovered the basics of human reproduction in 1843. Emil Knauer discovered hormones in 1890. Scientists found that the pituitary gland controls reproduction in 1926. Scientists at the University of Rochester discovered progesterone in 1928. These discoveries form the foundation of the story of the pill.

Margaret Sanger was convinced that her mother's early death was largely due to her giving birth to eleven children, even though the official cause was tuberculosis. This gave Sanger a life-long passion for family planning and birth control. She was able to stimulate research on an effective contraceptive through a wealthy socialite, Katherine Dexter McCormick. McCormick was empathetic since doctors had diagnosed her husband with schizophrenia and she feared it was hereditary. As a result, she vowed never to have children and was deeply interested in birth control.

Sanger arranged a meeting of herself, McCormick, and Gregory Pincus, head of the Worcester Foundation for Experimental Biology. McCormick's promise of funding resulted in Pincus focusing his energies on finding a pill that would prevent pregnancy. Pincus organized a team and gave the task of leading the laboratory studies to Min-Chueh Chang. The goal of his research was to explore whether the manipulation of the hormones usually found in a woman could prevent pregnancy. At this time, a number of researchers were working with progesterone and estrogen to improve infertility in women. A team of researchers from the University of Pennsylvania demonstrated in 1937 that ovulation in rabbits could be prevented by injections of progesterone. Chang tested more than two hundred different progesterone and progestin compounds before finding two that seemed effective and afforded easy production. Celso-Ramon Garcia and John Rock then conducted clinical trials. Although tests showed that the pill was successful in preventing pregnancy while not interfering with pregnancy after stopping the regimen, there were some undesired bleeding problems. Adding a small amount of estrogen to the pill controlled the bleeding problems. The FDA first approved the pill for the treatment of menstrual disorders in 1957. Approval for birth control followed in 1960.

The foregoing illustrates the melding of Phases Three and Four in the determination of the appropriate ingredients of an effective birth control pill and its eventual production. Moreover, this example illustrates the decadal nature of the technology cycle in the life sciences or health sciences arena. It took more than eight decades to lay the scientific foundation for developing the pill. It took nearly another decade for researchers to discover that injecting progesterone into rabbits prevented pregnancy. Two more decades transpired before the pill was available in the marketplace.

1962 — First Communications Satellite

Arthur C. Clarke, a British science-fiction writer, proposed in 1945 that a satellite orbiting above the earth could relay television signals between different stations on the ground to provide global coverage. Bell Telephone expected that saturation of their transatlantic cables would occur by 1960. Thus, John R. Pierce at the Bell Telephone Laboratories began campaigning for the development of communications satellites in 1956 (a year before Sputnik I). The Federal Communications Commission gave permission in 1961 for Bell Telephone to begin Project Telstar, the first commercial communications satellite. NASA agreed to launch the satellites for $3 million each. Bell assigned more than 400 employees to the project at one time or another.

More than eight hundred other companies supplied products and services. Telstar 1 weighed in at just over 175 pounds and was just less than three feet in diameter. Solar batteries, which provided all of 15 watts, powered it. It could handle 600 simultaneous telephone calls or 1 television channel. The satellite's signal on earth was less than one-thirtieth of a household light bulb. The ground stations required to receive and process the satellite's signal were monsters. Bell Telephone's antenna was horn shaped and weighed 380 tons. They placed the antenna inside an inflated dome to protect it from wind and weather. The dome was approximately 200 feet in diameter and 150 feet high, making it the largest inflatable structure ever built at the time. Live television pictures of U.S. Vice President Lyndon B. Johnson and other officials gathered at the Carnegie Institution in Washington, D.C. became the first television transmission to cross the Atlantic. The first television program entitled "America, July 23, 1962," showing scenes from fifty television cameras around the United States was seen by an estimated one hundred million viewers throughout Europe. This is an example of a corporation at its best in performing Phases Three and Four of the technology development cycle.

1969 — Internet

Some perceive the Internet as the world's largest distributed machine. Moreover, its invention was also distributed. In response to the stunning launch of Sputnik I by the Soviet Union in 1957, the Department of Defense created the Defense Advanced Research Projects Agency (DARPA) to perform research in command, control, and communications systems. (DARPA's name was ARPA until 1972.) One task given DARPA was the development of a network that would survive a nuclear attack. J. C. R. Licklider, Director of Behavioral Sciences, Command & Control Research for DARPA, wrote the first known memo outlining some of the functional requirements and challenges of establishing an "Intergalactic Computer Network" in 1963. Paul Baran of the RAND Corporation wrote a seminal paper on the subject in 1964. He proposed the concept of a distributed network with no central control or hubs and redundant communication links. Each node would keep track of simple information such as network connectivity and network loading to route messages most effectively. Since each node was equal to all others, the surviving network could continue to operate and route communications around damaged elements. His second ground-breaking proposal was to break up messages into a number of pieces or packets, route these packets independently through the network, and then rejoin them at the destination computer.

Robert Taylor, then director of DARPA's Information Processing Techniques Office, started the ARPANET project in 1966. He recruited Larry Roberts from the Massachusetts Institute of Technology's Lincoln Laboratories to be DARPA's project manager. He ran the ARPANET program until 1973 when DARPA's director decided to transfer it from DARPA to the Defense Communications Agency. (The official transfer occurred in July 1975.) Roberts thereby became known as the "father of the ARPANET." Although the ARPANET's goal was to link DARPA's researchers together, Larry became aware of Baran's paper and chose the concepts put forth in the paper for the basic architecture of the ARPANET. Wes Clark, another computer scientist working on the project, suggested the concept of the Interface Message Processors (IMP). Bolt, Beranek and Newman (BBN) won the contract to develop the IMP. In October 1969, the ARPANET was born when two computers using the IMP and associated packet communications protocols successfully passed the first message between them. Ray Tomlinson of BBN introduced email in 1971 and the file transfer protocol (FTP) followed in 1973. Bob Kahn invented the Transmission Control Protocol (TCP) and along with Vincent Cerf, the Internet Protocol (IP). TCP/IP replaced the original ARPANET protocols in 1983 and became the basic protocols of the Internet. The ARPANET was a prototype in every sense of the word. Hence, its development provides an example of the third phase of the technology development cycle. Again, this is an example of a decadal development cycle.

The National Science Foundation (NSF) began building its own network in the late 1980s to provide scientists everywhere access to "mainframe" computers. This NSFNET displaced the ARPANET in 1991. The advantages and cost savings of email supplied the impetus for companies to install the hardware and interfaces to connect to the growing computer networks. The Federal Networking Council formally named the Internet in 1995 when it defined the Internet as a global information system logically linked together by the TCP/IP or its follow-up systems. Some other notable contributions to the development of the Internet include Bob Metcalfe's invention of the internet local area network protocol, Douglas Engelbart's invention of the first hypertext system, and Marc Andreesen's invention of Mosaic, the first browser.

1978 — Cell Phone

The cell phone capitalizes on a number of technologies, as was pointed out in Chapter 3. However, the concept of a mobile phone dates back to the 1920s when experiments were performed using a single frequency. This did not allow for true two-way communications. In 1949, Bell Telephone developed a system known as Mobile Telephone Service (MTS) that used two radio frequencies. Eventually they offered MTS in all the metropolitan areas of the United States. Drawbacks were numerous including an operator had to place the call back at the "home office," quality was poor, and there could be only twelve simultaneous mobile telephone calls in any one metropolitan area. Those desiring to become MTS subscribers had to wait sometimes more than ten years. Finally, the Federal Communications Commission requested proposals for a high capacity, spectrum efficient mobile system in 1968. Both Bell Telephone and Motorola proposed cellular-type systems where the use of computers would enable the repeated use of an area's frequencies. In 1978, a Bell Telephone subsidiary deployed such a system in Chicago and American Radio Telephone Service installed a similar system in Washington/Baltimore area. These two prototype systems proved the feasibility and affordability of cellular service.

Richard H. Fefrenkiel of Bell Laboratories invented and patented the cellular structure and its basic operational concepts underlying today's cell phone systems in 1978. By monitoring the signal strength of a mobile phone at the current cell's receiver, as well as those at neighboring receivers, the system can seamlessly switch the cell phone from one cell to another. This approach provided improved quality over the old MTS system and permitted many thousands of simultaneous conversations to take place within a metropolitan area using essentially the same bandwidth that the MTS used. Many others have brought extremely innovative improvements to all aspects of the cell system, including the handset, "cell towers," and making other services available. Again, this provides a good example of industry demonstrating its great capacity to perform Phase Four of the technology development cycle. In addition, the cell phone development did not happen over night but was the result of decades of research and development.

1981 — Personal Computer (PC)

IBM invented the Personal Computer (PC) and gave it its name. Prior to this, the computers of its genre were simply microcomputers. As previously indicated the PC was IBM's third try at such a machine. Faced with competition from Apple and other microcomputer makers and predictions of 40% growth during the 1980s for microcomputers, IBM desperately needed the PC. Frank Carey, IBM's CEO at the time, gave the task of designing and building the PC in a year to William Sydnes and a team of twelve engineers. Sydnes recognized the need to separate the development of the PC from IBM's corporate structure and mentality. Outside vendors supplied many of the parts and all the software. These were major breaks from IBM tradition. After all, IBM viewed itself as unsurpassed when it came to software. Sydnes chose Intel Corporation to supply the microprocessor or "brains" of the computer. He selected Bill Gates to provide the operating system and compiler. In a surprise to many including many IBM employees, Sydnes and his team delivered the computer within schedule on August 12, 1981 with a price of $1,565 for a basic PC. A fully configured PC cost about $4,500. Since Sydnes insisted on an open architecture (i.e., hardware and software interface specifications were provided to all developers), software applications and specialized hardware boards mushroomed. Consequently, the IBM PC seized nearly thirty percent of the market in its first year. The PC changed the home as well as the office. In just three years, nearly ten percent of American households owned a computer. By 2000, a majority of households had computers. Today, less than a quarter of American households are without a computer, and two thirds of those with computers have broadband access to the Internet. WOW!

The foregoing discussion provides only a hint as to the vastness of American's golden age of technology. This discussion provides some good illustrations on how the different phases of the technology development cycle are accomplished. The examples demonstrate the essential role industry plays in product development or Phase Four of the technology development cycle. They also illustrate the decadal nature of the technology development cycle.

Chapter 10. The Decline

"Facts don't cease to exist because they are ignored." — Aldous Huxley

How can one think there is a decline of technology in America, when we are bombarded daily with news of new technology? A cell phone is technologically obsolete before the end of the contract with the service provider. A computer may be a technological dinosaur even though it still works perfectly. Even automobiles have become marvels of technology superseding itself. High-tech digital cameras have replaced film cameras. Advertisements hype the latest technological marvels. The financial news is loaded with information on technology and companies. Moreover, the long-term trends on investment in research and development are all reported to be positive. Nearly everyone has heard or read of the quickening pace of technology and the explosion of new products. So, Chicken Little: How is it that the sky is falling?

Before proceeding, a definition of a decline in technology in America is required. As used in this book, a decline is defined as a significant decrease in the number of new products and services originating in the United States per unit of gross domestic product (GDP). In other words, if fewer innovations based on U.S. research and development reach the marketplace per unit of GDP, that would constitute a decline. (This is analogous to the way the finances of the technology cycle were considered in Chapter 5.) Another way to look at it is that a decline is when the U.S. loses its world leadership in innovation.

The above definition does not include any aspect of market share, competitive position, loss of dominance, or rankings with other nations. Numerous publications and organizations including the National Science Foundation and the American Association for the Advancement of Science have taken up the drumbeat regarding this country's shrinking position relative to all manner of measures. These measures include publications in scientific journals, number of graduates at various levels in science and engineering, number of workers engaged in science and technology, and various cuts to funding of research and development. While this makes good press and may even stir the public's emotions, these clarion calls for concern are in reality nothing more than declarations of the inevitable.

For example, as China develops its university system there is an inevitable increase in Chinese professors publishing papers in academic journals. Since the development of China's university system began with almost nothing, the annual percentage increases are staggering. On the other hand, the United States' university system is very mature and thus the number of professors and papers they publish is relatively stable. The unavoidable result is a proportionate decline in journal articles by American professors.

The United States has had a dominant position in everything related to technology for the past century. This does not mean that America can or even should maintain the position. Other nations have recognized the advantages of a "technology-based economy." Japan is a prime example. It has used technology-based products to become the number two economy in the world. It will soon lose this position to China. As has already been observed, the three ingredients required to establish a technology-based economy are extremely gifted people, education, and funding. Since gifted people make up a certain fraction of a population, then China and India have far more "raw" talent than does the United States or other countries of the world. As China, India, and the rest of the world educate their gifted people in the sciences and engineering, America's relative position regarding numbers of scientists and engineers will diminish, potentially to a position based on relative population size. The various countries' ability to educate their gifted people determines the rate at which this occurs.

As the foregoing illustrates, the relative position of the United States will decline as other countries prosper and invest in technology development. This is all good. The result will be a greater number of new products or innovations coming to the global marketplace. As countries such as India and China develop their own intellectual capital, they will value it and take steps to protect it. The result is that they will protect others' intellectual capital so that others will protect theirs. There is no limit to ideas and innovation. The innovations of others do not impoverish us. The computer notebook and the cell phone benefit users in other countries just as much as they do users in the United States, which was their innovative source. Similarly, Americans have benefited from subsequent innovations in the cell phone that have originated in other countries. A problem arises only if the United States does not obtain its proper share of innovations based on population or GDP.

Hence, the appropriate measures of technology development pertain to the proportion of innovations or new products relative to the total population or GDP. These measures are difficult to determine due to the difficulty in identifying what constitutes an innovation or new product. Further, as discussed in previous chapters the important innovations are the revolutionary ones that generate entirely new industries. Finally, these are poor measures on which to base decisions because they are like "driving in the rear view mirror." That is, decisions affecting these measures were made decades prior to any observed changes in the measures. This is a result of the decadal nature of the technology development cycle discussed in Chapter 3 and further reinforced in Chapter 9.

Discerning trends while they are in their infancy and there is still time to take action is much more challenging than when they are blatantly obvious. This is very much the case for American technology. As seen in Chapter 5, the total investment in R&D by the U.S. has remained relatively constant at approximately 2.5% of GDP over the past 45 years. Further, investments in basic research (Phase One), applied research (Phase Two) and development (Phases Three and Four) have been very stable as a percentage of the GDP. Hence, it is difficult to make a case that a decline has begun in the U.S. based on investment alone. The case for decline rests in the details of the underlying structure. It also rests on understanding the means by which technology passes from one phase to another and the impact this has. The details will reveal that the decline has begun in Phase Two of the technology development cycle. There are some indications that a decline has begun in Phase One, as well. As a result, it will be decades before the full impact will be evident. That is, it will be decades before a reduction in new and improved products flowing into the marketplace based on American innovation relative to the total GDP makes it blatantly obvious.

A brief discussion of the passage of technology through the development cycle is necessary as a first step in understanding the details of the underlying structure. One of the findings in "Chapter 4 — The Technology Players" was that largely, different people and organizations perform the various phases of the technology development cycle. Furthermore, key people move for at least awhile from one phase and organization in the cycle to the next. John Bardeen represents in the case of the transistor a typical example of a Phase Two researcher who moved between Phase One research at the university and Phase Two research at Bell Laboratories. Others on the Bell Laboratories' "transistor" team went to Fairchild and later formed Intel Corporation. Companies have recruited many researchers from their laboratory to help them exploit an invention. This may be a limited involvement such as a consulting role. Sometimes the researchers became the entrepreneurs who founded the company.

In his book, *The Innovator's Dilemma*, on managing disruptive technologies, Clayton M. Christensen provided examples of how new companies have used members of the development team to exploit the new disruptive technology. The company in which the technology base for the product originated often is unable to capitalize on the development. One example that he examined in the book is the computer disk drive. CDC was the world leader and supplier of disk drives for mainframe systems. It developed the technology base for the disk drives in personal computers including notebooks. It was unable to capitalize on this development. Key employees left CDC and joined companies that were able to capitalize on the CDC developed technology base. Again, the transition of the technology from one phase to the next — in this case, Phase Three to Phase Four — was accomplished by key individuals involved in the Phase Three development at CDC moving to companies to perform Phase Four development that brought the technology to market. One of the observations of "Chapter 4 — The Technology Players" was that each succeeding phase's development requires capabilities different from those previously. In the disk drive case, product development required expertise in conceiving a product design that facilitated manufacturing. In addition, experts in the design of the manufacturing tools were required. These are just two of the additional skills required to take a prototype to product. One finds these stories repeatedly. After all, the real stake in the new technology lies with the people who have contributed to its development.

A newly graduated Ph.D. going to work in a research laboratory developing new devices is a most effective means of transferring Phase One research at the university into Phase Two research in the laboratory. In this way the innovator, college professor, transfers his knowledge and expertise to the next phase of the development cycle. Still most people stay within their comfort zone of a single phase of the development cycle.

A cluster of high technology companies in the environs of MIT furthers the argument regarding the transfer of technology through the technology development cycle. This is the case for the areas surrounding all of the great research laboratories. Either the people that started these companies came from those same research laboratories or they wanted to draw on the research performed at them. In addition, researchers and developers that work in the same technical areas and live in the same geographical areas tend to know one another. These relationships form another mechanism for moving a technology down the development cycle. (Silicon Valley affords a prime example of this.) It only takes one or two key people to facilitate the transition of a technology from one phase to the next. Moreover, this human chain is largely responsible for the effective transition of technology from one phase to another.

Though we have examined the development of a single technology from idea to its incorporation into a product, many "new" products incorporate a spectrum of technologies, each having their own development cycle. The personal computer and cell phone are just two examples. With each of these products comes the need for an infrastructure to produce these products. Oftentimes, the manufacturing and testing of the products incorporating a new technology require the development of additional technologies. Designs and test requirements for a new technology based product are not simply "tossed over the fence" to an organization totally unfamiliar and unequipped to handle the manufacturing and testing of the product. People familiar with the design of the product and its underlying technology need to "guide" the development of the equipment that will produce and test it. This has resulted in the establishment of a supporting industrial base, such as, in the case of microelectronics, the companies that make the machines that make or test the micro-devices. Again, the human links are essential in the transfer of "knowledge" from one aspect of the development process to another.

Moving technology down the development cycle is hard and inexact. Many factors are involved and it has been the subject of considerable study. This is not the subject of this book. The argument that a decline has begun depends on the realization that the human and geographical linkages are very important in moving a technology through the four phases of the technology development cycle. A human chain with strong bonding between those involved in adjacent phases of the technology development cycle depicts the cycle's execution. Thus, a decline in research activity in any one phase will lead to a decline in the rate of innovations reaching the marketplace — a decline in technology as a whole. Therefore, the United States cannot just rely on performing the last one or two phases of technology development within its borders in order to maintain a robust technology based economy. The winnowing of technologies through the development cycle discussed in Chapter 2 exacerbates the effect of a decline in research in an early phase of technology development. Thus, a shrinking Phase One or Two effort in the United States constitutes the beginning of the decline in American technology.

Let us first consider the possible indications of a decline in Phase One research or the basic research that the universities and colleges primarily perform. Recently, the National Science Board of the NSF has raised the flag. They have acknowledged the global nature of basic research and recognized that the country, which makes a discovery, enjoys an enormous initial advantage in exploiting the discovery. Federal funding of basic research has declined slightly since 2005 when considered as a fraction of GDP. Similarly, industry funding of basic research has at best kept even over the same period. This follows a rise in Government funded basic research that resulted from the decision to double NIH's budget in 1995 and from the budget fallout of the terrorist attacks on September 11, 2001 (see Chapter 5).

More significantly, NIH's portion of the Federal Government's basic research funding went from less than 45% of the total to approximately 55% of the total. This has resulted in a 20% decline in federal funding of basic research in everything else. NIH's mission and its research are devoted to improving the nation's health. This rightly has general appeal and support. It is not clear that increasing Government funding for basic research in the health sciences will not result in a corresponding decrease in industry funding. The Government, the universities and their associated research hospitals, and the pharmaceutical industry have established a level of collaboration, which reinforces this doubt. Moreover, as previously observed, there is no guarantee that a company will benefit from its own basic research. This additional funding has not shown staying power, as approximately half of the increase in NIH funding has been lost since 2003 (Figure 5.8). In conclusion, basic research in all areas other than the health sciences has declined.

Continuing to consider indicators of decline, the decrease in articles on science and engineering in peer-reviewed journals by authors residing in the U.S. has been significant. Based on NSF's *Science and Engineering Indicators 2008*, there has been a greater than 30% reduction in the number of articles per billion dollars of GDP during the period of 1995 to 2005. The decline was approximately 10% when considered as the number of articles per million U.S. workers. The total number of articles has actually increased but as stated earlier the important measure is relative to GDP or population. The actual number of articles published in physics by American authors has decreased 10% during the decade of 1995 through 2004. This decrease in published articles is primarily due to authors from industry writing fewer articles.

There is no perceptible decline in the number of researchers involved in Phase One — either in the physical sciences or in the life sciences. According to the National Science Board's report, *A Companion to Science and Engineering Indicators 2008*, the U.S. position in patent filings "suggests sustained U.S. leadership for inventions." Although the current decline in federal funding of basic research is the first multi-year decline since 1982, "Federal policy is to increase support for physical sciences

research in future years." The American Recovery and Reinvestment Act of 2009 provided a significant boost in the current budget for Phase One research. In addition,
the proposed budget for fiscal year 2010 would increase basic research. Although
these actions are positive relative to basic research they by no means establish an end
of the trend begun in 2005.

Clearly, the case for a decline in Phase One basic research is not clear-cut. Current
Government declarations and actions could reverse the downward trend if continued.
On the other hand, the currently declining areas need to persist, and some other indicators need to shift towards a decline, in order to make a strong case for a decline in
basic research. Certainly, the situation regarding Phase One is cloudy and one cannot
rule out a decline.

It is in Phase Two research (device phase) that a decline in research activity of at
least a decade duration can be detected. Now let us consider the indicators of a decline in Phase Two research. First, one of the findings in Chapter 5 was that industry
has become the dominant source of funds for R&D. Industry is even more dominant
for R&D outside of the medical science arena. This is in itself not necessarily bad.
However, it will become evident that industry has lost much of its ability or willing-
ness to perform the Phase Two research that leads to the revolutionary devices of the
future.

Second, R&D performed at the Government's laboratories has declined more
than 50% since 1970 based on funding received (Chapter 5). Since the DOD funding
category for the laboratories is 6.1, 6.2, and 6.3 (Chapter 1), most of their work falls
into Phase Two. After the end of the Cold War, funding for new weapons systems
declined dramatically. (The Iraq War has brought an influx of orders for existing
weapons systems and benefited much of the remaining defense industry, but it has
had the devastating effect of further restricting R&D funding to efforts with an immediate application to the war.) The defense industry went through a major restructuring and consolidation between the end of the Cold War and the beginning of the
Iraq War. During this period, industry went after all available funding from the DOD.
The large companies turned to sources they previously shunned including Phase Two
research. The companies employed massive lobbying efforts to achieve these objectives. Consequently, a goal of the DOD's laboratories became spending approximately
70% of their funding with industry. (The DOD originally established the laboratories
to perform research needed by the services. Buying research from industry is a very
recent occurrence.) This had two negative effects. First, it further reduced the funds
retained by the laboratories to use for their in-house activities including research.
The impact was that of a funding cut. Second, the technologists at the laboratories
had to use their time to perform contracting functions — writing requests for proposals, evaluating proposals and monitoring the work of contractors — instead of
performing their own research. The reduction of internal funding and the change in
assignments has dramatically reduced research performed at the DOD laboratories.
In addition, studies initiated by Congress have pointed to a perceived excess capacity
in DOD laboratories and suggested restructuring the laboratories so that they would
be Government owned and contractor operated. In this latter case, industry would
perform all of DOD's research other than that done by universities. Recalling from

"Chapter 4 — The Technology Players" — the rich heritage of innovation of the Naval Research Laboratories and the other DOD service laboratories, the decline in technology development by DOD's laboratories is a tragedy for Phase Two of the development cycle.

The "industrialization of Government research" has not been unique to the DOD. It has affected agencies such as NASA. NASA has terminated "block" funding of technology work at its center laboratories. It has replaced the technology development that its centers previously performed on an assigned basis with various competitions, most of which are open to all comers. With these competitions has come the pressure on NASA to award industry a greater proportion of the R&D dollars. The contraction and consolidation of the military industrial contractors that occurred after the end of the Cold War certainly had a part in this change at NASA as it did with the DOD laboratories. With the need to survive, NASA's research funds became fair game for these contractors. Unfortunately, when the researchers at the NASA centers fail to obtain funding for their efforts, then they must go elsewhere and their research ends. For example, JPL received from NASA approximately $100M on an assigned basis for Phase Two research in FY2000 and today it is less than $50M, mostly obtained on a competitive basis.

Furthermore, competition for Phase Two funding does not foster risk taking and long-term efforts. No matter how one cuts it, the winners of funding are those who can demonstrate the best value for the Government. That is, winners are those that can identify measurable benefits of their research, demonstrate the risks of the proposed work are reasonable and manageable, prove the approach to the research is sound, and argue that success is likely. That just is not the real life situation for Phase Two research as was pointed out in Chapters 2 and 4 where failure occurs more often than success.

Competing for research funding is an environment in which research becomes incremental and unimaginative. In other words, the competitive environment turns the researcher into "surviving" financially. Improving the materials and processes used to build a device is much more likely to meet the requirements of a competition than some "wild new" idea that may take a decade or more to work out with few, if any, applications apparent — as was seen in Chapter 3. Similarly, proposing an enhancement to work that has already been funded and is in a proven interest area of the sponsor is more likely to be a successful bid than an "out of the box" or "off the wall" idea. Such a chilling environment for innovation is not conducive to funding research ideas that could really have an impact similar to those of NRL's radar developments of the past.

One such competition, the annual Director's Innovative Initiative of the National Reconnaissance Office (NRO) provides an excellent example of the foregoing discussion. This competition was established with the goal of providing research funding for "wild blue yonder" or "out of the box" ideas that could eventually have a significant impact on the NRO mission, if successful. Bob Pattishall, the Advanced Systems & Technology Director at the time, initiated the program in 1998 with a statement that a 10% success rate was most acceptable. While ten years is really too short of time to assess such an effort based on Chapter 3's findings that the development cycle typically takes several decades, criticisms and changes have begun. The agency sees that the success rate has been too low and is taking steps to remedy the situation. One step is to require the proposals to show how the proposed new technology can become part of a system development within five years. This blatantly violates the decadal nature of the technology development cycle. Only technology that is fairly far along in its development can claim to meet such a requirement. In addition, the awards favor industry with only four out of the 29 awards made in 2007 going to Government laboratories and federally funded research and development centers (FFRDCs). Industry received 19 and the remainder went to universities. In 2008, the results were that out of 27 awards industry received 24, universities received one, and Government laboratories and FFRDCs received two.

DOD's Defense Advanced Research Projects Agency has the mission within DOD to fund the "high payoff, high risk, disruptive technologies," in other words the innovations, for DOD. Quoting from DARPA's Strategic Plan, "DARPA typically accounts for about 25 percent of DOD's science and technology (S&T) budget. This is in line with the common industry practice of devoting about 75 percent of R&D funding to product improvement but allocating 25 percent for new ideas, products, and markets." Further, by its own admission the vast majority of its focus is on efforts with a near term payoff. Charts in its Strategic Plan indicate at least 80% of DARPA's funding goes to near term programs. It touts bringing ideas from basic research to fruition in military systems, but that is clearly not its focus. Quoting DARPA's Strategic Plan again, "DARPA invests about 97 percent of its funds at organizations outside DARPA, primarily at universities and in industry. Over time, this investment leads to new capabilities in industry and steadily reduces the risks of the underlying technology. At some point, a company becomes sufficiently confident of the capability ... to propose the technology to DOD users or acquisition programs." The absence of any mention of Government laboratories or FFRDCs is most telling. In fact, one former Director routinely made a point at DARPA TECH (an annual convention in which DARPA presents its program to the world) that less than 7% or approximately $200M of its funds went to Government sources (Laboratories) and FFRDCs. Of this, no more than half goes into Phase Two research, which means less than $100M goes to fund Phase Two developments at all Government laboratories and FFRDCs. This is approximately the level of funding NASA provided JPL for Phase Two research in 2000. DARPA has only reduced funding of the service laboratories and DOD FFRDCs since then. The effect has been to reduce the service's laboratories to skimming some management fees off DARPA research programs by serving as DARPA's executive agents. This keeps some technologists employed but does not support any research.

DARPA recruits program managers, who have a research program in mind. DARPA gives them approximately five years to realize their research objectives. As seen in Chapter 3, this is excessively little time to achieve major results. The program managers are encouraged to take risks — a typical DARPA hard problem is one, which requires "a miracle" to occur. To take a risk in the R&D world is to undertake an effort that may not yield the anticipated or hoped-for outcome. That is, the effort may be a failure. Now this all sounds good and noble until a significant amount of money has been spent on an admitted failure. Hindsight never makes failures look good. The news media and Congress can be relentless. The visibility and availability of information coupled with the demands for success and for high returns on investment from Congress and the public are a great deterrent to taking the risks that agencies such as DARPA should be taking. Still, DARPA does indeed take risks but its management retains an eye on the impact of failure on the agency. The bottom line is that innovation is being restricted within DOD when it comes to Phase Two of the technology development cycle.

A very notable and vivid example relative to risk taking comes from another agency, NASA. Dan Goldin tried to take NASA out of the billion-dollar, once-a-decade unmanned space mission into a "faster, better, cheaper" approach when he became the administrator in 1992. The intent was to execute a number of cheaper missions in the decade. The result would be a launch every couple of years and he declared publicly that it was okay to fail occasionally. This was fine until JPL tried to undertake two missions to Mars for the price of one. Unfortunately, the low cost of the previous Pathfinder Mission served as the basis for setting the price of the two missions. In an attempt to meet all their objectives within cost and schedule, both missions took irresponsible risks in the performance of pioneering work. Failure of those missions was not acceptable to the public and Congress. They demanded the changes necessary to assure such failures would never happen again. A much more disciplined approach to risk management was just one response to this demand. As an example, the Mars Science Laboratory (MSL) delayed its scheduled launch date, which originally was in 2009, by two years in order to reduce some of the identified risks. In fairness to Goldin, the "faster, better, cheaper" approach arguably did result in a greater science return per dollar spent than the more costly, deliberate, and risk averse approach that was taken previously. The point of this example is that spending significant tax dollars on a failure really does matter. Recall from Chapter 2 (on the great winnowing process of the technology cycle) that research and development is mostly about failure. One cannot be averse to failure and pursue earth-shaking R&D at the same time.

NASA touts itself as an organization devoted to science and technology. However, is it really? Approximately half of its $15B annual budget goes to shuttle operations today. This is not helping technology development. Approximately, another quarter of NASA's budget is going towards the development and building of a new crew vehicle and launcher. These have to be "human rated" safe systems. Only proven and tried components can go into them. These programs are new technology adverse. (These programs are tough enough to implement without introducing the complications of a new technology.) Once, the new crew vehicle and launch systems are put into service, there will be the operational costs of these systems. Do not expect them to absorb less of the NASA budget than the Shuttle has. This represents a tremendous shift from when NASA was brand new and there was no proven basis on which to build. In the beginning, there were no continuing operations. Everything was new and involved extensive technology development.

Other than a small allotment of funds to aeronautical research, essentially all of the remainder of NASA's budget is devoted to robotic missions — Earth orbiting spacecraft and probes to other bodies in the solar system. (NASA supports some earthbound and airborne data collection efforts to validate space borne observations.) These missions support the comprehensive study of the Earth, the exploration of the solar system and the study of the universe. Generally, greater than half of the cost of any robotic mission is building and launching the spacecraft. The builders of these spacecraft are averse to the introduction of new technologies, which have a propensity to cause schedule slippages and cost overruns. Cost overruns do not set well with management, Congress, and the public. Hence, highly reliable, well-known and frequently used technologies are employed everywhere possible. The only time new technologies find their way into missions is when no other way is possible. Long gone are the days when most of what NASA did was new and depended on vast amounts of new technology (e.g., the Apollo Program). New technologies do make their way into the instruments because those instruments are essential to the sought after science, whose primary constituents are the academic researchers in the universities throughout the country and the world. Once the spacecraft is operational, there is the cost of operations, which takes up the vast majority of the remaining mission cost.

Further exacerbating the situation regarding Phase Two research, NASA has integrated technology development within its various mission programs. As indicated, the various missions comprising these programs are risk averse and pursue new technology only because it is essential to the mission. In addition, NASA requires that the technology base of a mission be at least at TRL 6 (Chapter 1) before the start of a mission. This precludes Phase Two efforts, which end with the technology at TRL 4. Thus, Phase Two efforts within the programs are separate from any mission and are not likely to benefit any mission for decades (Chapter 3). Bottom line is that NASA funds a very meager Phase Two program of the technology development cycle. Institutionally, there is no longer a proponent.

This leaves the Department of Energy (DOE) as the last bastion for science and technology in the Government. DOE's Strategic Plan backs this up with the following statement: "The Department serves a critical role within the U.S. science enterprise as managers of the largest system of National Laboratories and major scientific user facilities." In fact, DOE employs approximately 19,000 scientists at these facilities. Furthermore, DOE's strategic goals in science and technology are noble: (1) achieve the major scientific breakthroughs in energy research, (2) provide the infrastructure to enable the first goal, and (3) integrate basic and applied research to accelerate innovation. In round numbers, DOE's annual budget is approximately $32B per year and has been relatively stable. DOE spends approximately $4B towards the science and technology strategic goals. Unfortunately, funding of R&D in the DOE has been essentially flat in constant dollars since the mid-1980s. Since the GDP has more than doubled in this period, then the percentage of GDP going to fund R&D in DOE has been cut in half (see Figure 5.9). R&D funding in DOE declined significantly from its peak in 1978 after the OPEC oil crisis to its mid 1980s level. Thus, DOE's funding of R&D has been in decline relative to the GDP for more than three decades.

The following quote comes from DOE's web site: "The Department of Energy is the single largest Federal Government supporter of basic research in the physical sciences in the United States, providing more than 40 percent of total Federal funding for this vital area of national importance. It oversees, and is the principal Federal funding agency of, the Nation's research programs in high-energy physics, nuclear physics, and fusion energy sciences."

Approximately 50% or $2B of the $4B science and technology budget is spent at universities for basic research, leaving at most $2B at its laboratories in the areas of basic energy sciences, advanced computing, biological and environmental sciences, high energy and nuclear physics, and fusion energy research. (This does not include the work in nuclear weapons research performed by the nuclear weapons laboratories managed by the DOE.) Further, one of the charters of DOE's National Laboratories is to perform the basic research that is beyond the scope, capabilities, or facilities of university researchers. This includes much of today's research in high-energy physics, nuclear physics, and fusion energy sciences. Two examples where essentially all of the research is in Phase One basic research are DOE's Stanford Linear Accelerator Center and The Thomas Jefferson National Accelerator Facility. It is impossible to ascertain the precise amount of Phase Two research undertaken in DOE's National Laboratories without a comprehensive review. However, reviewing the overview material on each laboratory's web site and overall budgets for each laboratory indicates that Phase One research comprises a significant portion of the research performed at DOE's National Laboratories. A generous estimate is $1B or half of the total National Laboratory's budget goes into Phase Two research. Moreover, this is devoted to a relatively small number of technologies (compared to the sum total of all physical science based technologies) that are of great importance to the relevant energy and environmental issues.

The rest of the Federal Government is inconsequential relative to funding Phase Two in the physical sciences (less than 5% according to Chapter 5). The National Science Foundation is a major source of funds for Phase One basic research — but not for Phase Two. The other Departments (e.g., Justice, HUD, and Education) and agencies (e.g., EPA) essentially have no need for such research. Thus, an optimistic estimate of Phase Two research conducted in the Government's laboratories and FFRDCs would certainly fall short of $2B per year. Again comparing this as a fraction of the GDP to what was spent during the Cold War era, a most significant decline in Phase Two research conducted by government's laboratories and FFRDCs is evident.

Based on the prior discussion, the preponderance of what little Phase Two research funding DOD and NASA have now goes to industry. DOE devotes a small portion (approximately 3%) of its funds to a very narrow scope of Phase Two research. Therefore, the nation as a matter of deliberate policy or by default has turned to industry for Phase Two research. Discussions in prior chapters pointed out the importance of the industrial laboratories such as those of AT&T, GE, Hughes, Sperry, Xerox, et cetera to Phase Two research in the United States. This was during the periods of the rise and the Golden Age of technology in America. Things have changed. They are no longer the powerhouses of Phase Two research they once were. These industrial laboratories still perform Phase Two research but not to the extent of the past.

AT&T was broken up in 1984 and left to compete with MCI and other long distance carriers. AT&T could no longer afford the luxury of the Phase Two research it funded at Bell Laboratories. After all, AT&T had never been the big benefactor of such research. AT&T spun-off Lucent Technologies, which comprised the equipment-manufacturing arm of Western Electric and Bell Laboratories in 1996. AT&T management evidently saw the manufacture of telecommunications equipment and its associated R&D as relatively unimportant to their plans for AT&T. Management has turned Bell Laboratories into a product development laboratory. It had to contribute to the bottom line. Gone were the research projects with no definable benefit to the corporate parent. Gone were those with too long a time horizon. Gone are most of the Phase Two research programs and their associated researchers. Subsequently Lucent was merged into the French company Alcatel. An American institution of distinction has been lost to industrial globalization.

Xerox's PARC became an independent research and development company on January 4, 2002. It is now dependent on selling its services to other companies. Similarly, Hughes Research Laboratories transformed to HRL Laboratories, LLC on December 17, 1997. On January 2001 Raytheon, Boeing, and General Motors owned the partnership. It performs research and development for its owners, Government agencies, and selected commercial companies. These two organizations are now dependent on relatively short-term contracts that require the achievement of specific results. Clearly identifiable benefits to their sponsors are requisite. These conditions do not support Phase Two research whose characteristics are uncertain results, unknown benefits, indefinite timelines, and an unlikely future relative to finding its way into a future product. It is almost certain that the next "laser" innovation will not come from these laboratories as currently structured.

IBM's Watson Laboratories have experienced a similar fate. When IBM ruled the world of big computers, margins were high and research was part of the total mystique. IBM's research laboratories vied with AT&T's Bell Laboratories for the breakthroughs in building the first devices ever (Phase Two research). At least two IBM researchers have received Nobel Prizes. Along came the mini-computers with mainframe capabilities and the personal computer age and IBM stumbled. At one point, some Wall Street experts were writing IBM's obituary. Louis V. Gerstner, Jr. took the helm and restructured IBM. The lean and revitalized company has done extremely well in the present competitive environment. Watson Laboratories are strongly focused on supporting the new IBM where the bottom-line rules. Again, these conditions do not encourage the kind of Phase Two research program that was once the hallmark of the Watson Laboratories. Yes, IBM has come back and R&D funding within IBM has returned to historic levels but every indication is that it's more product and service focused and for the most part tied to a near term return of investment.

Clearly, the situation has changed at the four premier laboratories of Bell Laboratories, Xerox PARC, Hughes Research Laboratory, and Watson Laboratories to where support for Phase Two research is no longer, what it once was. This does not necessarily imply that industry supported Phase Two research is in decline overall. It is necessary to dig deeper to draw such a conclusion. Unfortunately, industry does not provide the needed information that applies exclusively to Phase Two research levels and hence directly support such analysis. Various Government reporting requirements do not make such information available. Further, for competitive reasons industry maintains considerable secrecy regarding their R&D programs and expenditures. Therefore, one has to use a considerable amount of peripheral information in order to make the inference.

First, industry lacks incentives to perform Phase Two research and in fact has a number of disincentives. As previously noted, those companies, which have sponsored Phase Two device development, have rarely benefited by producing products incorporating the devices that resulted from such research. It is impossible to rationalize such research activities and organizations such as an old time Bell Labs or Xerox PARC to a board of directors or to a group of financial analysts from Wall Street. No board of directors or CEO can withstand the consequences for "such wasteful spending" of the shareholders investment.

Further, the CEO's and boards of directors have no hope today of personally benefiting from successful long term research even if the companies were successful in financially benefiting from Phase Two research. As is all too well understood, current-quarter "numbers" dominate corporate values on Wall Street and are key factors in determining corporate executives' compensation and tenure. There is little value placed on a future that is decades away that is the case for products emanating from Phase Two research. To make matters worse, a CEO's longevity at a company has become very short. D.C. Denison wrote in a 2001 article in the National Post, "a generation ago, it was not unusual for an executive who reached the top job to serve for decades. Jack Welch, the chairman and CEO of General Electric Co., held those jobs for 20 years by the time he retired." Denison went on to quote John T. Challenger, the head of a Chicago-based firm that tracks CEO Departures, "CEO turnover has been accelerating for the last 10 years. CEOs find themselves in very difficult situations these days, from dealing with economic uncertainty to employees who want better salaries. The CEO is in the middle of all those battles, which makes it tough to survive." Business Week (December 2000) reported, "two thirds of all major companies worldwide have replaced their CEO at least once since 1995, according to a recent survey by consultant Drake Beam Morin Inc." A study entitled, "The Era of the Inclusive Leader," on CEO turnover released in 2007 by Booz Allen Hamilton provides some sobering findings, including:
- CEO turnover has increased nearly 60% from 1995 to 2006.
- One in three departing CEOs depart involuntarily.
- CEO tenure correlates strongly to investor returns.

A number of studies have placed the average tenure of CEO's in the neighborhood of eight years and the median at approximately five years. These findings certainly reinforce the short time frame used for corporate planning and decision-making.

The so-called technology companies are no better. The ones, which still have one of their founders at the helm, have shown no real propensity to establish such research capabilities. Microsoft, for example, has failed to demonstrate that it is capable of developing innovations, which are revolutionary or paradigm shifting. Microsoft borrowed its Windows operating system from Apple's Macs, which Apple took from Xerox's PARC. Microsoft took the basis of its Office Suite from other innovators. Its web browser came after the invention of Netscape. Microsoft's skills have been in turning prototypes into products, developing user documentation, packaging, and marketing. Sun Microsystems built a business around the networking concept Andy Bechtolsheim, a Sun founder, developed while a student at Stanford. The long time CEO and now chairman of the board, Scott McNealy, has at times seemed more interested in fighting in the courts with Bill Gates and Microsoft than developing new products and his business. (One can argue that while Scott McNealy was waging this assault in the courts, IBM established itself solidly or took over the market that Sun had established for itself.) Sun now finds itself no longer viable as a stand-alone company. Consequently, Oracle is acquiring it. Steve Jobs has done a fine job at the helm of Apple by bringing many innovative products to the market. However, examining Apple's corporate documents fails to yield any hint of Phase Two research. They are doing very well exploiting the device developments of others.

Protection of intellectual property provides another disincentive for Phase Two research. Patents expire after twenty years. As previously noted, a patent for a device developed in Phase Two research is likely to expire before products or industries exploiting that device will have come to maturity. Thus, there is little likelihood of any significant royalty stream coming into play for those developing the most innovative devices. This serves as a double whammy since the original developers of a device are not the ones to conceive of and build the products exploiting it. This has always been the case. The royalties have gone to the product developers, as was the case with Edison and the rest of the inventors of his era. As conditions at the beginning of the golden age of technology that were conducive for industry to perform Phase Two research eroded, industry and Government changed funding roles (see Figure 5.6). Today, Government funds more than 60% of Phase Two research. Certainly, lack of a return on investment is a sufficient reason to minimize corporate funding of Phase Two research.

Ownership of patents for work done under Government funding is impossible for most individuals and corporations. Universities, not-for-profits, and small businesses may elect to retain rights to inventions made under federal funding agreements (grants, contracts). The results of all others in the performance of Government funded research belong to the Government. (Under certain partnerships, companies may obtain exclusive licenses.) Relatively few patents are applied for and obtained for the results of Government funded R&D. The lack of protection of intellectual property is a significant disincentive for taking products to market that are based on the results of Government funded research and development. The benefit to the government contractor for performing Government funded R&D is not in the commercial marketplace but rather in gaining an edge in a much larger "production contract" from who else but the Government. Again, the short terms of "leaders and decision makers" in both Government and industry provide a strong incentive to look for the near term contract award. The major loser in this scenario is truly innovative and revolutionary Phase Two research. In conclusion, the foregoing provides significant indicators that Phase Two research is in a state of decline within industry.

The humanistic side provides additional indirect indicators of the decline in Phase Two research. Let us consider how Americans value their scientists and engineers. Are their appropriate incentives to encourage America's brightest and most capable young people to pursue an education and career in science and engineering? Are scientists and engineers honored by society or looked upon as some sort of freak — geek? Among answers to these and similar questions are some additional clues that a decline has indeed occurred.

The National Science Board's (NSB) study, *Science and Engineering Indicators 2004*, provides some insight into the human perspective, particularly regarding public perceptions and attitudes. As with news in general, the television is the public's primary source of information on science and technology. Science and technology news and programs do not attract the viewers that other shows attract. No science and technology related story made the top ten news stories in the years 2000 through 2002. Not even successfully mapping the human genome or the anthrax scare could break the top ten. The category of science and technology ranks ninth among news programs on television. It follows such categories as community affairs, crime, health, and sports. Backing this up, the vast majority of Americans consider themselves not very well informed about science and technology.

The work place for scientists and engineers reflect this "apathy" towards science and engineering. During the decade between 1979 and 1989 median real salaries for scientists and engineers holding a bachelor's degree or higher declined by 0.6% to $42,000 per year while that of all people with a bachelor's degree or higher rose by 27.5%. Changes in salaries for scientists and engineers reflect the population as a whole (those with and without a degree) from 1987 to 1992. While median real salaries decreased by 3.4% for all workers from 1987 to 1992, those of scientists and engineers not in the biological sciences decreased between 2.7% and 3.0% depending on the specific discipline. Starting real salaries for new college graduates with a bachelor's degree in science or engineering declined approximately 10% during this period. This contrasts with physicians and lawyers who saw the median real salary increase by 8.0 to 17.0%. The number of scientists and engineers in the work force declined 3–6% during this period depending on discipline. This was at a time when the work force grew by 4%. In contrast, the number of lawyers in the work force grew by nearly 13% and physicians by 23%. Clearly, scientists and engineers no longer have the prestige, the influence, or the import they once had in the business world. These statistics contrast sharply with the perception of an ever more rapidly expanding technology base, which depends on scientists and engineers in order to expand.

TABLE 10.1 — PERCENTAGE CHANGES IN DEGREES AWARDED CITIZENS AND PERMANENT U.S. RESIDENTS IN 1985 TO 2002

Discipline	% Change for Bachelor's Degrees	% Change for Master's Degrees	% Change for Doctoral Degrees
Engineering	-21.0	1.5	47.9
Agricultural Sciences	42.7	39.0	-42.9
Biological Sciences	56.7	19.8	20.5
Computer Sciences	22.3	65.0	87.8
Mathematics/ Statistics	-18.5	-4.0	9.0
Physical Sciences	-41.6	-48.2	-13.3
Totals	4.0	9.4	11.6

Based on data extracted from Science and Engineering Indicators 2008 and "Science and Engineering Statistics"

Trends in the education of scientists and engineers in the United States provide another indicator of a decline beginning to occur in the technology cycle. Since the automation of original thinking and innovation appears to be still far in the future, the United States remains dependent on people to perform the research and development of the technology development cycle.

First consideration is given to the trends in the number of degrees awarded. The high water mark for bachelor's degrees awarded in engineering is 1985. The period between 1985 and 2002 is of interest because it is long enough to show some long-term trends and it includes slightly more than a decade since the fall of the Soviet Empire. Table 10.1 presents the percentage change in the number of degrees awarded to residents and permanent residents in 1985 versus 2002 for the disciplines of interest. The uniformly bright spot is in the biological and computer sciences where there have been high double-digit increases at all degree levels. The bursting of the dot-com bubble and the exporting of IT jobs could have a negative effect on the future relative to those pursuing degrees in computer sciences. The physical sciences have been a disaster with significant double-digit decreases at all degree levels. The mathematics/ statistics and engineering disciplines both show a nearly 20% decline in bachelor's degrees. They do show increases in the awarding of advanced degrees. The agricultural sciences exhibit significant increases at the bachelor and master levels but show a significant decline at the doctoral level. The realization that the population increased over this same period by more than 20% aggravates this situation. This means that the United States is falling behind compared to its population in those areas where the percentage change is less than 20%. Even with the strengths in the live sciences and computer sciences, the totals are falling behind compared to population growth. The foregoing foretells a future shortage of scientists and engineers to propel America's technology development cycle related to everything but the live sciences. This includes everything from new electronic products to new energy sources and systems to new systems to protect the environment.

Universities have kept their programs in science and engineering going by educating foreign students. In 2004 between five and ten percent of the bachelor's degrees in the engineering and the mathematical sciences including computer science went to foreign nationals. Forty to fifty percent of the master's degrees in these areas went to foreign nationals. In the case of PhDs, fifty to sixty percent of the degrees in the mathematical sciences and engineering went to foreign nationals. This does not include the additional foreign students that have obtained permanent residency in the United States. The number of foreign students studying science, technology, engineering, and mathematics (STEM) has been growing at an 8% rate recently. The numbers are large with more than 40,000 graduate students from India and more than 30,000 from China pursuing advanced degrees in STEM at U.S. universities in 2007.

Between 1990 and 2000, the number of foreign-born Asian workers in science and engineering positions grew from approximately 140,000 to approximately 460,000. Vivek Wadhwa, AnnaLee Saxenian, Richard Freeman, and Alex Salkever report in a study, *Losing the World's Best and Brightest*, that in the past approximately 90% of Asians and two thirds of foreign graduates have remained in the U.S. after graduation. Their report indicates that this is changing. They found that more than 85% of foreign students anticipate eventually returning to their homelands. Nearly half of the Asians students wish to return home within five years. On top of this, Paul Saffo wrote in an article about the growing trend of foreign universities and companies recruiting American scientists and engineers to move abroad. Coupling this with the fact that those with PhDs and master degrees perform much of the Phase Two research, American universities may well be educating those who will be at the heart of technology development in competing countries. The greatest benefits fall to those who design and produce the new innovative products and not to those who produce them at commodity prices.

Here are some very sobering statistics regarding foreign-born scientists and engineers to conclude the discussion of human resource indicators. Twenty-five percent of the science and engineering workers in the United States are foreign-born. At least one foreign-born founder helped start one quarter of all engineering and technology companies between 1995 and 2005. Foreign-born individuals helped start eBay, Google, and Intel.

The American Recovery and Reinvestment Act of 2009 provides a bump up in R&D funding in the amount of $19 billion. Just over $11 billion goes to NIH, $3 billion goes to both NSF and DOE, $1 billion goes to NASA, $0.6 billion goes to NIST and $0.3 billion goes to DOD. Essentially all of this is for basic and applied research with the lion's share going to basic research (i.e., approximately $16 billion of the $19 billion). An additional $3.5 billion is to be spent on facilities and capital investment at universities. Universities and Phase One research are the big winners. This amounts to approximately a 15% increase in government spending on R&D. This additional funding brings some agencies' (e.g., NIH) basic research funding back to historic levels but some still lag (e.g., DOE and NASA). Applied research still woefully lags. The current Obama administration has indicated its desire to restore Government R&D funding to pre-decline levels. These are certainly positive signs but the 2009 stimulus package is a one time event and does not represent a turn around in the annual Federal budget regarding R&D spending. Other national priorities, including health care, social security, Medicare and the wars in Iraq and Afghanistan, with their immediacy, will likely take precedence over technology development.

In this chapter, we were not successful in finding a "smoking gun" pointing to the beginning of the decline of technology in America. However, the sum total of all the indirect indicators provides a most powerful argument that the decline in technology development has begun. The following findings relative to Phase Two research are a product of the considerations in this chapter:

- Phase Two research in Government laboratories and FFRDCs has declined on a GDP basis.
- No incentives exist for industry to perform Phase Two research and many disincentives are present.
- Corporations use Government funded Phase Two research to obtain additional Government contracts rather than to develop new products and industries.

• The lack of patent protection for inventions made under Government contract provides a disincentive to their incorporation into a new product or service.

• Corporate focus and management tenures are too short to foster Phase Two research.

• Salaries of physical scientists and engineers have not kept pace with other professionals.

• The numbers of scientists and engineers employed outside academic institutions have decreased significantly.

• Those receiving degrees in the physical sciences and engineering have dropped dramatically.

• Foreign-born scientists and engineers are dominating the U.S. workforce.

• Foreign countries are recruiting U.S. educated scientists and engineers, thereby further reducing America's ability to develop technology.

This situation can only result in a decline of the technology output of the United States on a per capita or GDP basis. These findings are certainly adequate to conclude that a decline in Phase Two technology development in America has begun and that it will ultimately lead to an overall decline of American technology. The consequences of such a decline are pursued in the next chapter.

Chapter 11. Economic Impact of a Decline

"These are the times that try men's souls." — Thomas Paine

At this point, one may justifiably say, "That's interesting, but so what?" After all, everything seems to go in cycles, eras, epochs, et cetera. Technology has had its time in the spotlight; next, it will be something else. If this were the case then only those impacted by the decline would have much interest in this story. That is, those employed in technology development comprise the main group of people impacted by a decline. However, the impact of a decline of technology in America is far greater because the decline affects the economic well being of all Americans.

Clearly, economics provides the basis of the observations put forward in this chapter. Thus, the chapter relies heavily on the observations and works of others for authenticity. The chapter comprises three segments: technology's past impact on the economy, information technology's impact on productivity, and the impact on the economy of the outsourcing of high-tech jobs.

For a considerable period (centuries) prior to the beginning of the twentieth century, Britain was host to the number-one economy in the world. Consequently, its residents enjoyed the world's highest standard of living. Then, the United States overtook and surpassed Britain's global economic leadership early in the twentieth century. By the start of World War I, the United States had taken over the lead in the production of coal, pig iron, steel, heavy chemicals, and the fields of heavy industry. Nearly a century of unprecedented economic growth followed with no other country coming close.

How was this possible? The United States did not have the advantages that Britain enjoyed — the Empire, the economic base, and the tradition. The U.S. did not achieve it by mimicking jolly old England. Certainly, most students learned that the United States possessed copious amounts of natural resources. Most students have also heard about the heritage of the Puritan work ethic. This most assuredly contributed to America achieving some sort of parity with England.

However, how did the United States get so far ahead? At least one historian, Thomas P. Hughes, attributed it to the rise of technology in America in his book, *American Genesis: A Century of Invention and Technological Enthusiasm 1870-1970*. In his book he wrote of innovation and inventors. He even suggested that one of the things foreigners admire and study about America is its innovation. Interestingly, Americans tend not to have this same regard for America's innovation. Americans hold tenaciously to America's traditions related to the Constitution, the Bill of Rights, capitalism, and the vast opportunities afforded its people. History seems to have relegated Whitney, Edison, and Bell to the status of folk heroes such as Davy Crockett, Wyatt Earp, and the Texas Rangers. Today, a large body of Americans has more disdain for its technologically astute corporations — Microsoft, IBM, Hewlett Packard, et cetera — than respect and admiration. A poll conducted by the Marist Poll for the Knights of Columbus found that three-quarters of Americans believe the moral compass of industry is wrong, 90% believe corporate executives make decisions based on what is good for them, and two thirds believe the "public good" is not a significant motivating factor in business decision making.

The United States has provided the world with a stream of new technology-based products, services, and processes for the past century. This has led to the United States economy having been the top dog during this span. Further, those countries, which lead in bringing new products to market in proportion to their population, will be the ones with the highest standard of living. How is this so?

It is not just the invention and commercialization of the light bulb, the telephone, the vacuum tube, transistor, or the laser that provided the engine for America's economy. It is what came with the commercialization of these inventions. Each of these inventions gave rise to an entire industry. In the case of the light bulb, the industry was associated with the invention, design, and manufacture of the system for generating and distributing electrical power that in turn led to a myriad of electrical appliances. In the case of the telephone, a whole communications industry was born. With the vacuum tube came the electronics industry including radio and television, and with the transistor came the semiconductor industry.

Discussed previously, the cell phone industry represents a recent example whose basis includes a number of fundamental innovations by American researchers. It is true that the manufacturers of cell phones have produced electronic devices previously and many of the service providers have been the traditional telephone companies. However, new major corporations such as Qualcomm Corporation have become essential members of the industry based on providing unique cell phone technology to the equipment manufactures and wireless service providers. Likewise, IBM and others existed prior to the personal computer but many companies, both software and hardware, have evolved or come into existence as part of the industry base of the personal computer and its essential partner, the world-wide web. Notable examples include Microsoft, Dell, Ebay, Google, Yahoo, and America Online.

The American pioneered GPS system is responsible for an industry involved in the production of hardware, software, and services for mapping and navigation. This is a very young and rapidly changing industry. A familiar application is the equipping of automobiles with GPS based navigation aids. Another is the combining the worlds of computers and GPS to revolutionize cartography and create a family of evolving systems referred to as Geographical Information Systems (GIS). The bottom line is that new industries have come into existence to provide the systems required to support these revolutionary products.

The foregoing examples provide an indication of the impact that technology has had on the American economy. Immediately after a technology's entry into the marketplace, the resulting industry becomes the high-tech industry of the period. Its employees enjoy the relatively high pay of being high-tech workers. The language has changed to describe the situation but this has been the case for more than a century.

Let us leave the discussion of specific examples and look at the overall impact of technology on the U.S. economy. In 2008, there were approximately 600,000 high-tech businesses (or 8% of all businesses) in the United States according to the National Science Foundation. Entrepreneurs form nearly 84,000 new high-tech companies in the United States annually. These high-tech companies employ approximately 13,400,000 workers (or 12% of all workers). Approximately 5,000,000 of these workers are scientists and engineers with at least a bachelor's degree.

The total economic impact of technology development on America is even greater than creating completely new industries and high-tech companies, as great as that is. Alan Greenspan made this point in a speech he gave to the National Governor's Association on July 11, 2000: "With the rapid adoption of information technology, the share of output that is conceptual rather than physical continues to grow. While these tendencies were no doubt in train in the 'old,' pre-1990s economy, they accelerated over the past decade as a number of technologies with their roots in the cumulative innovations of the past half-century began to yield dramatic economic returns."

In the same speech, he went on to say, "The process of innovation is, of course, never ending. Indeed, the substitution of physical capital, in which new technologies are embodied, for manual labor is an ongoing trend that began nearly two centuries ago when work in craft shops shifted to factories and then to assembly lines. However, the development of the transistor after World War II appears in retrospect to have initiated a special wave of creative synergies. It brought us the microprocessor, the computer, satellites, and the joining of laser and fiber optic technologies. By the 1990s, these and a number of lesser but critical innovations had fostered an enormous new capacity to capture, analyze, and disseminate information. Indeed, proliferation of information technology throughout the economy makes the current period appear so different from preceding decades. This remarkable coming together of technologies that we label IT has allowed us to move beyond efficiency gains in routine manual tasks to achieve new levels of productivity in now-routine information-processing tasks that previously depended upon people to compute, sort, and retrieve information for purposes of taking action. As a result, information technologies have begun to alter significantly how we do business and create economic value, often in ways that were not foreseeable even a decade ago."

FIGURE 11.1 — PRODUCTIVITY CHANGE IN THE NON-FARM BUSINESS SECTOR, 1959–2008

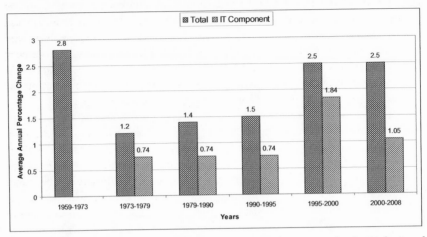

Based on data extracted from "Explaining a Productive Decade: An Update" and "Productivity Change in the Nonfarm Business Sector, 1947-2008"

Robert D. Atkinson and Andrew S. Mckay stated in a study entitled, *Understanding the Economic Benefits of the Information Technology Revolution*, "Technological innovation, particularly in information technology, is at the heart of America's growing economic prosperity." They further stated: "The integration of IT into virtually all aspects of the economy and society is creating a digitally-enabled economy that is responsible for generating the lion's share of economic growth and prosperity."

According to the Census Bureau non-farm productivity increased in the U.S. at approximately 1.5% between 1973 and 1995 (Figure 11.1). Historically, the average increase in productivity was 2.8% for the period of 1959 to 1973 as depicted in Figure 11.1. Although the significant decrease in productivity after 1973 and its gradual return to historic levels is important to understand for economists, it has no apparent bearing on the issue of technology's overall economic significance. Since then the increase has been 2.5%. A number of researchers have estimated the information technology (IT) impact on the change in productivity. As one might expect, there is general concurrence but the exact values cover a limited range of dispersion. Figure 11.1 depicts the results presented in the report, "Explaining a Productive Decade: An Update", by Stephen D. Oliner and Daniel E. Sichel since their results cover the period from the very beginnings of IT to the present (1973–2008). The Joint Economic Committee of Congress concluded in a study entitled "Information Technology and The New Economy" in 2001: "Information technology contributed significantly to the productivity revival. At least half of the one-percentage point increase in labor productivity growth is attributable to IT. In all likelihood the contribution from IT is even greater than this conservative estimate." Of interest is that Oliner and Sichel attributed the entire 1.0% increase in annual change in productivity for 1995-2000 to IT. They also showed a significant decrease in the IT component since 2000. Clearly, IT has played a most significant role in improving the nation's productivity.

As already documented, United States workers and businesses were pioneers. However, America has never been alone. Europe has had its innovators including Guglielmo Marconi, Sir Robert Watson-Watt, Heinrich Hertz, Lord Kelvin, Michael Faraday, James Maxwell, and Otto Hahn. One might say that Americans have been overwhelming in executing the complete technology cycle. Americans have been willing to set out for new frontiers and thereby have reaped the rewards of being pioneers. In addition, America has historically been favorable to the formation of new businesses. Indeed, technology has been and is vital to America's economy.

Initially, the capability to design and build new high-tech products resides with only a very few. Moreover, as documented previously, each revolutionary technology such as the light bulb or the transistor leads to a myriad of new products and services. Initially, the availability of skilled workers, facilities, and machinery limits the production capacity and its ability to keep up with demand. This generates a premium in wages and prices. As the product matures, an ever-increasing number of people and businesses with the capability to design and produce a given product evolve. This gives rise to its eventual commodity pricing — very close to the marginal cost of production. Examples abound. All electronic devices have followed this behavior. Clearly, greater wealth is generated early in the product cycle while profit margins are high, than after it has become priced as a commodity.

Historically, the manufacture of a product has moved to countries where labor costs are lower than where the product was invented as it reached the commodity stage. Hence, yesterday's high-tech products — light bulbs, small electrical appliances, radios, televisions, personal computers, cell phones, etc. — are manufactured in so-called third world or emerging countries. For some, this poses a threat to America's economic well being. They see the high-tech jobs in the U.S. as moving offshore. This has received much research and debate without achieving a consensus.

There appears to be a pattern that generally follows the example of memory production. In summary, Japanese industry went hard after the production of memory chips, which had been essentially the sole domain of U.S. manufacturers. They succeeded only to lose out to other less costly Asian sources. Meanwhile, U.S. industry regained their leadership position in the semiconductor manufacturing by emphasizing products involving logic and control circuits, which require significantly more engineering and sophistication in their production. Researchers at the Rand Corporation wrote in their report, "High-Technology Manufacturing and U.S. Competitiveness", "U.S. manufacturing activities that have remained in the United States tend to be the most advanced and complex manufacturing, typically requiring close coordination with engineering and design staff. But more routine manufacturing, in which every possibility for a gain in efficiency must be pursued, tends to locate overseas for economic advantages."

Currently this "hand me down" approach is under attack. The leaders of other nations recognize the benefits of being the pioneers in the world of new technology based products. Japan, South Korea, China, and India are just a few examples whose behavior indicates an understanding of this point. In addition, the globalization of corporate America has led to companies seeking innovation wherever they can get it.

The March 2005 issue of "Technology Review" provided an important and alarming example of the competition that America faces to retain its world leadership in innovation and technology development. Microsoft opened its Advanced Technology Center in Beijing, China in November 2003 with 20 employees. Approximately 100 employees culled from more than 50,000 applications had joined the Center by late 2004. Among the primary goals of the Center is the goal of "incubating technology created in China in order to spread it to the rest of the world." If the center is successful, it will pioneer the bringing of new products to the Chinese market based on Chinese based technology and from there to the rest of the world using Microsoft's money. Where will the new industries spun off from this pioneering reside? Where will the rewards of being pioneers go? Betting on China would be a sure thing if the observations in this book have any validity.

As pointed out in the previous chapter, there is no denying that China will eventually become a dominant technology development player. Furthermore, as long as U.S. technology development efforts keep pace on a population or GDP basis, America's standard of living will only improve — not just from its own efforts but also from those of China and all others who invest in technology development. The concern is that global corporations will shift their R&D efforts from the U.S. to offshore thereby "robbing" the U.S. of its proper return on its investment in technology development.

Another possible concern is the emerging U.S. policy regarding international science and engineering (S&E) partnerships. The National Science Board of the NSF established a task force to address this issue in 2005. The task force's finding were published in the report entitled, "International Science and Engineering Partnerships: A Priority for U.S. Foreign Policy and Our Nation's Innovation Enterprise". The report stated: "New security threats, globalization, and the rapid increase in health and environmental challenges have generated a need to reassess the U.S. Government's role in international S&E and diplomatic institutions. The U.S. Government needs to adapt rapidly to these changes so that our economy remains competitive, our national security remains sound, and our valuable resources are utilized effectively and efficiently in support of discovery and innovation. A critical mechanism for achieving U.S. goals in this development is international S&E partnering to serve new diplomatic purposes. Effective international S&E partnerships advance the S&E enterprise and energize U.S. innovation and economic competitiveness, but they also have great potential to improve relations among countries and regions and to build greater S&E capacity around the world."

The task force noted several changes in the global S&E enterprise including the aftermath of September 11, 2001; globalization of the economic, social, technological, cultural, and political spheres; and the global nature of many societal challenges. September 11 dampened the flow of ideas; globalization means America no longer dominates in all technologies; and the global nature of societal challenges refers to such concerns as global warming, environmental change and degradation, weather forecasting, and global epidemics. The National Science Board made numerous recommendations towards creating a coherent and integrated U.S. international S&E strategy. Certainly, considerable good can result from implementing such a strategy as long as it does not lead to a decline in America's investment in its own internal technology development. America needs to keep as many of those "most advanced and complex manufacturing" activities possible in the United States.

The changes that the U.S. automobile industry faces may be only the beginning of what the United States, as a whole will face, as the impact of the decline in American technology becomes more apparent and widespread. Labor unions have had to accept changes in their contracts with Detroit automakers. The effect of these changes is reduced labor costs, not through labor saving innovation, but by reducing the hourly compensation of autoworkers. The auto industry is closing a number of factories. General Motors will shed more than 50,000 workers beyond those already terminated prior to 2009. Many consumers and experts perceive Detroit-made automobiles as inferior to almost all others. Consequently, Detroit-made automobiles sell for less than the competition. American technological leadership has largely been missing for decades.

Detroit's automobiles were at one time the best made and most reliable in the world because of LeLand's passion for precision manufacturing. Precision manufacturing was retooled and became known by various names including Quality Circle, Six Sigma, and Total Quality Management (TQM), but quality is a result of precision manufacturing. TQM is essentially an obsession from the CEO to the lowest level worker and includes all suppliers and the customers. This is reminiscent of the story of LeLand rejecting an entire shipment of ball bearings from Sloan's company that were to be used in his engines because the ball bearings did not all meet the specifications. Japanese automakers began making better quality automobiles than Detroit by developing new and improved manufacturing tools and processes. They took the lesson LeLand taught Henry Ford and Alfred P. Sloan about the importance of precision manufacturing, dusted it off and updated it. Many have credited W. Edwards Deming of the United States with teaching the Japanese the importance of quality and customer satisfaction. The American auto industry knew this at one time. The notions of competing with more of the same and offering no more than the market demands are at the heart of the current problems facing the Detroit automakers. Exceeding customer expectations is a winning approach. Innovation could be a critical part of a permanent solution for Detroit automakers. How many involved are considering this option? The Obama Administration seems to have done so in forcing the industry to produce much more fuel-efficient cars through new mileage standards and offering loans to the automakers towards achieving those standards.

One may wonder whether America's automobile industry is not the canary for all of America's economy. Consider what has been happening to Hollywood. More and more production of content for American audiences has moved to foreign locations including India, South America, Canada, and England. Foreign entities supply the cameras and other equipment used by Hollywood. Will Hollywood become the next Detroit? On the other hand, consider Silicon Valley. China and other emerging countries now produce many of the innovations of Silicon Valley. Even Apple's innovative I-pod and I-phone started with their production located in foreign lands. What is Silicon Valley's future? What are the criteria for a product or service to be "made in the U.S.A."?

Outsourcing of jobs has become a big news item of considerable debate as to its impact on the American economy. One can find well-known and respected economists on both sides as to whether the net outcome is beneficial or deleterious to the U.S. economy. During a trip to India in March 2004 to explain that outsourcing had created a political problem in the United States, then Secretary of State Colin Powell stated in response to a question, "... outsourcing is a natural effect of the global economic system and the rise of the Internet and broadband communications. You're not going to eliminate outsourcing; but at the same time, when you outsource jobs it becomes a political issue in anybody's country. Outsourcing means a loss of U.S. jobs, so that means that these jobs have to be replaced."

Information Technology and Business Processes Outsourcing (IT/BPO) represents a business area involving what most people consider desirable jobs. Data on which to draw conclusions is very limited because IT/BPO has only been significant since 2000. So far, India has been the overwhelming winner with approximately 60% of the total IT/BPO worldwide. The U.S. represents approximately two thirds of India's IT/BPO. Thus, taking a closer look at India provides a fair picture of the whole. India's IT/BPO revenues have grown from $1.8B to $31.9 B in the decade from 1998 to 2007. Employment has risen from 42,000 in 2000 to approximately 500,000 in 2006 while India's labor pool of highly skilled workers available for employment in IT/BPO has grown from 190,000 to 16.3 million. Experts expect that India's employment in IP/BPO will reach 1.1 million workers by 2012 and that it is nowhere close to being constrained by the availability of qualified workers. Companies that turned to IT/BPO have experienced a 40-50% savings over having the work done in the United States. This is directly a result of the fact that labor costs in India are approximately one-tenth of those in the United States for equally competent workers. The principle areas of IT/BPO are customer care including the operation of call centers, health care including customer billing, finance including a wide range of information management, and human resources including personnel record keeping. Currently call centers comprise 70% of India's IT/BPO.

Estimates on the number of U.S. job losses due to IT/BPO are difficult to quantify due to the difficulty in obtaining that precise information from businesses. Estimates range from essentially zero to hundreds of thousands per year. William Greene has addressed this issue in his paper, "Growth in Services Outsourcing to India: Propellant or Drain on the U.S. Economy?" According to Greene, Forrester Research estimates that 3.3 million jobs will have been lost to IT/BPO by 2015. Conventional economic wisdom holds that if a large number of less expensive and more highly skilled workers are available around the world then competition should drive down U.S. wages for IT and business process workers. Richard D'Aveni of Dartmouth College stated in a roundtable discussion on the impact of outsourcing that was sponsored by the Academy of Management on May 18, 2004, "... the excess labor supply abroad is going to have [a] significant impact on the wages in service industries, just as it has had on manufacturing wages over the past 20 years."

As the debate over outsourcing has grown in importance, a polarization has occurred. The two opposing camps are those that accept outsourcing's inevitability and do not want intervention, and those who find it completely unacceptable and want effective government intervention. In a speech to the New American Foundation and the Electronic Industries Alliance on May 11, 2004, Senator Joseph Lieberman pointed out that neither group can solve the outsourcing problem since "neither gets to the heart of the outsourcing problem — America's failure to innovate. To stop offshore outsourcing and preserve American jobs, America needs to rise to the international competition and grow again through innovation. Leaving it all to the markets won't work. Hiding behind a wall won't work. Only education, innovation, investment, trade, training, and hard work will give us the growth and jobs we want and need."

This is not talk about the outsourcing of low pay, low-skill jobs to India. This is about America's future. The United States is outsourcing research and development, the innovation that Sen. Lieberman is talking about, to India. IBM, General Electric, Cisco, Intel, Motorola, and Texas Instruments are among the U.S. multinationals that have established major corporate research and development centers in India. Forecasters expect outsourced R&D to grow from $1.3 billion in 2003 to $9.1 billion in 2010. Since this prediction predates the current economic slump it will most likely be missed. However, the point is that the poor economic conditions will only delay the date of 2010 by a year or two. Outsourcing R&D will only hasten the decline in American technology.

This is just the tip of the iceberg of R&D related challenges facing the U.S. The United States now ranks 17th in terms of R&D tax incentives. It is fifth among nations based on R&D investment as a percentage of gross domestic product (GDP) and the percentage of workers involved in R&D. (Note that the United States is not keeping up on a GDP or population size basis.) U.S. companies invested $28.8 billion on R&D in foreign countries in 2003. IBM has advanced research laboratories in Switzerland, China, Israel, Japan, and India. Procter & Gamble employs more than 7500 researchers in 20 global R&D centers, including China. Approximately 150 of the U.S. Fortune 500 companies have recently set up R&D facilities in India and many of the rest are considering doing so. The American Electronics Association's publication, "We Are Still Losing the Competitive Advantage: Now Is the Time To Act," quoted Timothy E. Guertin of Varian Medical Systems, Inc., "While U.S. Government investment in long-term basic research continues to shrink, other nations are increasing their investments, which support foreign-based competitors. Many of our company's current medical devices were based on fundamental research funded in part by the military and the National Cancer Institute a decade ago. Investments in scientific research today will be the foundations of America's competitiveness and military readiness tomorrow." Clearly, this does not bode well for America's future economy.

To make matters worse, America is not preparing for the evolving global situation in the education of its young people as was discussed in the previous chapter. "We Are Still Losing The Competitive Advantage: Now Is The Time To Act", also quoted Randolph E. Gunter, PhD, and President of 21 Century Learning Solutions, Inc., "China and India have more honor students than the U.S. has kids — they are not catching up, they have passed us. Improving K-12 math and science education is the solution to most competitive issues. Why? Because appropriate education equates to appropriate 21st century skills which equates to good paying jobs; China and India understand this, we don't. We must immediately and appropriately train and educate our 4th to 8th grade math and science teachers so they can start preparing America's digital kids for an increasingly flat world." China now graduates nearly six times more engineers than does the United States. India graduates nearly 50% more engineers than does the United States. While alarming, this should be expected to occur at some time based on prior discussions. However, even small South Korea with 1/6 the population has passed the United States in engineering bachelor's degrees awarded. The U.S. now produces a lower percentage of degrees in science and engineering (17%) than the world average (27%). To make matters worse, more than 50% of the degrees awarded by American universities in mathematics, computer science, and engineering go to foreign nationals. These last three facts should be an alarming call to change. Many U.S. corporations have cited the availability and superior education of workers as a primary reason for them to have or to consider outsourcing of high-tech jobs or establishing R&D centers in India and elsewhere.

If America did not face enough of a challenge, there are those who view technology as inherently evil or bad rather than being a tool, which can be used for benefit or for harm. The French philosopher Jacques Ellul saw technology as a threat to human freedom and was concerned that a technological tyranny would emerge over humanity. Lewis Mumford, the American historian of technology, shared many of Ellul's ideas and strongly opposed the concept of constant growth in the economy. Many share in these fears. To them, technology is responsible for many of the ills facing us today including the threat of nuclear war, pollution of the earth, congestion, and global warming, to name a few. The growth in the number of people, who share these perspectives, may pose the greatest threat to America's commitment and success in research and development. To these people, having fewer "technological gadgets" is an improvement in one's standard of living and absolutely is not a lowering of it.

Finally, the collapse of the financial sector may provide some insights into the impact of the decline in American technology. The U.S. Financial sector accounted for about fifteen percent of all domestic corporate profits between 1973 and 1985. During the 1990s, the financial sector profits swelled to twenty to thirty percent of the corporate profit pie. Prior to the collapse, financial sector profits had grown to more than forty percent of the total. Along with this growth, salaries also outpaced the rest of industry. From 1948 to 1982, average compensation in the financial sector was 99-108% of the average compensation for all domestic industries. After that, the financial sector's employee compensation shot up to more than 180% of that for all industries.

The products that gave rise to such spectacular growth included high-risk mortgages, derivatives, and other high-risk financial instruments. Of note is the fact that the financial community considered many high-tech companies with new and innovative products as too risky an investment to attract some of this money after the dot-com bust. A company with the potential of exponential growth and the rewards of high profit margins could not compete with a mortgage that the lender knew from the outset that the borrower could not afford and could only repay by reselling the property for a significantly higher price after a few years. This represents a total lack of confidence in American technology and its ability to create wealth. Maybe, the financial sector understands the decline and is taking action accordingly, and in so doing, hastens the decline of American technology by denying funding to its new ventures. As an aside, estimates of the loss of American wealth due to the debacle in the financial sector exceeded ten trillion dollars.

This leaves the United States with a choice of one of two paths to follow. One path is to produce as many products and services as possible at competitive prices in the global marketplace. This can only happen if the production costs are reduced to match those of other countries or if the United States imposes tariffs or regulations to raise the cost to U.S. consumers of the imported products and services. Trade restrictions have undesirable consequences including other countries imposing barriers against products and services for which the United States excels. Let us assume a free trade solution of reduced production costs. Ultimately, this means lower wages for American workers and a reduced return on investment for the producers as Detroit is all too aware. A general decline in the standard of living relative to the rest of the world befalls the United States as one product or service after another repeats this episode. This path lacks any redeeming features.

The alternative path is to give birth to new technology based products and services that give rise to the rewards of being pioneers in new industries. Meanwhile, the normal transition of production to countries with lower costs benefits all consumers. This requires that the United States have within its borders an aggressive and robust technology development cycle funded at levels commensurate with countries making the greatest R&D investments on a GDP or population basis. This requires the proper support of R&D here in the United States: funding, people, and education.

In summary, we have discussed the impact that technology has had on creating new industries in the United States and the resultant creation of wealth. We've noted technology's contribution to recent improvements in American productivity. These discussions have highlighted the importance of being the pioneers in bringing products and services to the marketplace. They have brought out the potentially deleterious impacts of the outsourcing of high-tech jobs. These discussions have identified the risks to the American economy of outsourcing research and development. They have pointed to America's decline relative to the rest of the world in science and engineering education and its potential impact on U.S.-based R&D. Clearly, technology is an integral part of America's economy and its impact is large.

CHAPTER 12. RELYING ON A SERVICE ECONOMY IS UNACCEPTABLE

"Build a better mousetrap and the world will beat a path to your door." — Ralph Waldo Emerson

Much of the discussion on the rise and the subsequent decline of technology in America rests on examples drawn from the manufacturing sector of the economy. One may argue that as manufacturing becomes less important in the evolving economy then research and development is diminished in importance as well. After all, economic theory holds that as economies mature they move up the ladder from agrarian to manufacturing (industrialized) to service. By some accounts, the service sector already makes up approximately eighty percent of today's economy and it is time to give up the old paradigms. The fallacy of this argument will be uncovered in this chapter.

The advantages and disadvantages of America's service economy has received much press (usually negative) relative to such issues as the outsourcing of high paying jobs to Mexico, China, India, and the Philippines; illegal immigration; and the bankruptcy of General Motors and other manufactures in the current recession. To many, the service sector comprises the personal services or menial jobs such as housekeeper, gardener, or hairdresser. However, it is much more.

The service sector is defined officially as comprised of the following business categories: utilities; construction; trade (wholesalers and retailers); transportation and warehousing; information (including software, telecommunications, movie and broadcast); finance and insurance; real estate; professional, scientific and technical services (including computer system design and scientific R&D services); management of companies and enterprises; administrative and support (including waste management and remediation); educational services; healthcare and social assistance; arts, entertainment and recreation; accommodations, and food services; public administration; and other services. Alternatively, it is everything that is <u>not</u> agriculture, manufacturing, or ore/mineral extraction. (By international agreement, the economy is divided into four sectors for tracking trade. They are agriculture, manufacturing, ore/mineral extraction, and services.) Furthermore, today IBM is not just a manufacturer of computer hardware. It has recast itself into a provider of business solutions in which the computer hardware is only a small part of the service they provide. No wonder the U.S. has a service economy.

TABLE 12.1 R&D BY ECONOMIC CATEGORY

Industry	Total ($millions)	Percentage of Total	Federal ($millions)	Company ($millions)
Manufacturing	124,078	62.2%	13,328	110,750
Nonmanufacturing	75,461	37.8%	5,790	69,671
Trade	24,959	12.5%	30	24,929
Information	16,830	8.4%	540	16,290
Finance, insurance, and real estate	4,024	2.0%	0	4,024
Professional, scientific, and technical services	22,577	11.3%	4,628	17,949
Health care services	536	0.3%	59	477
Other non-manufacturing	6,515	3.3%	513	6,002

Taken from Table 2.1 of "Measuring Service-Sector Research and Development, Final Report"

It is clear from the foregoing definition of the service sector that a number of the categories including those of information; professional, scientific, and technical services; and health care employ research and development to achieve new and improved products and services. Table 12.1 presents a summary of the levels of R&D performed in the various sectors for 1998. The previous chapter already chronicled the economic impact of information technology. Therefore, R&D spending in furthering the information technologies associated with computing, software and data networks is vital to maintaining America's economic well being. (These fall within the industry categories of information; professional, scientific, and technical services; and other non-manufacturing of Table 12.1.) . In fact, the services sector is responsible for nearly 40% of all R&D. There is no doubting that R&D is important to the service economy.

The argument hypothesized at the beginning of the chapter depreciating R&D's importance presumes that the manufacturing sector of the economy is much less important than it use to be. This is not necessarily the case. The value of goods manufactured in the U.S. has consistently trended higher since before 1950 through present times with the only declines having been in times of recession. Manufacturing employment has remained relatively constant from 1950 through 2000 even while achieving the largest productivity gain of any sector. It has only been since 2000 that a twenty percent decline in manufacturing employment has occurred. This has been attributed to productivity gains, a weaker demand for manufactured goods, foreign competition, and currency valuations. Displacement of American workers by foreign workers poses a potential concern.

FIGURE 12.1 U.S. TRADE BALANCE

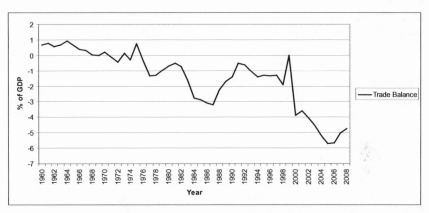

Based on data extracted from "U.S. Trade in Goods and Services - Balance of Payments (BOP) Basis"

The U.S. trade balance is the sum total of all its exports less all its imports. Figure 12.1 presents the U.S. trade balance as a percentage of Gross Domestic Product (GDP). The U.S. has consistently run a deficit since 1975. Up until 2000 the deficit remained between zero and a (negative) three percent of GDP. Since 2000 the deficit has been as much as six percent of GDP with a slight improvement the last couple of years. Is this a concern? Certainly if companies produced goods and services representing the trade deficit here at home instead of in foreign countries then there would be additional employment for American workers. Looking at the trade deficit from the perspective of the economic definition of wealth as all goods and resources having value in terms of exchange then the trade deficit represents a transfer of wealth from the U.S. to foreign entities such as governments, businesses and people. Currently, much of the deficits are held in the form of U.S. "greenbacks" and debt instruments. Eventually, it has to balance out through the U.S. running a positive trade balance with its trading partners for a period of time or through foreign ownership of America's assets — real estate, corporations, tools of production and/or intellectual property. America has already experienced foreign ownership of its assets to a very limited extent. One might imagine in the extreme a situation where Americans' standard of living actually deteriorates.

One might question whether or not intellectual property represents wealth from an economic perspective (i.e., has value in terms of exchange). The extent to which technology has created wealth has been amply demonstrated in this book. The know how to provide superior products and services represented by patents and copyrights truly represents value in terms of exchange. The (unpatented) formula for Coca Cola represents an extremely valuable piece of intellectual property. Interestingly, it has been relatively recently that economists have seen intellectual property as representing wealth. Adam Smith didn't see it back in 1776. Knowledge about how to produce things was considered available or free to all. It wasn't until two centuries later in the 1980s when Paul Romer developed and expounded a viable model of the economic value of "ideas" (intellectual property). As a result, economists extol the importance of technology in creating wealth. It doesn't take an investor with the keen eye of Warren Buffett, or a rocket scientist, for that matter, to recognize that trading America's wealth in intellectual property for some consumer goods (e.g., clothes) is akin to trading Manhattan for a few beads.

FIGURE 12.2 TRENDS IN U.S. EXPORTS

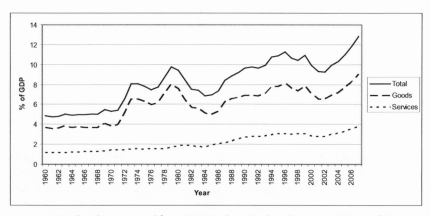

Based on data extracted from "U.S. Trade in Goods and Services - Balance of Payments (BOP) Basis"

Therefore, it behooves the United States to develop and improve its products and services so that the rest of the world will want and value them sufficiently to eliminate its trade imbalance. Let us begin by examining the U.S. export business. Figure 12.2 depicts the historic trend of U.S.'s exports as a percentage of GDP. Total exports have risen from approximately 5% in 1960 to in excess of 10% for most of the current decade. This means that exports have grown at twice the rate of the American economy as a whole. Furthermore, products (referred to by the economists as "goods") still represent approximately seventy percent of U.S.'s exports. This means that the proportion of total exports that goods or products represents has declined slightly more than ten percent in nearly fifty years. Clearly, products will be in America's export mix for some time to come.

Figure 12.3 depicts a refined composition of U.S. exports for the year 2007. The fact that capital goods excluding automobiles represents nearly 30% of the total exports and consumer goods represents less than 10% really stands out. It indicates that even though the U.S. invented many of the modern consumer goods, it cannot compete in the global marketplace to produce them. Indicative of this is the fact that IBM sold its $12 billion a year PC business to China's Lenovo. Furthermore, capital goods excluding automobiles largely comprise the machines for the manufacture of goods. Do not these machines represent America's know-how, America's technology, America's intellectual property? Are not Americans giving away their future for some clothes, a few electronic baubles and some oil?

FIGURE 12.3 COMPOSITION OF U.S. 2007 EXPORTS

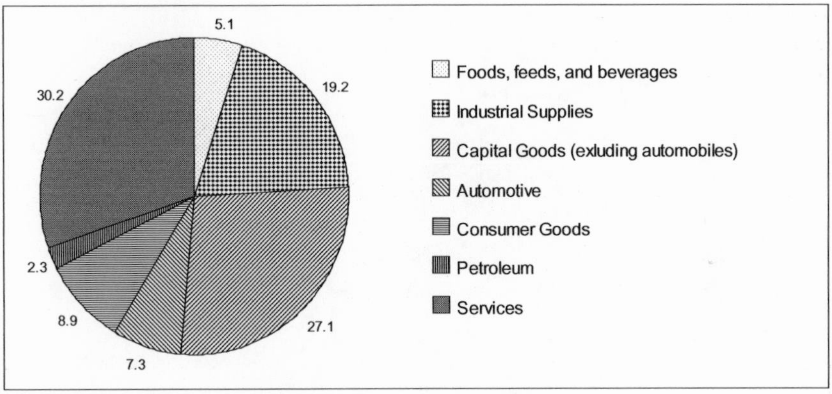

5.1
30.2
19.2
2.3
8.9
27.1
7.3

☐ Foods, feeds, and beverages

▦ Industrial Supplies

▨ Capital Goods (exluding automobiles)

▧ Automotive

▤ Consumer Goods

▥ Petroleum

■ Services

Based on data extracted from "2007 Economic Census"

Since the export of services represents 30% of total exports and America's economy is a service economy then it would appear that increasing the export of services provides the sought after answer. One must not jump without looking. Recall that the nature of most services such as retail trade, health services, food services, education, construction, and accommodations necessitate that the provider have personal contact or at least be near to the recipient. In addition, nine of every ten companies with fewer than twenty-five employees are in the service sector and they employ ninety percent of the workers employed by small companies. Most of these small companies are not a source of export.

Figure 12.4 depicts the composition of service exports for those segments contributing at least two percent of service exports. The travel and passenger fares segment, which represents foreign travelers visiting the United States, is the largest segment by far with more than 25% of the U.S.'s service sector exports. Other major segments are royalties and license fees, other transportation, financial and management, and consulting. Each of these contributes at least 5% of the service exports. Film and television rentals, research/development/testing, and education each comprise a little more than 3% of the service exports.

One might contend that America is now in the information age given that information workers make up more than half of the U.S. workforce. That is, their primary job involves the acquisition, storage, manipulation, and/or communication of information. Thus, it is surprising that computer and information services make up only 2.7% of America's service exports as depicted in figure 12.4.

The possibilities for increasing exports significantly in each of these major service segments are considered next. These possibilities lead to an assessment of the role that technology could play in achieving such increases. This in turn provides insights for increasing R&D funding.

FIGURE 12.4 COMPOSITION OF 2007 SERVICE SECTOR EXPORTS

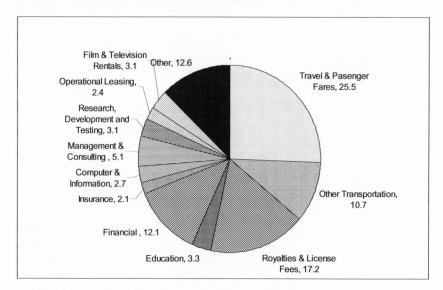

Based on data extracted from "2007 Economic Census"

Travel and passenger fares include all the services tourists make use of during a trip including transportation, accommodations, fees to attend attractions, and food. Increasing travel and passenger fares revenue involves attracting more visitors to come to the United States and/or having them stay here longer when they do come. Of course, the travel services have to be able to accommodate an increase in visitors. Providing them is principally a matter of investment. Creating a demand depends on foreigners having the discretionary resources to spend on such travel and effective marketing. Generally, technology is not going to help on this one.

Licenses and royalties represent the second largest area of service export. This represents the selling of intellectual property to foreign enterprises. These foreign enterprises use these licenses to provide goods and services to their domestic markets and/or for the export of goods and services to other nations including that of the U.S. In general, this appears to be a losing proposition for the United States. Americans are foregoing the benefits of providing those goods and services directly. America is selling its intellectual capital for a mere pittance. Investing America's dear R&D resources in order to license the results to foreign enterprises appears to make absolutely no sense. (R&D is leveraged within the economy. That is, relatively small investments in R&D yield much larger levels of economic activity. Furthermore, significantly increasing total exports through licenses and royalties requires much higher levels of R&D. This in turn requires many more technology researchers and developers. However, American universities are not able to recruit and train enough scientists and engineers to meet America's own internal needs.)

The export of financial services makes up the third largest source of service exports. American corporations are very competitive in the international marketplace when it comes to account management, credit card operations, and collection management. Financial institutions are making greater use of advanced technology in the areas of data mining, database management, and network security. Others outside of the financial institutions develop these technologies and the financial institutions apply them to their needs as they become available. Although Table 12.1 shows that financial institutions invest significantly in R&D, these investments are largely directed outside the financial arena.

In fact, the top ten financial companies with approximately 25% of the total financial sector receipts reported no significant R&D expenditures in 2003. Furthermore, many of the financial companies' investments in R&D do not meet NSF's criteria for research or development. The top ten financial firms with the greatest R&D expenditures in 2003 were an investment technologies firm, a holding company, a global media and technology company, a technology design and patent leasing company, a designer of wireless technologies company, a bio-detection platform leasing company, a technology-based trading company, a managed health care and consulting company, a patent manager and software design company, and a licensor of semiconductor chip connections. According to the National Institute of Standards and Technology (NIST) report, "Measuring Service-Sector Research and Development, Final Report," apparently none of these companies' R&D expenditures is in technologies that support the financial services segment.

Furthermore, the NIST report pointed out that consortiums and vendors conduct many of the development efforts in support of financial services. There appears to be considerable sharing of infrastructure and basic capabilities. One thing made very clear by the NIST researchers is that the current financial services industry is not technology driven.

Before leaving the discussion of the financial services sector exports, one may wonder what the fiasco in sub-prime mortgages and derivatives wrought on the world by America's financial institutions will have on future exports of their services. The weakening of this sector certainly reduces its global leadership position. Time will only tell.

The fourth largest segment, other transportation, is associated with the level of international trade. Increasing the level of global trade increases other transportation. The distinguishing factors are generally time of transit and cost. Cost differences are associated with relative efficiencies and labor costs. Transport power-train efficiencies and the efficiency of loading/offloading operations govern transit times. Gaining a significant advantage here through improved technology is relatively marginal because of the maturity of transportation systems.

Management and consulting is the fifth largest exporting segment in the service sector with approximately 5% of the service exports. Foreigners seek U.S. expertise in the areas of accounting, advertising, legal services, and management. It is a growing export area and certainly is not technology driven. It is very hard to imagine this segment of the service sector making up the trade deficit.

Education offers significant opportunities for export. The U.S. remains unchallenged in the areas of management training, technical training, and English language training. The export market for these services essentially encompasses all business sectors. Remote learning and computer-assisted training represent continuing opportunities for research and development. Still education represents only slightly more than 3% of the U.S.'s services exports.

An important fraction of education exports comes from foreign students attending U.S. educational institutions. These exports, sometimes referred to as transparent exports, are delivered here at home. Furthermore, all the businesses providing goods and services to these foreign students are also exporting their goods and services. This is the same as the businesses, which provide goods and services to foreign travelers here in the U.S.

Film and television rentals also contribute 3% of the U.S.'s service exports. Integration and adoption of high quality three-dimensional capabilities could enhance these exports considerably. Certainly, movies and television shows are nothing but intellectual property.

Information services contribute 3% of the U.S. export of services. Information services include such items as email, network services, data interchange, data processing, electronic information services such as those provided by Google in support of electronic commerce, and professional consulting regarding computer and information services. The world considers the U.S. as the leader in providing these services. Unfortunately, those qualified in the computer and information sciences relatively easily mimic these services. Only a robust R&D effort will maintain this leadership position.

Intellectual property is the basis of six of the top eight business segments relative to the export of services. These segments represent more than 40% of U.S. services exports. Most of them are dependent on technology development in order to remain viable in the marketplace. It is most unlikely that any one segment can grow sufficiently to eliminate the trade deficit.

Furthermore, the perishability of intellectual property exacerbates the challenge of eliminating the trade deficit. Content in the information services tends to have a relatively short shelf life. Once people have seen most movies and made their purchase of the DVD there is little residual demand. Reverse engineering of software applications is much easier, in general, than developing the original software. Expertise is no better off. Utility patents protect intellectual property for a period of twenty years from the date of application with the patent office. It is truly amazing that Coca Cola's recipe remains a secret and thereby retains its value after nearly one and a quarter centuries. However, expertise generally becomes common knowledge at some point. Clearly, after intellectual property becomes common it has essentially no economic value. It has been drained of its wealth.

This implies that the United States continuously needs to create an ever-increasing wealth of intellectual property. This requires that it constantly expand its technology development or research and development efforts. One could look at the trade deficit as a direct result of research and development not keeping pace with the economy. America needs more, not fewer, highly developed scientists and engineers.

Unfortunately, Americans are not stepping up and meeting the challenge. Consider these numbers. More than half of the slightly more than 6,600 PhD engineers that the U.S. turns out annually are foreign nationals. Educating foreign students in the sciences and engineering use to be a good investment for the United States because they tended to get jobs here, become permanent residents, and eventually even become citizens. Today, that is not the case as opportunities in their home country lead to many returning home.

Compare this situation with the approximately 15,000 physicians, the 40,000 lawyers, and 120,000 MBA's that U.S. universities anoint annually. Frankly, most of these 175,000 recipients of advanced degrees produce very little intellectual capital. Is the United States making the best investment decisions by creating six attorneys and nearly twenty business managers for every doctoral engineer? The rest of the world is not following the United States. China and India are investing heavily in their educational system to compete favorably in the information age.

It would appear from current trends that the U.S. would be lucky to hold its own as far as the export of services with their high content of intellectual property. Thus, the export of goods, as well as services, will remain important in order to eliminate the U.S. trade deficit. In addition, the production of goods at home means fewer imports that need to be offset by exports. Technology development in both the goods and services sectors is essential to America's economic well-being. Being a service economy is indeed not the answer to dealing with a decline in technology development.

CHAPTER 13. RESEARCH OPPORTUNITIES ABOUND

"Watch out for emergencies. They are your big chance." — Fritz Reiner

The previous three chapters have established that a decline in technology research has begun, technology has been essential to the American economy and relying on a service economy to lessen America's dependence on technology is simply not possible. One might question whether there are sufficient research opportunities to justify revitalizing America's technology development efforts. After all, can new industries be created that will provide enough high paying employment opportunities? The answer is not only yes, but America's well-being depends on it. The ensuing discussion explores some of these vital research opportunities.

America faces three main issues relative to the environment. Managing the Earth's carbon cycle is essential to reining in the exponential growth of carbon dioxide in the atmosphere. Protecting, cleaning up, and enhancing fresh water supplies are required in order to assure adequate supplies of healthy water for the country's population and its agriculture. Managing human and animal waste is fundamental to preserving a healthy food supply.

Global warming and man's contribution to the increase in carbon dioxide in the Earth's atmosphere has been a hot topic of newspapers, television, conversation, global politics, and even a movie. Out of all this, all but a very small minority of die-hards agree that man cannot persist in continuing to dump ever-increasing amounts of carbon dioxide into the atmosphere. Most people recognize a need to manage the Earth's carbon dioxide cycle. Frequently, positions have been taken and much written with very little science to support them.

Interestingly, there is very little known about a portion of the Earth's carbon cycle. Man's contribution to carbon dioxide in the atmosphere is pretty well known. (Man has increased the carbon dioxide levels by approximately 40% since the inception of the industrial revolution.) Precise quantitative information is extremely limited regarding the sinks that remove carbon dioxide from the atmosphere. The atmosphere accounts for approximately 2% of the total carbon in the Earth's carbon cycle. The land's biomass contains approximately 5% and the ocean 93% of the carbon contained within the carbon cycle. The land's biomass and the ocean comprise both sinks and sources of carbon dioxide. The current understanding of the transfer of carbon between the land's biomass and the atmosphere and between the ocean and the atmosphere is sufficiently incomplete so that what happens to between twenty and thirty percent of the carbon dioxide released by man into the atmosphere is unknown. This is equivalent to trying to manage a company or one's personal finances when a quarter of the expenses are unknown.

The bottom line is that a much better understanding of the Earth's carbon cycle is required in order to manage it effectively. First, someone has to collect data on the levels and locations of sources and sinks of carbon dioxide in the atmosphere with sufficient resolution and time scale as to permit scientists to model the carbon cycle accurately.

Second, scientists will need to build, test, and refine models of the carbon cycle until they accurately reflect its dynamics. This in turn will permit the accurate prediction of the impacts of specific actions aimed at reducing carbon dioxide levels in the atmosphere. Unfortunately, a NASA satellite that would have provided the necessary data regarding the carbon cycle failed during the launch phase in February 2009.

Regrettably, there is no means of curtailing the increase in carbon dioxide in the near term. Thus, there is a need to find methods of inhibiting the release of carbon dioxide into the atmosphere at major sources. The general approach, referred to as carbon sequestration, is to capture the carbon dioxide and pump it underground where conditions are suitable for long-term entrapment. Some believe that sequestration could capture and prevent as much as fifty percent of the carbon dioxide created by the burning of fossil fuels from entering the atmosphere. Sequestering the carbon dioxide requires that it be selectively captured from the source's exhaust, which comprise many gases. Scientists have been pursuing this research with some announced successes. However, as previously discussed, it is a long road from a laboratory demonstration of a principle to a commercially viable product. Success would result in a completely new industry devoted to the manufacture and installation of sequestration facilities on a global scale — at home and abroad. Clearly, understanding and arresting global warming presents many research and development opportunities. Certainly, some are of global scale. Many have the potential for enormous consequences.

Historically, everyone has taken pure healthy drinking water for granted. Certainly, governments have taken steps to assure clean and safe drinking water for their populations. This is not the case for many parts of the globe. Congress has passed laws and the Environmental Protection Agency (EPA) has established regulations on the levels of contamination allowed in American's drinking water. This has resulted in the regulation of in excess of ninety contaminants. All these laws and regulations do not assure a safe and dependable water supply.

Many chemicals are carcinogenic. In excess of 1400 infectious organisms, of which many are waterborne, are pathogenic and new ones are constantly emerging. Infectious diseases account for more than a quarter of the deaths worldwide. Contamination of the water supply can happen after water treatment through leaks, breaks in the system, and repairs and maintenance. Lead contamination in school drinking fountains in Los Angeles has been a recent problem. Contamination of the watershed is rampant.

Use of fertilizers and insecticides in agriculture contaminate the watershed. Ammonium perchlorate or simply perchlorate is both a naturally occurring chemical and a key ingredient in solid state rocket fuel. It is present in fertilizer imported from Chile. Other sources of contamination include research, manufacturing, testing, and employment of rockets, roadside flares, and fireworks. Whereas scientists have not yet identified perchlorate as a carcinogenic, they have found it to affect thyroid function. Testing has detected it in water supplies across the country. It has contaminated large aquifers in California. It has been found in milk and many foods.

Chlorine compounds used to control biological materials in drinking water are themselves considered contaminants with adverse health effects in some elements of the population. The EPA lists sixteen inorganic chemicals, more than fifty organic chemicals, and three radioactive elements as contaminants, which scientists consider harmful and for which the EPA has established standards.

Agricultural irrigation itself can lead to watershed contamination. The great Central Valley of California is one of the highest producing agricultural areas in the world only through the extensive use of irrigation. The problem arises in leaching the soil, which has built up deposits of water-soluble salts over millennia prior to turning it to agricultural use. In a case in the Central Valley of California, one of these salts contained selenium, which can have deadly effects when concentrated sufficiently. The selenium built up in a wastewater lake to the level where it was responsible for the deaths of waterfowl. Significant research into the transport mechanisms and the evaluation of a number of remediation approaches resulted in a solution. Methods and techniques (intellectual capital) developed for this situation could be useful in a wide variety of similar situations.

Understanding and monitoring contamination levels, controlling contamination, and remediation are problems of major proportions. Remediation of contaminated watersheds and aquifers presents a most challenging technical problem due to the volumes involved and the relatively low concentrations of contaminants — often parts per million or parts per billion.

Assuring adequate water supplies presents another set of R&D opportunities. Desalination and cleaning up brackish water for human consumption are just two areas for R&D. Reverse osmosis appears to afford the most cost-effective means of desalination. Although a few companies and communities have built and operated commercial desalination plants there is still a need for improvements in the membranes at the heart of the reverse osmosis technology. In addition, materials used in the water handling equipment could be more resistant to the salt water.

It should now be clear from our discussions that providing an abundant and healthy water supply presents numerous R&D opportunities. Significant business opportunities await those who invent cost effective filtration materials, desalination membranes, and remediation analysis tools. Significant export opportunities will also abound given the global nature of the water problem.

Managing human and animal waste is a growing environmental problem and current methods are inadequate to solve it. Increased densities of agricultural operations point to the problems of managing farm animal excrement. Insufficient or non-existent strategies to prevent animal feces from contaminating ground water have led to regular salmonella outbreaks caused by irrigating fresh produce with contaminated water. A pig farm of 100,000 hogs produces as much manure as a city of a quarter million residents and has no sewage treatment facility. Farmers generally use cesspools to treat the manure. These cesspools are major sources of watershed contamination and are responsible for the release of nearly 200 tons of ammonia into the atmosphere annually. Similar observations apply to large bovine operations. R&D efforts are exploring the use of manure for energy production. Clearly, the United States needs to make vast improvements in the management of animal waste.

Piling human solid waste in landfills, dumping partially treated sewage into the ocean and streams, and allowing storm drains to flow directly into the ocean and streams are having dire consequences. Disposing of human waste in such a manner contaminates watersheds, fouls the beaches, and poisons fish and wildlife. Scientists have traced a disease that threatens the California sea otter population with extinction to cats' excrement, which contains the protozoa eggs responsible for the disease. They believe that storm and irrigation runoff carries the protozoa eggs into streams and into storm drains that flow directly to the sea.

The biggest contaminants of the oceans and streams are nitrogen and bacteria that come from sewage, industrial plants, and farming. These higher levels of nitrogen result in greater growth of algae, bacteria, and plankton. This and over-fishing have resulted in a 90% reduction in the large fish populations in the ocean. Red tides (specific algae bloom), toxic algae, the destruction of corals, and an abundance of jellyfish have replaced them. As some have said, the oceans are evolving backwards towards being a primordial soup. The oceans provide 16% of the animal protein consumed globally. In Asia, this reaches 28%. The oceans represent an irreplaceable food source. The world cannot afford to let them die.

This calls for affordable waste management on a global scale. With 50% of the earth's population living within 60 kilometers of the coast, proper treatment of sewage and urban runoff is vital to protecting the oceans. The current practice of dumping sludge on the ground or in landfills sets the stage for the leaching of nitrogen products back into the watershed and the oceans. However, early twentieth century technology and laws govern sewage treatment. The impact of "treated" sewage outflows into streams and the ocean was unknown back then. Every country needs to do water reclamation beyond a trivial scale. The world needs a better solution. Innovative R&D could result in much more palatable solutions to sewage treatment.

Without touching on the subject of the air one breathes, the foregoing discussion gives a hint of some of the monumental R&D opportunities in the environmental area. The need for solutions is evident. Unquestionably, the nature of many of the problems and their solutions mandates Government action on a global scale.

Feeding the global population will continue to be a growing challenge. The challenge involves improving production efficiency relative to the use of labor and natural resources, achieving sustainability, and decreasing the environmental footprint. The foregoing discussed some of the improvements needed relative to the environmental impact of food production. It articulated the need for alternatives to the excessive use of fertilizers, water, and pesticides. It also noted the need for improvements in the treatment and disposal of animal waste.

Genetic studies have opened a myriad of research opportunities. Genetic engineering has proven to be a practical method for improving disease resistance, nutritional content, salt tolerance, drought tolerance, yield, taste, texture, and appearance in agricultural crops. Genetic engineering has resulted in a reduced dependence on insecticides, fertilizers, and other agrochemicals. Experts believe that they have seen only the "tip of the iceberg" of genetic research.

Farmers have abandoned thousands of once cultivated acres due to irrigation induced salt build up, other contamination, soil depletion caused by wind and water erosion, et cetera. The Central Valley of California is just one example where this has occurred. Water usage in farming tends to be very wasteful except in very arid regions such as in Israel. Developing farming methods, which facilitate the permanent use of the agricultural eco-systems, are both necessary and afford tremendous research opportunities.

Many believe that nanotechnology has the potential to revolutionize food production by providing new tools for improving the detection of diseases, the molecular treatment of disease, and enhancing the ability of plants to absorb nutrients. Smart sensors and smart delivery systems will enhance the farmer's abilities to combat viruses and other pathogens. Expanding current research in nanotechnology applications to agriculture will bring to fruition these exciting possibilities.

The Department of Agriculture facilitates and funds research and development in support of agriculture. It works in very close collaboration with the farmers. Hence, the Department's research program encompasses such areas as international competitiveness, farm economics, sustainability of rural farms, and marketing. The Department of Agriculture would need to adjust its R&D program to pursue the above cited research opportunities more vigorously.

Globalization and urbanization have created new threats to public health. Recall that approximately 50% of the world's population lives in cities within 60 kilometers of the coast. Many are overcrowded, suffer from severe air pollution, and lack adequate infrastructures and sanitation systems. This coupled with the increased international trade in food and the extensive movement of people throughout the world creates new threats to public health on a global scale. Global warming, habitat destruction, deforestation, and loss of biodiversity resulting from urbanization and the quest to feed the exploding human population compound the problem. Globalization has also brought with it the threat of bioterrorism. No one is exempt from these threats to public health. The need to understand these threats and develop appropriate responses to them on a global basis presents a myriad of research opportunities with almost unimaginable payoffs. (The consequences of a global pandemic debilitating and killing a significant portion of the world's population are nearly impossible to postulate.)

Continuing to consider research opportunities with a global as well as local impact, we now explore some of the research opportunities in the production and use of energy, the lifeblood of modern society. Finding and exploiting on a global scale an alternative to fossil fuels as an energy source could help stem the buildup of carbon dioxide in the atmosphere as well as provide an enduring replacement for petroleum based fuels. Since oil's use as a fuel is primarily for transportation and fixed power stations then the need is for alternative means of powering automobiles, buses, trucks, trains and airplanes.

For many including a number of environmentalists and politicians, electric vehicles are the answer. Politicians have passed laws that consider them zero emission vehicles. This is not necessarily the case. The situation with electric vehicles is endemic to America's energy and transportation problems in which a solution must resolve the political, environmental, resource, and technical issues. An incident that occurred approximately fifteen years ago helps illustrate this. A young woman came to our door seeking signatures for an initiative that would have furthered the pursuit of electric cars in California. My daughter, Karen, was in junior high school at the time and was at my side.

After the young woman had extolled the virtues of electric vehicles to garner my signature and I continued to decline, she asked me why I did not do so. Briefly, I explained that the electricity to charge the batteries in an electric automobile currently came in the most part from coal, petroleum, and natural gas fired electric generating plants and these are not zero emission facilities. Therefore, one may think of the electric vehicle as having a very long exhaust pipe emitting its share of pollutants at the power plant. In addition, the batteries used to power electric vehicles employ environmentally unfriendly chemicals that eventually need disposal. Continuing from basic principles, electric cars are inherently energy inefficient compared to gasoline ones. Comparable electric cars have to be significantly heavier than their gasoline-powered counterparts since the best electric storage batteries are a hundred times heavier than gasoline for storing the same amount of energy. (The lighter power train of an electric car partially offsets the significant weight of the batteries.) Since heavier cars are less fuel-efficient than lighter ones, weight does matter. Making matters worse, there are multiple changes of energy states inherent in electric cars. Simply, the energy state changes are fossil fuels to heat, heat to mechanical energy, mechanical energy to electricity, electricity to chemical energy in the battery, chemical energy to electricity, and electricity to mechanical energy, which moves the car. By the second law of thermodynamics, each change in energy state is inefficient to some degree (looses some energy). In contrast, a gasoline-powered vehicle converts heat from burning gasoline to mechanical energy, which moves the car. The young woman was rather "blown away" and said she was going home to read about what she heard. The incident made an impression on Daughter Karen, who has subsequently gone on to become an environmental scientist. With the encouragement and assistance of Government, Detroit and others continue to pursue and bring to market electric vehicles despite its environmental and efficiency issues. The best technology is not always the winner.

Biofuels and hydrogen appear to be the front-runners other than electricity to replace the gasoline in cars. Alcohol made from plant starch (e.g., corn) is one biofuel. A most significant drawback of using plant starch is that it represents only a small part of the biomass of the plant (e.g., the grain). Producing alcohol consumes considerable amounts of energy in the form of fertilizer and heat to cook and distill the alcohol. The fermentation process converts half of the sugar to CO2 — not good for the atmosphere if it is released. Furthermore, acreage used for alcohol production could produce food (either for human or livestock consumption). In fact, there is not enough available land on which to produce corn to reduce gasoline consumption significantly.

Consequently, much debate and scientific analysis of the net energy balance and environmental impact of various liquid fuels has resulted. For example, does alcohol take more energy to produce than it contains? The answer somewhat depends on the amount of energy allocated to the residue animal feed, which is high in protein. One must also consider the power train of the vehicle (e.g., conventional engine or fuel cell/electric motor). The environmental impact includes the fraction of energy that is not renewable (e.g., fertilizers made from natural gas), CO2 and other gases released to the atmosphere, and the effect growing the feedstock has on the land.

Currently, each fuel has its advocacy group. Many believe that producing fuel from the cellulose, which comprises the largest constituent (30–60%) of the biomass, is the solution. There are currently two principle means of conversion. One is a thermal gasification where heat applied to the biomass in the presence of oxygen or steam under pressure creates methane. Running the methane through the established Fischer–Tropsch process converts it into diesel fuel. Obtaining a high enough efficiency in terms of the energy content of the fuel compared to the energy used to make it is a major challenge to commercial viability. In addition, there are a number of environmental concerns with this method, due to the copious use of energy for the conversion.

The other is biological where various organisms are used to convert the cellulose to sugar, from which alcohol can be made using fermentation, or to methane/oil directly. Designing the right organisms through genetic engineering constitutes a significant amount of current research. Also, developing continuous operations rather than batch processes seems to be mandatory due to the volumes involved. Being able to sustain the growth of the organisms is a challenge since the organisms' waste products can kill them if not removed. Minimizing the time required to complete the conversion is important in order to keep costs down. Much research is being done in this arena with a limited number of field demonstrations being planned to establish a particular approach's feasibility.

The scale factor regarding the conversion of biomass to liquid fuel is daunting. Let us assume a 20% efficiency for the conversion of biomass into a liquid fuel. This is neither theoretically impossible nor is it a foregone conclusion. Then to provide the feedstock to a small refitted petroleum refinery that processes 100,000 barrels a day would require the processing of approximately 900,000 tons of biomass a day. The U.S. consumes approximately 9 million barrels of gasoline per day for motor vehicle use. Thus, replacing oil, which is used for producing gasoline, with biomass would require nearly 100 of the biomass conversion facilities, each with an output of 100,000 barrels of feedstock per day. On a nationwide basis, 90 million tons of biomass would have to be collected and processed daily.

Hydrogen advocates will claim that they have the ultimate answer. They view hydrogen as the ultimate clean fuel. This however depends on how it is used, whether in an internal combustion engine or a fuel cell. If it is burned in an internal combustion engine there will still be NOx formed. As is the case of the electric car, one has to consider the process of producing the hydrogen. Currently, the most common method is to combine natural gas with steam at a very high temperature and water at a lower temperature to get hydrogen and CO_2. Currently the CO_2 is released to the atmosphere but in principle could be sequestered if this technology is developed sufficiently. The process has nearly a 90% rate of efficiency.

A Norwegian company has developed a process for producing hydrogen from hydrocarbons which produces just hydrogen and carbon black. This process is less than 50% efficient if only the methane is used. Coal can similarly be processed to produce hydrogen. (Actually syngas which is hydrogen and carbon monoxide can be further processed to increase the amount of hydrogen produced and oxidize the carbon monoxide to produce CO_2.)

Fermentation of organic matter using bacteria can also be used to produce hydrogen from various feed stocks such as biomass. Algae grown under certain conditions will produce hydrogen. Algae has been genetically engineered to produce hydrogen more efficiently. Recently, photosynthesis efficiencies of 7–10% have been achieved.

Finally, hydrogen can be produced through the electrolysis of water. This requires copious amounts of electricity which itself may or may not be produced in an environmentally friendly manner.

Challenges with most of these processes include achieving adequate efficiency, making it cost competitive with petroleum based fuels, scaling up to commercial production rates, and maintaining an environmentally friendly process. There is considerable research and development ongoing but many predict it will be decades before gasoline will be replaced entirely by one or more of these fuels. There remain many research opportunities with the potential for creating a whole new industry related to producing and possibly distributing the replacement fuel for gasoline.

Nearly half of the world's electrical power including that of the U.S. is generated using coal. The global consumption of coal produces more than 12 billion metric tons of carbon dioxide annually. On top of this 25% of the globe's electricity is generated by burning oil and natural gas. Although coal reserves are likely to last centuries, the need to eliminate essentially all carbon dioxide emissions remains. There are three basic options for hydrocarbon-fired power plants: (1) sequester the carbon dioxide, (2) convert the hydrocarbons to hydrogen using a carbon dioxide free process, and (3) generate electricity another way. The first two options were discussed previously in this chapter.

Alternative means of producing electricity include wind, ocean waves/tides, solar, hydro, and nuclear including nuclear fusion. Approximately 15% of the world's electricity comes from hydroelectric plants. The availability of sites and the environmental and political impacts limit their expansion. Hydroelectric generation is very mature resulting in a very low payoff for R&D.

Recent advances in turbine design and control systems have made wind generation facilities more attractive. One may question whether diminishing returns have not set in for R&D in the wind generation of electricity. Whereas solar has been around for a while, there is a need to improve efficiencies and reduce the total investment costs to make solar a real alternative to fossil fuel fired generating plants. Current R&D expenditures appear to be rewarding.

This leaves ocean and nuclear options as fertile opportunities for research and development. Oceans potentially represent a huge energy source. The only problem is that the energy density is very low. Various options include tidal power, wave power, ocean thermal energy conversion, ocean currents, ocean winds, and salinity gradients. As with wind-powered turbines, the ability to generate electricity from the ocean is not generally continuous. Nor is it pervasive. Few places exist in the world where the difference between high and low tides are sufficiently great to permit cost effective electrical production. The same is true for each of the other means of using the ocean for generating electricity.

The British, French, and Spaniards first used tides to run a waterwheel in the 11th century. Today, France operates a 240-Megawatt power plant off its coast. The next largest facility is more than ten times smaller. There is an ocean current driven test facility off the coast of Hawaii. There are a few additional ocean wave generating test facilities, whose relocation is relatively easy. Other than this, the ocean remains a major untapped resource. Several companies are developing systems to generate electricity using the ocean as a power source. The environmental impacts including those on fish populations and local water circulation caused by significant ocean-based electrical generation are largely unknown. Ocean power generation could be a new frontier for R&D.

Fusion has been the Holy Grail for clean power generation for decades. Other than the false announcement by some Utah researchers of cold fusion in a jar, research has involved large and expensive facilities. Oak Ridge National Laboratory in partnership with the Princeton Plasma Physics Laboratory and the Savannah River National Laboratory are leading the United States' participation in an international effort called the International Thermonuclear Experimental Reactor (ITER) to be built in France. It uses superconducting electromagnets to initiate and contain the reaction. Lawrence Livermore National Laboratory is working on a laser based technique to compress and heat the hydrogen ions sufficiently to cause their fusion into helium ions to occur. They have built the world's largest laser at the cost of $3.5 billion with the goal of mimicking the temperatures and pressures at the center of the sun. These are very big ticket items and well beyond the scope of small companies and groups to undertake. As in the case of ITER, they are beyond the ability of many countries to fund. Never the less, this research offers tremendous possibilities for the future and if successful, it will provide significant opportunities for U.S. industries to participate in the developing and building of a nuclear fusion power industry.

Normal nuclear power plants based on fission produce 15% of the world's electricity. France produces nearly 80% of its electricity by nuclear — highest percentage of any nation. The U.S. produces the most electricity by nuclear but only 19% of its total production. The last nuclear power plant to go online in the U.S. was Watts Bar I, which went online on February 7, 1996. There are many reasons for the decline of nuclear power on a global basis. One reason certainly has been the growing problem of disposing of the nuclear waste. The design of today's nuclear reactors is such that approximately 97% of the fuel remains unburned in the spent rod upon its removal from the reactor during refueling.

The U.S. had a program to research and develop what is called a mixed oxide fuel cycle. This involves the reprocessing of the spent rods to separate the waste and the reusable fuel. Fuel rods would then contain a mixture of this recovered fuel and a small amount of new fuel. Thus, reprocessing would dramatically reduce the amount of waste requiring storage to a few percent of what it is now. Fears such as those concerning the safety of reprocessing operations and the possibility of the diversion of bomb making materials brought the mixed oxide fuel program to a halt in the U.S. Today, Britain, France, and Russia have extensive reprocessing facilities. France leads the world in reprocessing 25% of its spent nuclear rods. Japan, China, and India are pursuing reprocessing. Many believe that that innovation can resolve reasonable concerns regarding safety and security. Research and development can lead to better solutions. To this end, the U.S. announced a new initiative in 2006 that would establish an international effort to reprocess fuel in such a way as to inhibit nuclear proliferation, while making nuclear power available to developing countries.

Aside from reprocessing, researchers and engineers have proposed new reactor designs, which would improve the safety and effectiveness of nuclear power production. The U.S. Government has provided limited funding to pursue some of the improved reactor designs. One company has come up with a concept that would allow the use of what was previously an unusable isotope of uranium in its reactor. This coupled with reprocessing could provide the world with nuclear generated electrical power for centuries. Clearly, there is much room for research and development in the nuclear energy field.

This chapter has uncovered immense research and development opportunities in some of the major problems facing society. Optical and quantum computing beckon researchers in the computer sciences. Vastly expanded computing capabilities will open new vistas for the information and knowledge sciences. Nanotechnology beckons researchers with new and exciting possibilities. Bioelectronics may provide a whole new generation of electronic products. Possibilities include lighting systems reaching 90% efficiency or brand-new high efficiency television screens. As energy becomes more costly and concerns for the environmental impact increases there will be a growing demand for products and services, which are more efficient and environmentally friendlier. This opens the door for more research and development. This will lead to the creation of new industries and the re-creation of old industries. Those with better ideas will flourish.

CHAPTER 14. RESEARCHERS AND ORGANIZATIONS FOR THE FUTURE

"Boldly go where no man has gone before." — Gene Roddenberry

The previous chapter established the need for expanded research and development and explored some of the opportunities for innovation. This chapter considers a few of the people and organizations that may have a significant impact on America's future well-being. As learned earlier, it is nigh on impossible to predict who is going to make the big discovery or invention. Recall that only one, out of a great many ideas, ever makes it through R&D into the marketplace. Moreover, out of those that do make it to the marketplace only a few are very significant — change paradigms or create new industries. In an interview for an article in *Technology Review*, "Making Gasoline from Bacteria," Craig Venter, a researcher in biofuels, aptly stated, "We need a hundred, a thousand solutions, not just one. I know at least a dozen groups and labs trying to make biofuels from bacteria with sugar."

As Craig indicated, there are many researchers and innovators who are pursuing their passions and are at least as worthy of mention as those that are represented in this chapter. Selecting the researchers and organizations that this chapter acknowledges was neither scientific nor comprehensive. The Internet sites of *Scientific American*, *Technology Review*, and *Popular Mechanics* provided the lists of top innovations and innovators. Literally hundreds of innovators are worthy of inclusion. The actual researchers and organizations selected for inclusion were those that addressed opportunities discussed in the previous chapter, had the potential of significant impact, offered an engaging story, and when considered with the others represented a cross section of research. Each of the selected people or organizations was sent a copy of a proposed vignette about them and their research with a request to correct and enhance the vignette. More than half of those contacted responded, which led to significant improvements in the content of this chapter. The intent of the vignettes is to excite one about the future possibilities for American R&D. Therefore, here are the stories of twenty researchers and organizations arranged in alphabetical order.

Greg Allgood and Children's Safe Drinking Water Program

Dr. Greg Allgood has been concerned about safe drinking water since his days as a Master's student in Public Health at the University of North Carolina, Chapel Hill. He went on to get his Ph.D. in toxicology from North Carolina State University. He has spent 21 years at Proctor and Gamble (P&G) working on treating water for much of the time and now leads P&G's Safe Drinking Water Program. He is also the chair of the communications working group of the World Health Organization's International Network to Promote Household Water Treatment and Safe Storage. John Hopkins University Bloomberg School of Public Health's Center for Communication Programs recognized his contributions by presenting him with the 2006 International Health Communication Gold Medallion.

The Children's Safe Drinking Water program focuses on providing safe drinking water through a novel household water treatment product. Among the attributes of this product are ease of use and affordability. The quest of P&G researchers since 1995 has been to improve on chlorine water treatment, which kills bacteria and viruses but does nothing to parasites. Their achievement was to develop a powder that is as effective in water treatment as large multi-stage municipal water treatment plants. *Popular Mechanics* in citing the product as one of the ten New World-Changing Innovations of the Year for 2008 stated that the mixture contains chlorine, which kills the bacteria and viruses, and a compound, which causes suspended solids, metals and parasites to clump together so that they can then be filtered out with a cotton cloth. *Popular Mechanics* quoted Eric Mintz, chief of the CDC's diarrheal diseases and epidemiology section, in their article, "The visual improvement is dramatic." Most important of all is that it costs only pennies to treat a gallon of water. The product failed to be a commercial success and was about to be abandoned by P&G when Dr. Allgood convinced the company to set up the nonprofit Children's Safe Drinking Water Program for the product instead. The Program with the help of UNICEF and the World Health Organization has helped purify more than 250 million gallons of water in more than forty countries.

Theodore Betley

Breaking the bonds that tie is the challenge of getting hydrogen fuel from water. As discussed previously, electrolysis is the brute force approach and as such is energy intensive. Dr. Theodore Betley is pursuing the way plants do it during photosynthesis. That is, his goal is to take water, add photons or energy, and efficiently extract hydrogen. This requires working at the molecular level. Ted has mimicked nature by arranging catalyst doped small clusters of metals within a nanocrystal. This has enabled him to replicate the multi-step process that nature uses to break down water efficiently to make sugar during photosynthesis. He is now pursuing a catalyst, which yields an acceptable efficiency. Still to come is the commercial production of these engineered nanomaterials. Having grown up in Michigan, Ted went to the University of Michigan and earned a degree in chemical engineering. Notably, two of his undergraduate internships were at the Ford Motor Company and Exxon. He received his Ph.D. from the California Institute of Technology in inorganic chemistry related to iron mediated nitrogen reduction. From there he spent a couple of years at the Massachusetts Institute of Technology researching water oxidation catalysis. He currently is an Assistant Professor of Chemistry and Chemical Biology at Harvard University. *Technology Review* honored the significance of his work with a Top Young Innovator under 35 Award in 2008.

Stephen del Cardayre and LS9

Dr. del Cardayre is through and through a biochemist, having received his bachelor's degree from the University of California — Berkeley and Ph.D. from the University of Wisconsin-Madison, in biochemistry. His Postdoctoral training was in Microbial Biotechnology at the University of British Columbia. Prior to becoming the Vice President of LS9 for research and development, he was directly involved in the development, application, and commercialization of technologies for the engineering of biocatalytic processes for the pharmaceutical and chemical industries.

LS9 is exploring the conversion of biomass into synthetic petroleum using genetically engineered microbes. They are using techniques from synthetic biology to modify the way that bacteria make fatty acids. Stephen del Cardayre has declared that, "the company can make hundreds of different hydrocarbon molecules. The process can yield crude oil without the contaminating sulfur that much petroleum out of the ground contains. The crude, in turn, would go to a standard refinery to be processed into automotive fuel, jet fuel, diesel fuel, or any other petroleum product that someone wanted to make." The company hopes to have a pilot plant in operation soon and be providing synthetic crude to refineries within five years. If successful, LS9 will breathe new life into the petroleum industry.

Central Michigan University Research Corporation (CMU-RC) and Dendritic Nanotechnologies Inc.

Central Michigan University Research Corporation and Dendritic Nanotechnologies have developed a ground water purification system based on a dendritic polymer developed by Dendritic Nanotechnologies. (A dendritic molecule is one that is repeatedly branched like a tree.) CMU faculty and Dendritic Nanotechnologies staff are collaborating on refining the polymer for the removal of perchlorate from ground water. Additionally, CMU will perform all testing and Dendritic Nanotechnologies will manufacture the resulting polymer. Perchlorate pollution is widespread throughout the U.S. with 27 Department of Defense facilities known to have perchlorate contamination. Perchlorate interferes with iodide absorption by the thyroid gland in women. Since ground water accounts for approximately fifty percent of the nation's municipal, domestic, and agricultural water supply, perchlorate contamination potentially affects the health of millions of women. This breakthrough technology offers the potential of a cost-effective means of ground water remediation.

Michelle C. Chang

Dr. Michelle Chang's interests are very diverse as indicated by the fact she received bachelor's degrees in both biochemistry and French literature from the University of California, San Diego. She was both an NSF and MIT/Merck Foundation Fellow while pursuing her Ph.D. at the Massachusetts Institute of Technology (MIT).

She has been at the University of California, Berkeley ever since. She is intent on contributing solutions to the world's environmental, energy and health problems. She is a recipient of the Arnold and Mabel Beckman Foundation Young Investigator Award. Central to her research is the employment of synthetic biology methods to engineer a microbe's enzymatic process so that it provides the desired product, whether it is a hydrocarbon fuel or a pharmaceutical. She is providing the fundamental understanding of how living organisms control the enzymatic processes.

Yet-Ming Chiang

Dr. Yet-Ming Chiang immigrated to the United States with his family when he was six years old. After high school, he went off to the Massachusetts Institute of Technology (MIT) and has been there ever since. A year prior to receiving his ScD in ceramics he joined the faculty in MIT's Material Science and Engineering department and later became the youngest person in that department's history to achieve tenure. Dr. Chiang has had quite an entrepreneurial bent having founded two rather diverse companies. American Superconductor is the first company he co-founded with David A. Rudman, John B. Vander Sande, and Gregory J. Yurek. American Superconductor produces high temperature superconducting wire. This wire can handle 150 times the current of a copper wire of the same dimensions. Superconducting transmission lines enable a much more efficient national power grid. In 2001, he founded his second company, A123 Systems, with Dr. Bart Riley and Ric Fulop. A123 Systems has become one of the world's leading suppliers of high-power lithium ion batteries in a mere eight years. The basis of the company's battery is nanotechnology that Dr. Chiang developed at MIT. A123's battery offers high power, safe chemistry, long life, and environmental soundness, at relatively low cost compared to traditional lithium ion batteries. With five times the power and ten times the life of current batteries and their safe chemistry, A123's batteries are finding their way into everything from hand tools to automobiles. Unique and rather miraculously, the recharging of A123's batteries to 90% of full charge takes only 5 minutes. Dr. Chiang is indeed shaping America's technology future.

Peter L. Corsell and GridPoint

Peter L. Corsell is an unlikely individual to be a leader in technology. He received his bachelor's degree from the School of Foreign Service at Georgetown University. After graduating, he served with the U.S. State Department in Cuba and as a political analyst with the Central Intelligence Agency. His listing among the recipients of the prestigious TR35 2008 Young Innovator Award attests to his technology leadership role. Peter founded GridPoint to create technologies that would accelerate the adoption of renewable energy sources and increase energy efficiency. GridPoint has developed software and hardware that allows the electric utilities to match electrical generation and consumption by controlling many of the devices such as water heaters, furnaces, and air conditioners on the grid. Peter has stated that "Consumers should be able to buy 74° and the utility company then sells them 74°," By controlling the precise time of operation of heating and cooling systems, the utility can match the load to the supply while still providing the customer the desired room temperature. GridPoint's Smart Grid also facilitates the integration of renewable energy sources

such as solar cells and wind turbines into the Grid. Peter's passion for the environ-
ment and society is evident by his Chairmanship of the World Economic Forum's
Global Agenda Council on Sustainable Energy and his membership on Newsweek's
Global Environment and Leadership Advisory Committee. He also serves on Xcel
Energy's Smart Grid Advisory Board and the Corporate Board of the Environmental
Media Association. Clearly, if Mr. Corsell has his way the world will become more
energy efficient and environmentally sensitive.

Gen-Probe Incorporated

Gen-Probe has consistently made Forbes list of the best 200 small companies.
Though it is small in size, it is big in impact. The company is a world leader in the
development, manufacturing, and marketing of diagnostic tests for the screening of
donated blood and for the detection of human diseases including those causing sexu-
ally transmitted diseases (STDs), tuberculosis, strep throat, pneumonia, and fungal
infections. The company has invented a fully automated, high-volume system for performing their innovative tests. This system facilitates the testing and diagnosing of
these diseases in the underdeveloped regions of the world where one or more of these
diseases may be prevalent. The company is currently developing tests for prostate
cancer, drug-resistant hospital infections, and the virus that causes cervical cancer.
Dr. Lyle J. Arnold leads the company's research and development. He has at least 36
U.S. patents issued with more pending. He received a BS in Chemistry from the University of California at Los Angeles and a Ph.D. in Chemistry/Biochemistry from the
University of California at San Diego

Julia R. Greer

Just as physics has provided the underpinnings of many twentieth century innovations, Julia R. Greer is laying the physics foundation for tomorrow's nanotechnology applications. Julia has taken an interesting path to her current position as an
Assistant Professor at the California Institute of Technology (Caltech). She began
life in Moscow, Russia and attended both a science and mathematics (magnate) high
school and the preparatory division (high school) of the Moscow Conservatory of
Music. After immigrating to the United States with her family in 1992, she attended
high school in upstate New York where she exchanged tutoring in mathematics for
English interactions in order to learn English. She went on to MIT where she got
her bachelor's degree in chemical engineering with a minor in music performance.
She gained practical experience at Intel while working on her doctorate at Stanford
University in materials science and engineering. She was a post-doctoral fellow at
Palo Alto Research Center (PARC) before arriving at Caltech. She is the recipient
of a number of awards including the Top Young Innovator under 35 Award in 2008.

In the world of nano materials, Julia has found "a world out there that is only beginning to be discovered. It is now apparent that when we are dealing with the sizes
on the order of one billionth of a hair, there is new physics and its laws need to be for-
mulated and understood..." There is no doubt that this new physics will provide the
underpinnings for such diverse applications as data storage at terabits per cubic inch,
high-efficiency solid-state engines, single-cell diagnostics of complex diseases, and
the development of ultra-light yet super-strong materials for vehicles. In Julia's mind,

the physics she is exploring will lead to the development of revolutionary new materials with unprecedented properties. Applications include biocompatible materials for implantable devices such as pacemakers and new materials that can withstand extreme thermo-mechanical environments for use in nuclear power plants. Julia performs as a concert pianist when not pursuing the physics of the very small.

Brad Hines and Soliant Energy

Brad Hines graduated from the Massachusetts Institute of Technology (MIT) with Bachelor and Master's degrees in Electrical Engineering. He spent the first 14 years of his career working at the Jet Propulsion Laboratory, initially in a small skunk works-style group, then later on massive space projects such as the $1B Space Interferometry Mission. As his career moved upwards through the NASA hierarchy, he began to realize that the heft of a large organization wasn't the best place to express his creativity, and looked for a challenge that would allow him to exercise both technical and management innovation to bring something valuable to the world, to produce something that could really benefit people.

Brad spent a few years exploring different opportunities before deciding to make the leap into solar energy. He perceived that it was a field where technology was changing quickly and where the global context was increasing its importance rapidly. From a technology standpoint, the particular field of photovoltaic solar concentrators drew upon many of the same technologies he had used in developing space telescopes at NASA. These technologies involved the fields of optics, electronics, thermal control, high reliability engineering, tracking mechanisms, and embedded control systems. Therefore, Brad left JPL for a southern California startup, where he cut his teeth in the solar industry and became Vice President of Engineering.

He then founded his own startup, Soliant Energy, which is focusing its efforts on solar panels that employ ultra-efficient solar cells combined with modest solar concentrators made of plastic. Space systems where the efficiency is worth the very high price are traditionally the only application of ultra-efficient solar cell technology. Soliant Energy expects to achieve the high efficiencies of the space cells with the cost reductions of a solar concentrator and the mass production techniques of the automotive industry. Brad's team has designed a solar panel that fits in the same frame as current roof mount systems and anticipates selling the panels at a competitive price per kilowatt of power produced. The company is testing pre-production installations now, with launch planned for 2010. Soliant is only one of a number of companies that are pursuing various approaches to more cost-effective solar panels, and is not the first to apply the principle of solar concentration to ultra-efficient but high-priced solar cells. However, Brad's vision that has made Soliant unique is to make use of this technology to deliver market differentiation, by 1) delivering the most efficient solar panel on the market, and 2) delivering it in a package that is compatible with standard solar panel installation practice. Thus, Soliant provides innovations that enable the easy adoption of their products by the numerous existing commercial solar installers.

Intellectual Ventures

Intellectual Ventures has put forth a new nuclear reactor design that overcomes all the problems of conventional reactors if it proves to be technically and commercially viable. Among the problems they have overcome, include the heavy reliance on enriched uranium for fuel, periodically opening the reactor and refueling it, and storing or reprocessing the spent fuel. The Intellectual Ventures scientists' design requires only a small amount of enriched fuel. The "core" of their reactor design gradually converts nonfissile material into the fuel it needs. Theoretically, a reactor based on this design could run for a century without refueling. Most of the fuel would be uranium-238, which today is a waste material. Millions of pounds of uranium-238 already exist in stockpiles around the globe. *Technology Review's* article naming the Intellectual Ventures' design as one of the ten emerging technologies of 2009 quoted Charles W. Forsberg, executive director of the Nuclear Fuel Cycle Project at MIT, regarding the design that it presents "... the simplest possible fuel cycle and it requires only one uranium enrichment plant per planet." Although the basic concept has been around for decades, this is the first practical design that anyone has put forth. A number of issues need to be addressed in developing this technology, including those associated with safety under accident conditions. Intellectual Ventures believes that the first unit could be up and running by the early 2020s if its development is pursued. *Technology Review* named the Intellectual Ventures' design as one of the ten emerging technologies of 2009 that could change the way we live.

Lonnie Johnson and Johnson Electro-Mechanical Systems

"Once a tinkerer, always a tinkerer" is an apt description of Lonnie Johnson. As a child, he took his siblings toys apart to create something new. Later, as a high school senior, he built a robot he nicknamed Linex and entered it in the science fair at the University of Alabama. This got him to Tuskegee University where he earned a degree in engineering. After graduation, he worked at Oak Ridge National Laboratory and then joined the Air Force where he got into space work. This led him to the Jet Propulsion Laboratory (JPL) where he worked on the Galileo Mission to Jupiter, back to the Air Force for some more space work, and back to JPL to work on the Cassini Mission to Saturn.

While tinkering with a jet pump and a nozzle for a refrigerator cooling system, he accidentally sprayed a jet of water across the room. This led to his most famous invention, the Super Soaker squirt gun. It took him a couple of years to convince a toy company to build and market it. After finally making it to market, it became the number-one toy seller in 1991 and grossed in excess of $1 billion. Johnson's royalties from the Super Soaker gave him the independence to pursue his passion for invention. While working for the Air Force and JPL, he continued to extend some ideas on an environmentally friendly refrigeration system that he developed while building his high school robot. Reversing the concept of refrigeration, he turned to generating electricity based on the principle that temperature differences create pressure gradients. By using these pressure gradients to force ions through a membrane, he was able to generate electricity from heat with no moving parts. His approach is entirely different from any other thermoelectric device or fuel cell. Paul Werbos, who has provided National Science Foundation funding, has stated "This is a whole new family of technology." *Popular Mechanics* honored Lonnie's invention by naming it one of their top 10 inventions in 2008. Lonnie has patented more than a hundred of his inventions. Using his financial success to give back to his community, he provides space in his facilities for a high school robotics team and for the Georgia Alliance for Children, of which he is the chairman.

Jay Keasling

One might say that today Dr. Jay Keasling sits atop the biofuels field. He is Professor of Chemical Engineering at the University of California Berkeley, a Senior Faculty Scientist, Director of the Physical Biosciences Division at the Lawrence Berkeley National Laboratory, Director of the Berkeley Center for Synthetic Biology, and Chief Executive Officer (CEO) of the Joint Bioenergy Institute. Back in 2006, *Discovery Magazine* named him Scientist of the Year. His fellow professionals have recognized him by naming him a Fellow of the American Academy for Microbiology and the American Institute of Medical and Biological Engineering (2000). Jay and three of his students formed a synthetic biofuels company, Amyris Biotechnologies.

Jay began his journey in the disciplines of chemistry, biology, and engineering in the applied field of farming in Nebraska. From there, he went to the University of Nebraska for a bachelor's degree in chemistry and biology. After that he went to the University of Michigan and got a master's degree and doctorate in chemical engineering. After a stop at Stanford University for a post doctorate, he has been at the University of California, Berkeley.

After building a tool kit for engineering microbes to produce various products, he took on his first big problem, producing an affordable and effective antimalaria drug. An effective one already existed, artemisinin, with a 90% cure rate, but it came from the sweet-wormwood plant and was slow and expensive to produce. Keasling's team took a simple yeast cell into which they grafted some wormwood genes and then modified some other yeast cell genes to achieve a microorganism that converts sugar into artemisinin. As a result, the cost of manufacturing a dose was pennies rather than dollars. He has taken steps to prevent anyone from profiting from this innovation and has entered into an agreement with the pharmaceutical company Sanofi-Aventis to produce and sell the drug at cost.

Amyris Biotechnologies intends to capitalize on Jay's technology in the production of biofuels. They have engineered some microorganisms to turn sugar cane into fuel. They are constructing a pilot plant in Emeryville, California and have teamed with Crystalsev, one of Brazil's largest distributors of sugar and ethanol, to push Amyris' technology into full production. They have signed on Santelisa Vale, the second largest ethanol and sugar producer in Brazil, to be the first to use the technology.

The Department of Energy established the Joint Bioenergy Institute, of which Joel is the CEO, to provide Government research on converting lignin and cellulose into fuel. It comprises a partnership of three national laboratories and three universities and has an annual budget of approximately $25 million.

Vic Knauf and Arcadia Biosciences

Arcadia Biosciences is committed to improving the production efficiency, quality, and nutritional benefit of the food everyone eats by employing ecologically sound technologies. One of the company's technologies allows farmers to grow crops with much less use of nitrogen while maintaining the same yields. Another technology provides strains of plants that are salt tolerant, which is important for arid regions dependent on heavy use of irrigation. The company is exploiting a technology that combines normal plant breeding with a screening procedure at the gene level to develop strains of plants possessing desired attributes. This avoids having to label the resulting product as "genetically modified." The company is developing toma-toes, which are richer in antioxidants, and better tasting. Safflower oil contains GLA (gamma linolenic acid) which appears to have a therapeutic benefit. Safflower oil with higher levels of GLA is now possible.

Dr. Vic Knauf leads Arcadia's research staff. Dr. Knauf earned a BS in biology from the New Mexico Institute of Mining and Technology and an MS and Ph.D. in micro-biology and immunology from the University of Washington. Among his credits are 27 patents and more than 50 professional papers. He co-founded a company prior to joining Arcadia that Arcadia subsequently acquired. This acquisition brought the gene level screening technology to Arcadia. Under his leadership, Calgene released the world's first five genetically engineered plant products.

Clifford Kubiak

University of California, San Diego professor, Clifford Kubiak, has demonstrated making carbon monoxide out of thin air. For the uninitiated, carbon monoxide is widely used to make plastics and other products. It is also a key ingredient in the making of synthetic fuels including methanol and gasoline. The process involves a silicon electrode, which absorbs light and converts it into electricity. This, in turn, helps drive a reaction that converts carbon dioxide in the air into carbon monoxide and oxygen. This is not a near term solution for removing carbon dioxide from the atmosphere because of the usual long and tortuous technology development process needed prior to the existence of any commercial plants employing this process. It will even be longer before there are a significant number of plants. However, Kubiak has stated, "any chemical process that you can develop that uses CO2 as a feedstock, rather than having it be an end product, is probably worth doing." He added, "… if chemical manufacturers are going to make millions of pounds of plastics anyway, why not make them from greenhouse gases rather than making tons of greenhouse gases in the process?"

Dr. Kubiak received his bachelor's degree in chemistry from Brown University and his Ph.D. in chemistry from the University of Rochester. From there he went on to do a post-doctoral at the Massachusetts Institute of Technology. He is a recipient of an Alfred P. Sloan Foundation Research Fellow. He recently discovered a class of molecules that exhibit a two-state switching mechanism similar to that of transis-tors but are approximately a thousand times smaller and a thousand times faster than today's smallest transistors. The molecules discovered by Kubiak are the only known molecules that exhibit two stable interchangeable states and one trillion per second switching times. Dr. Kubiak has brought us another technology development effort, which could have profound impact on the future. One can only wonder what other such discoveries in basic science he will make.

Joel Selanikio and DataDyne.org

Joel began his career after graduating from Haverford College with a degree in sociology, and began working on Wall Street as a computer consultant. Looking for something more, he went to Brown University and got an M.D. He then participated in the Epidemic Intelligence Service Program of the U.S. Centers for Disease Control and Prevention (CDC). Dr. Selanikio led the response to numerous foreign and domestic outbreaks including serving as Chief of Operations for the Health and Human Service Secretary's Emergency Command Center in the aftermath of 9/11 while an officer in the Public Health Service. He has combined his passions for computer science and public health in co-founding DataDyne.org to promote new technologies and open-source software development for public health. Dr. Selanikio has received many awards including the 2008 Stockholm Challenge Award along with DataDyne.org.

DataDyne.org is employing mobile information technologies to create sustainable information flow in developing countries and to break down the barriers to data utilization. With a billion people in the world with no data records, the challenge is significant. To this end, DataDyne.org has developed EpiSurveyor, a free, open-source software suite that makes it simple to collect data using handheld computers and mobile phones. Reflecting Dr. Selanikio's passions, "DataDyne believes that programs like EpiSurveyor which combine an open-source model with leverage of the burgeoning mobile computing network have the ability to radically change the nature of developing country public health practice by putting the tools for efficient public health data collection and analysis completely into the hands of developing country health practitioners themselves, and by eliminating the dependence on expensive international consultants." Innovations and commitments such as that of Dr. Selanikio will indeed have a major beneficial impact on global health.

George W. Taylor and Ocean Power Technologies

Dr. George W. Taylor was educated primarily in Australia, receiving his Bachelor and Doctor's of Electrical Engineering degrees from the University of Western Australia and a Ph.D. in Electrical Engineering from the University of London. His first entrepreneurial adventure was the co-founding in 1971 of Princeton Materials Science, Inc., which designed and made liquid crystal displays and electronic watches. After selling out to Fairchild Semiconductor Corporation, he went into the consulting business. Then in 1994, he and Dr. Joseph R. Burns co-founded Ocean Power Technologies to pursue a dream of harnessing the "boundless energy of the world's oceans." Although ocean energy densities are an order of magnitude denser than wind energy densities, they are still relatively low. In order to harness these densities in a cost competitive system, it is necessary to successfully integrate a number of technologies including those of materials (the ocean's salt water is hard on many materials), large structures, energy conversion systems, control systems, and sensors. In accomplishing this, Dr. Taylor and the company have come up with a patented floating buoy system employing an innovative power take-off capability. They believe they can produce 10-megawatts of power in a 30-acre area of ocean. They believe they can achieve a 30-45% load factor, which compares favorably with wind energy, which is 25-35%, and solar energy, which is 10-20%. The U.S. Navy has contracted with them to build and demonstrate a unit off the shore of a Hawaiian Island. With in excess of 50% of the world's population living near the ocean, a significant fraction of the world's electricity may someday come from the ocean in an environmentally friendly way.

Craig Venter and Synthetic Genomics

Dr. Craig Venter has already made his mark on science and technology. He has published more than 200 research articles and participated in the mapping of the human genome. *Time Magazine* has listed him as one of the 100 most influential people in the world. Dr. Venter and Nobel Prize laureate, Dr. Hamilton O. Smith, co-founded Synthetic Genomics with the purpose of "developing and commercializing genomic-driven solutions to address global energy and environmental challenges." This purpose is not only a challenge to his Company's staff, but also to genomic researchers at large. He stated in a 2007 interview with *New Scientist*, "Over the next 20 years, synthetic genomics is going to become the standard for making anything. The chemical industry will depend on it. Hopefully, a large part of the energy industry will depend on it." The design and assembly of genes and whole chromosomes from chemical components of DNA is a new field of science. Synthetic Genomics is seeking to design, synthesize, and assemble specifically engineered cell level bio-factories to meet Craig's challenge.

Craig was far from a good student in high school. In fact, he may have topped the list for least likely to succeed. After graduating from high school, he devoted himself to a life of surfing, sailing and being an all around beach bum. Uncle Sam's call to serve in Viet Nam bought this life to an abrupt end. This experience gave him a new purpose and urgency in life. After his tour with Uncle Sam, he completed his college education in six years with a Ph.D. in physiology and pharmacology. Since then he has had a knack for making the tools of molecular biology do great things. His achievements include decoding more genes than anyone else has done in the world, pioneering the use of automated gene sequencers, and being first to sequence the genome of an entire living organism. The staff that Craig Venter has assembled at Synthetic Genomics may well come close to meeting their challenge.

Michael S. Wong

Michael S. Wong is currently developing nanomaterials to address problems in the environment, energy, and health through his Catalysis and Nanomaterials Laboratory at Rice University. Michael has stated that "treating nanoparticles (NPs) as building blocks and assembling them into useful structures is a powerful concept in 'bottom-up' nanotechnology, in which the dimension-dependent properties of the NPs can be handled and exploited in a usable form (such as porous oxides and microcapsules)." His efforts have resulted in the development of a nanometer size gold particle spotted with palladium that effectively breaks down trichloroethylene (TCE), an industrial degreaser that is carcinogenic and contaminates 60 percent of sites overseen by the U.S. Environmental Protection Agency's Superfund Project. Subsequently, he designed a method of growing them directly on the inner walls of hollow fiber tubes for the incorporation into water filters. He hopes to accomplish this very soon with prototype testing to follow shortly thereafter. Filters employing Wong's engineered nanomaterials may one day go a long way to ridding the earth's ground waters of industrial chemicals.

Ronggui Yang

Dr. Ronggui Yang grew up in China where he received his bachelor and master's degrees in thermal engineering and thermophysics, respectively. He came to the United States for graduate education. He received a master's degree in micro-electro-mechanical systems (MEMS) from the University of California, Los Angeles (UCLA). (MEMS involve the integration of mechanical devices, sensors, actuators, and controlling electronics on a chip.) From UCLA he went to Massachusetts Institute of Technology (MIT) to earn a Ph.D. Here, he performed research on energy transport and conversion at the nanoscale level and gained extensive experience in solid-state electronic materials and devices. Combining this exceptional educational experience with the collaboration of others having expertise in physics, chemistry, and the material sciences, has led to his discoveries in thermoelectric energy harvesting systems. Yang's systems harvest waste heat for useful electrical energy and thermal management systems and thereby improve the efficiency and reliability of electronic systems.

The discovery of thermoelectric materials occurred in 1821. By understanding what is going on at the nanoscale level and through applying nanotechnology manufacturing techniques, Dr. Yang has been able to create composite materials made of nanoparticles and nanowires, which have better efficiency than the best thermoelectric devices on the market today. In another innovation, Dr. Yang's team has encased a nanoscale wicking structure, which alternately vaporizes and condenses distilled water within it, to create a flexible sheet that transfers heat from one side to the other. This sheet or thermal ground plane, has better thermal conductivity than diamond, the best-known heat conducting material in nature, and could be integrated in electronic circuit boards and thereby used to relieve the critical overheating constraint in electronic systems. Ease of mass production further enhances Dr. Yang's technologies. One day one may see laser diodes and microprocessors cooled by one of Dr. Yang's flexible thermal ground planes. Alternatively, the waste heat from vehicle exhausts, factories, and industrial equipment may be harvested and turned into electricity based on the thermoelectric research of Dr. Yang and his fellow researchers.

A faculty member in the department of mechanical engineering at the University of Colorado at Boulder, Dr. Yang has authored and co-authored more than sixty papers, has received five patents, and made a number of invention disclosures. He has received numerous awards including the NSF Career Award in 2009 and the *Technology Review's* TR35 Award in 2008.

These twenty stories are inspiring and afford much hope for America's future. The fact that they are only twenty of the hundreds that have received national recognition or the thousands that are awaiting discovery is awesome. The realization that they and all those like them may not reach their potential due to insufficient funding is most sobering and dims one's hopes for America's future.

CHAPTER 15. EPILOGUE

"The future is purchased by the present." — Samuel Johnson

Having come to the end of the book, I hope the reader shares my admiration for America's technological achievements, appreciation for what they have meant to everyone, respect for those individuals who have played a vital role in their development, and a desire to accomplish something more than passive acceptance of an inevitable decline. The ten most salient points made in the preceding chapters are:

1. There are multiple phases to the technology cycle and that different people working in different facilities perform the various phases of the cycle.

2. It generally takes decades before a successful commercial product or process exploits a theory. In addition, a tremendous winnowing process occurs as things pass from one phase to the next of the technology development cycle.

3. The U.S. economy has been technology driven since before the twentieth century.

4. The rise of technology began with the private laboratories and shops of inventors such as Edison and matured with the establishment of the great corporate laboratories.

5. The Golden Age of technology in America roughly encompassed the period from the end of the First World War to the end of the Cold War and reached its apex in the corporate laboratories, in the Government laboratories, and with a torrent of new or improved products.

6. Every American has benefited with a better standard of living because of America's technological prowess. Much of America's most recent productivity gains are the result of the application of information technology.

7. There is no single indicator of a decline in American technology. Weakening Government funding of Phase One research at universities and colleges provides an indication of the start of a decline in Phase One. A decline in Corporate America's

Phase Two research combined with the considerable evaporation of the Federal Government's spending for Phase Two research indicates the possibility of a decline in Phase Two. This is backed up by a decline in the Phase Two research conducted by Government laboratories, in the proportion of university graduates majoring in science or engineering, in the failure of salaries for engineers and scientists to keep pace, and in the public's general lack of interest in science and engineering news. Together, the sum total of indicators of a decline makes a strong case for a decline in American technology.

8. A decline in American technology affects everyone.

9. Being a service economy does not diminish the relevance and importance of maintaining a robust technology development cycle.

10. There are plenty of opportunities for research and development and some of the researchers and organizations necessary to pursue them more vigorously are in place.

If the foregoing ten points are valid, then it is vital that the U.S. maintain a constant level of effort in all phases of the technology cycle in order to continue to realize the economic benefits from new products and services flowing into the marketplace. Therefore, the issue becomes one of identifying the best means for restoring funding for Phase One research in the physical sciences and for Phase Two research in all areas. Let us take a moment to summarize the prior chapters' discussions of America's current situation and then follow-up by identifying some opportunities for change.

As seen in Chapter 5, Phase Two research funding has historically come from three sources: independent researchers, corporations and the Federal Government. The day of the independent researcher was the latter part of the nineteenth century. Thomas Edison probably best epitomized the independent researcher as he was widely copied. The current cost of many modern laboratories and their equipment places Phase Two research outside the realm of affordability for the independent researcher. (In fact, maintaining an up to date micro-devices laboratory capable of producing the latest nano-devices is a significant challenge for a laboratory such as the Jet Propulsion Laboratory, which has an annual budget of approximately $1.5B.)

There are still independent researchers — they tend to be referred to as garage operations — and some great companies have resulted from their efforts. Apple Computing and Microsoft provide two outstanding examples. In fact, many of the information technology companies have been born in the innovator's garage. One may conclude that most of these garage operations have involved late Phase Three and Phase Four development efforts rather than the building of Phase Two devices due to the cost of building and maintaining research laboratories generally required for Phase Two research. For the most part, the corporate and Government research laboratories have built the first devices upon which the garage operators have developed their products. For example, the Apple Computing founders used the microprocessors developed by Intel and Motorola and integrated circuits developed by others.

Xerox's PARC and Hughes Research Laboratories have been set free as independent research companies — a modern version of the early twentieth century independent researchers. Unfortunately, they are dependent on finding funding from the corporate world or the Government. They lack significant funding of their own for research. As such, they have no choice but to perform that research and development for which they can find customers willing to pay. Consequently, these research organizations tend to become product development laboratories. It is beyond any practical imagination to think that independent researchers are able to muster annually the millions of dollars necessary to restore Phase Two research levels in the United States.

The corporate research laboratories dominated Phase Two research during the first half of the twentieth century. Moreover, the decline of Phase Two research in corporate research laboratories has been a result of the restructuring of corporate America and the difficulty in using return on investment to rationalize Phase Two research. AT&T was not the great benefactor of the transistor or the laser, although their Bell Laboratories developed the first devices. Arguably, the industry benefiting the most from these two devices has been the consumer products industry. It is very difficult to think about AT&T abandoning its core business of communications to become a consumer products company — a Sony, for example.

Clayton M. Christensen has researched and written extensively on the impacts and management of disruptive technologies and it fits well with the material of this book. However, most of his considerations fit into the context of Phases Three and Four of the technology development cycle. That is because most of his case studies are devoted to improving existing products — i.e., computer disk drives, dirt excavation equipment, et cetera. Admittedly, a new technology may be the basis of the product improvement. In contrast, the primary interest of this book is in how America can increase research on Phase Two devices, which lead to systems previously unknown. For example, the laser disk drive (i.e., CD, DVD), the personal computer, cell phone, and the GPS satellite/receiver have whole industries or sub-industries built around them that did not previously exist. Granted the manufacturers of phonographs and tape players have morphed into the manufacturing of CD and DVD players and the producers of the media placed on CDs and DVDs have similarly changed. However, an additional number of component suppliers have sprung up (i.e., the producers of the laser portion of the player). In addition, these revolutionary products rely on innovative devices that others have pioneered. In the absence of a change affecting Phase Two research, industry is not going to increase its funding of Phase Two research significantly.

The rest of the world has caught on and is developing research and development capabilities. U.S. foreign policy encourages it, American corporations invest in foreign research and development laboratories, and America's universities and colleges provide necessary educational opportunities. The U.S. will never have the field to itself as it once did, but it can still maintain a premier position. The United States remains by far the best place to start a new enterprise. The American university system remains the best in the world. Americans have the most freedom and best opportunities to pursue their individual dreams. Moreover, the United States certainly has the economic resources to support a vigorous technology development program. America has an abundance of the three necessary elements: people, educational system, and funding capability. All that is needed is a more supportive environment for technology development — particularly for Phase Two device research and to a more limited degree Phase One basic research.

The United States will have to develop some innovative approaches for improving the technology development environment once the need is generally recognized. This will require identifying all the constraints that the solutions must meet. Alternative solutions will come from the various people and organizations with a stake in the outcome. One can start by considering the changes, which have led to the decline, and suggesting some possible means of reversing these changes. Undoubtedly, greater awareness and increased discussion will lead to suggestions of a number of innovative and wonderful solutions. Here are some possibilities that might serve to start the discussion.

The Federal Government with its laboratories and Federally Funded Research and Development Centers (FFRDCs) is in a position to revitalize its Phase Two research role. As discussed in the chapter on The Decline, the Federal Government has become much more short sighted and has cut back Phase Two research at its laboratories and research centers since the fall of the Berlin wall. Federal funding of university research, which represents almost all of the U.S.'s Phase One basic research, has recently declined. Nevertheless, it really is in the interest of the Government to promote vigorous Phases One and Two research programs. The resulting products and services lead to an expanded economy and a much enhanced tax base. After all, growth industries with high profit margins and workers with good and growing incomes are the ingredients for a growing tax revenue stream. The Government has everything to gain for a relatively modest investment.

The investment is affordable and practical because industry will most willingly undertake the orders of magnitude more costly Phases Three and Four of the technology development cycle. For industry to perform this role in the technology development cycle, it needs to perform a modest amount of Phase Two research. This provides the essential connectivity of people involved in the different phases within the company that facilitates the passing of technologies from one phase to another. The Government certainly knows how to use incentives to get companies to do what is wanted.

The infrastructure is already in place — the DOD Laboratories, DOE Laboratories and its research oriented FFRDCs — to support a revitalized Phase Two research effort. Dedicating the military service laboratories once again to the conduct of vigorous research programs could benefit the Department of Defense's procurement programs as well as enhance the nation's technology development. The respective service's procurement organizations could once again assume the funding and monitoring efforts currently performed by these laboratories. Further, pay scales and rewards for innovation need to be such as to attract the most capable minds possible to perform Phase Two research. This seems very doable and requires no magic. One might say that our future well-being depends on it.

Revitalizing the Government's role in Phase Two research requires some modest restructuring of its R&D programs. DARPA could restructure its programs to place sufficient emphasis on Phase One and Two research. Funding for Phase Two research at NASA could be fenced at a level approximating 5% of its total budget without breaking its or the Federal Government's budget. DOE could refocus research at its laboratories on Phase Two research. EPA could enhance its research program significantly to address the myriad of environmental issues. Finding science based solutions to environmental problems and funding them appropriately is essential. Certainly, increasing NSF's funding is a meaningful way to increase support of research in the physical sciences. In short, the United States could take a significant step towards restoring Phase Two research by returning to what worked so well during the Golden Age of technology development — a vigorous Government funded and executed Phase Two research program. Moreover, the Government must not forget to take care of its essential funding of Phase One basic research.

It is more difficult to imagine the conditions under which Corporate America would return to being a major funding source of Phase Two research. It is inconceivable that the decadal nature of the technology life cycle will become significantly shorter. As a result, there is no return on investment for a decade or longer, if at all. Research affects income and cash flows negatively. Non-income producing assets sit on the balance sheet. The net result is generally a lower price of the corporation's stock. The foregoing explains why today's stockholders will not stand for a corporation to undertake a Xerox PARC.

Furthermore, patent protection expires before corporate America can exploit devices to their fullest. Certainly, some new devices will receive comments similar to those concerning the laser that it is an invention looking for an application. It is virtually impossible to predict how such a device will provide the commercial bonanza. Eventually, innovators and entrepreneurs will establish new companies and industries to exploit the revolutionary devices. Moreover, it is most inconceivable to imagine corporate investors developing the patience to reap the benefits of Phase Two research. Similarly, it is just as unlikely that the Government will return to the practice of protecting corporate revenues to promote the investment in Phase Two research. Today's world does not support the corporate based Phase Two research that once was conducted by the AT&T's, GE's, IBM's, Kodak's, and the Sperry's of the early twentieth century. However, all is not bleak. Corporations do respond to Government policies and incentives.

Since the technology development cycle involves decades, then twenty-year patents are generally of little value for the Phase Two researchers and those funding their research because the opportunity to derive income from patent licensing is almost non-existent. The fact that the sponsoring organization of Phase Two research rarely obtains the greatest commercial benefits of the research exacerbates the situation. These conditions suggest that changes in patent protections might encourage industry to fund Phase Two research. One possibility would be to set the expiration date of patents based on the first application of the patent in a successful product — say, twenty years after the introduction of the product into the market. This would assure licensing income for the inventors of fundamental devices. Basing patent protection on its exploitation in commercial products or services may be worth considering.

Another possibility would be to require evidence that implementation of the concept had occurred before granting the patent. This would eliminate the granting of patents for a concept when the submitter has no idea through which to implement it. An example of such a patent is the one given to Jerome Lemelson for the *idea* of an integrated circuit. (Jack Kilby and Robert Noyce were the actual inventors of the integrated circuit.) At the time of his patent application, Jerome Lemelson had no idea how to go about implementing the idea. Furthermore, the maturity of the underlying technology was insufficient to support the implementation of an integrated circuit. The granting of "concept" patents with no proof of implementation adversely affects the innovators who actually conceive and develop such devices. As an aside, Townes and Schawlow would not have received a patent for the laser under such a constraint. Of course, nearly infinite wording possibilities exist for making such a change in the patent law with just as many variations in what would be patentable. Nonetheless, considering possible changes in what is patentable could yield an approach that encourages more Phase Two research without negatively affecting Phase One basic research.

Providing specific exemptions in the anti-trust laws to producers of new products and services for a specific time could provide incentives for innovation. Such an act would declare Government's intent regarding industry's use of patents and innovation to achieve and maintain dominance in the marketplace. Such a move by Government would clarify the regulatory environment regarding the use of innovation-based practices to achieve global dominance. Past examples include AT&T, Sperry Gyroscope, and GE. Making the Government's intent explicit may appear to restrict competition and appear to be bad for the consumer but as has already been discussed, innovation is responsible for most of the growth in Americans' standard of living, America's GDP, and Americans' high paying jobs. Furthermore, the original author of the anti-trust laws did not intend to restrict the advantage that innovation or the offering of superior products and services afforded.

Tax credits afford the possibility of providing incentives to industry to invest in Phase Two research. There is considerable uncertainty in the effectiveness of this approach due to the long-term nature of the technology development cycle and the short-term focus of corporate management. In addition, with tax credits, there is still a cost associated with performing research and there remain the considerations of a reduction in return on investments, a reduction in gross profit margin, and an increase in under- or non-performing assets.

A radical approach to increasing funding of Phase Two research is to modify the paradigm. The new paradigm would be the collaborating of companies and universities in both Phase One and Phase Two research where the companies provide the funding and the universities provide the research. This is what has occurred quite recently relative to medical science research. Additionally, university researchers have embarked to a limited extent on Phase Two research efforts in some other areas of the sciences.

Achieving such a paradigm shift requires the recognition that Phase Two research is maybe more expensive by a factor of ten than Phase One research and that industry will require incentives to establish and fund Phase Two research at university owned and operated laboratories. One should also take into account the fact that the company, which sponsors the Phase Two research, is rarely the one that obtains the great economic benefit of the technology breakthroughs resulting from such research. In addition, the incentives could factor in the relatively inexpensive labor available to the university in the form of students, graduate assistants, and post-doctoral fellows.

Finally, this new funding source would be a godsend for America's universities including the public universities, many of which are in a precarious financial situation.

Employing the concept of granting patents for extended periods provides one means of changing the paradigm. One option is to grant patents to universities for the inventions of their staff members (professors) for possibly 50 or maybe even 100 years while retaining the standard period for all others. While this may seem outlandish to some, patents provide a means of protecting a form of intellectual property as do copyrights, which cover literary, scientific, and artistic works for the life plus 50 years after the death of the creator. The capability to provide exclusive rights for the applications of their patents for such extended periods would provide the universities with a new funding stream, which over time could be very significant. This coupled with the potential of having industry pay for the research would provide significant incentives to universities to enter into research agreements with corporate America. The incentives to companies to fund research at a university would be many, including: (1) the companies would have priority with regards to obtaining license agreements for patents obtained by the university; (2) they could share in royalties paid to the university on patents granted for research they funded; (3) they could enter into agreements with the university for priority access to patents resulting from other company's funding; and (4) the extended periods of exclusive licensing available only from the universities could enhance their competitive advantage through the use of patent protection for their products. Furthermore, this approach could improve companies' financial statements (e.g., research could be expensed rather than capitalized, laboratories for Phase Two research would be owned by universities and would not show up as assets on the balance sheet, and overall return on investment would thereby be increased). Companies could also obtain a growing long-term income stream through their share of royalty income generated by patents derived from the company's sponsored research.

Providing financial incentives to industry with or without changes in the patent laws might encourage industry to fund Phase Two research at the university. One incentive could be to allow industry to expense an amount greater than the actual funds provided to a university for research (e.g., 150%). This would shelter some profits from federal income taxes and thereby reduce some of the financial deterrents to investment in Phases One and Two research. Another incentive could be to allow a percentage of the royalties shared by the university with the funding company to be free of federal taxation. This has the potential to diminish the potential royalty income of the university. However, increases in industry-funded research at the university might well offset the lost royalty income due to sharing. In all cases, industry funded research at the university provides important financial support to faculty, students, and research laboratories.

This possible shift in research paradigm could contribute significantly to bringing Phases One and Two research back to the levels of the past without requiring significant Government financial support. As seen previously, the Government would benefit greatly from the increased tax revenues that the creation of new products and industries would generate. The universities and the companies funding research would remain free to enter into funding agreements and patent licensing agreements that make sense for them under the hypothesized changes. It appears that such changes could be a win for America. The country would win by reinvigorating Phase Two research and benefit from all that results from it. Universities would win by obtaining a new or enhanced funding stream. America's industry would win by remaining competitive in the global market. America's workers would win through the higher wages that leading industries could afford.

Global industrialization has brought about a concept that research, product development, production, sales, and customer support can be done in vastly different locations anywhere in the world that makes economic sense for the corporation. There is some evidence of this in the production of flat panel televisions and cell phones. However, as discussed in previous chapters the "high-tech" portions have remained near the engineering development centers. Therefore, it is important for America to retain its research and development efforts here at home, not in someone else's country.

So far, we have considered potential improvements for one of the three basic requirements of technology development — funding. The focus now turns to the second requirement of engaging the best and brightest people possible in technology development. These people need to be attracted to science and technology at an early age. An IEEE survey reported in *Spectrum*, "The Attractions of Technology [Engineering/Technology Survey – Professionals and Students]", states that essentially all of the respondents knew they wanted to be technologists by the age of 20. Sixty percent knew by the age of 15. The survey points out that a family member influenced more than two thirds. Knowing a technologist influenced a quarter of the respondents. A book or magazine was a positive influence for more than 40 percent. TV or movies influenced more than a quarter of the respondents. Numerous studies have articulated the influence of movies and television on adolescent behaviors, preferences, and career choices. Adolescents emulate to some degree their role models including those TV and movie characters with whom they identify.

TV and movies have consistently portrayed law officers, lawyers, and doctors as heroes with extraordinary competencies. This contrasts with the frequent portrayal of scientists as "mad" or "odd-ball." Dan Vergano wrote in an article titled, "TV, Films Boldly Go Down Scientific Path", on the portrayal of science and scientists for *USA Today* (March 30, 2009). He wrote, "In the past century, scientists went from somewhat remote heroes in films, such as 1943's *Madame Curie*, to more sinister figures in the Cold War, such as the title character in 1964's *Dr. Strangelove*, to more human characters, such as Jodie Foster's Eileen Arroway in 1997's *Contact*. Of course, mad scientists have always been popular, from 1931's Frankenstein to today's Fox show *Fringe*, blessed with its own nutty professor who works in a basement lab." He quotes astronomer and blogger Phil Plait, "Movies change to reflect the society around them, and the way science appears certainly reflects that." Today, Hollywood appears much more interested than in the past in getting the science right in its products.

It has been a long time since the people of science and technology have regularly been "front page" news. Jack Kilby, the co-inventor of the integrated circuit, passed away in 2005 with hardly a notice in the public media. That is because few people knew who Jack Kilby was. Yet, this man together with co-inventor, Robert Noyce, had more impact on the lives of people than most presidents, entertainers and sports stars ever have. Their invention of the integrated circuit has enhanced or enabled everything from kitchen appliances and automobiles to wristwatches. Most people know who Babe Ruth and Marilyn Monroe were and what made them famous. Who knows the same for Henry LeLand? Yet everyone in America today owes a debt of gratitude to LeLand

Public awareness of America's R&D heroes needs to be increased greatly if young people are to aspire to become scientists and engineers. One possible means to accomplish this is by funding and tasking the National Science Foundation in conjunction with the National Academy of Sciences with the mission of placing America's R&D heroes in the media spotlight. One way to do this is to follow a path of success. That is, create an awards extravaganza highlighting the annual achievements of the R&D heroes. Although, oftentimes today's R&D requires a team or small army of researchers, the entertainment industry can be emulated and the various contributors of success can be honored — the manager, the visionary, the supporting roles, et cetera. Granted, various entities do have awards to honor R&D accomplishments, but they are relatively unseen, out of sight, and out of mind. Without increasing the awareness of America's R&D heroes, the vast majority of the best and brightest are likely to become doctors and lawyers. Who will be taking care of the future of America's well-being?

The third and last requirement for a vibrant technology development enterprise is that of education. America's university system is the best in the world. Improvements are certainly possible and the major need of securing long term funding of America's universities has been discussed. However, there are real needs for improving education in America's primary and secondary schools. Math and science education poses a tremendous challenge. Math and science are hard to learn. Poor teaching causes many young people to turn away from becoming scientists, technologists, or engineers.

The National Science Board with considerable support of its Commission on 21st Century Education in Science, Technology, Engineering, and Mathematics (STEM) has addressed this at some depth. Some of the best and brightest participated in the preparation of the report. The report, entitled, *A National Action Plan for Addressing the Critical Needs of the U.S. Science, Technology, Engineering, and Mathematics Education System*, was unveiled on the 50th anniversary of the launch of Sputnik in the U.S. Capitol Building.

The National Science Board recognized "two central challenges to constructing a strong, coordinated STEM education system:

1. Ensuring coherence in STEM learning, and

2. Ensuring an adequate supply of well-prepared and highly effective STEM teachers."

The recommendations included several at the national level for directing attention to the issues and concerns related to STEM education and of coordinating and enhancing STEM education across the various programs. The Board also made recommendations regarding curricula, assessment metrics, and the dissemination of information. Finally, the Board addressed the challenge related to STEM teachers with recommendations on compensation, certification standards, and the preparation of teachers. Those interested in additional information on STEM education are referred to the Board's excellent report.

At the risk of being needlessly redundant, the ideas put forth in this book are for stimulating discussion and action where appropriate. A great debate will provide the ideas to develop a comprehensive approach for stemming the decline of American technology. Others concerned about America's loss of global technology leadership have put forth ideas, which have merit for consideration. The American Electronics Association has produced a number of papers on America's loss of competitive advantage with recommendations for regaining it. The membership of the Association, which David Packard founded, is probably at the center of the global challenge facing the U.S.'s technology industries. Consequently, they have probably been the most vocal in this arena of all the professional societies and trade organizations focused on the sciences and engineering. Their considerations and recommendations are certainly worthy of being included in any discussions regarding the maintenance of America's rightful position in the world of technology development and exploitation. This does not exclude other societies and trade groups from contributing to this discussion. They can provide a great deal of thoughtful input to a national discussion about America's decline in technology.

Besides the National Science Foundation with its National Science Board, the American Association for the Advancement of Science is a major resource regarding the issues facing the country relative to science and technology. They too have put forth ideas for strengthening America's technology muscle. Finally, readers of this book recognize the importance of a vigorous technology development enterprise in the United States and they represent a source of ideas.

In conclusion, America enjoys the largest and best economy in the world in large part due to the innovation of its researchers. For in excess of a century, America led the world in research and development. Much of the rest of the world has recognized the value of R&D for its future well-being. All phases of R&D comprise an integrated whole and are essential to a successful product development cycle. A decline may have begun in Phase One research but it almost certainly has begun in Phase Two research. The need to reinvigorate this vital part is real. We have explored some ideas in this chapter towards this reinvigoration but by no means do they comprise the totality of what is possible. Simply, we have considered all aspects of technology development — what it is, how it is done, what its importance is, what it needs, and how to provide for its needs. The future of America's technology remains with us.

> Change is the law of life. And those who look only to the past or present are certain to miss the future. — John F. Kennedy

BIBLIOGRAPHY

CHAPTER 1 — THE TECHNOLOGY DEVELOPMENT CYCLE

General

Exhibits: The Computer History Museum. February 5, 2009. ‹http://www.computerhistory.org/›.

Rothenberg, Marc, ed. *The History of Science in the United States: An Encyclopedia*. New York: Garland, 2001.

Biographies

"Arthur L. Schawlow, Autobiography". From *Nobel Lectures*, Physics 1981-1990, Editor-in-Charge Tore Frängsmyr, Editor Gösta Ekspång, Singapore, World Scientific Publishing Co., 1993. February 5, 2009. ‹http://nobelprize.org/nobel_prizes/physics/laureates/1981/schawlow-autobio.html›.

"Charles H. Townes, Biography". *Nobel Prizes in Physics*. Nobel.org. February 5, 2009. ‹http://nobelprize.org/nobel_prizes/physics/laureates/1964/townes-bio.html›.

Haven, Kendall, and Donna Clark. *100 Most Popular Scientists for Young Adults: Biographical Sketches and Professional Paths*. Englewood, CO: Libraries Unlimited, 1999.

"John Bardeen, Biography". From *Nobel Lectures*, Physics 1971-1980, Editor Stig Lundqvist, Singapore, World Scientific Publishing Co., 1992. February 5, 2009. ‹http://nobelprize.org/nobel_prizes/physics/laureates/1972/bardeen-bio.html›.

"Robert Hall, Biography". *Nobel Prizes in Physics*. Nobel.org. February 5, 2009. ‹http://inventors.about.com/od/hstartinventors/a/Robert_Hall.htm›.

"Walter Brattain, Biography". From *Nobel Lectures*, Physics 1942-1962, Amsterdam, Elsevier Publishing Company, 1964. February 5, 2009. ‹http://nobelprize.org/nobel_prizes/physics/laureates/1956/brattain-bio.html›.

"William B. Shockley, Biography". From *Nobel Lectures*, Physics 1942-1962, Amsterdam, Elsevier Publishing Company, 1964. February 5, 2009. ‹http://nobelprize.org/nobel_prizes/physics/laureates/1956/shockley-bio.html›.

Inventions

"A technical history of the laser". essortment.com. February 5, 2009. ‹http://www.essortment.com/all/historyoflaser_rsny.htm›.

Bellis, Mary. "History of Lasers". About.com: Inventors. February 5, 2009. ‹http://inventors.about.com/od/lstartinventions/a/laser.htm›.

Bellis, Mary. "The History of the Transistor — John Bardeen, Walter Brattain, and William Shockley". About.com: Inventors. February 5, 2009. ‹http://inventors.about.com/library/weekly/aa061698.htm›.

Carlisle, Rodney. *Scientific American Inventions and Discoveries: All the Milestones in Ingenuity — From the Discovery of Fire to the Invention of the Microwave Oven*. Hoboken, NJ: Wiley, 2004.

Haven, Kendall. *100 Greatest Science Inventions of All Time*. Westport, CT: Libraries Unlimited, 2006.

"Microwave Oven". Southwest Museum of Engineering, Communications and Computation. February 5, 2009. ‹http://www.smecc.org/microwave_oven.htm›.

"Solar Timeline". *Energy Efficiency and Renewable Energy*. Department of Energy. February 5, 2009. ‹http://www1.eere.energy.gov/solar/solar_timeline.html›.

‹http://www.eetonline.com/special/special_issues/millennium/milestones/bobeck.html›.

"The History of Solar". *Energy Efficiency and Renewable Energy*. Department of Energy. February 5, 2009. ‹http://www1.eere.energy.gov/solar/pdfs/solar_timeline.pdf›.

"Transistorized". PBS Online. February 5, 2009. ‹http://www.pbs.org/transistor/index.html›.

CHAPTER 2 — THE WINNOWING OF TECHNOLOGIES THROUGH THE DEVELOPMENT CYCLE

Inventions

"Encyclopedia". The History Channel. February 4, 2009. ‹http://www.history.com›.

"The History of Computing Project". The History of Computing Project. February 4, 2009. ‹http://www.thocp.net/index.html›.

Computer Memory History

Heads, Ananth and Ashwini Dwarakanath. "Emerging Memory Technologies". The Computer Science and Engineering Department of the Pennsylvania State University. February 4, 2009. ‹http://www.cse.psu.edu/~mdl/597e/memories1.pdf›.

Huong. Gregory T. "10 Emerging Technologies. Universal Memory" *Technology Review*. MIT. May 2005. February 4, 2009. ‹http://www.technologyreview.com/computing/14407/page6/›.

Hutchby, James A., Ralph Cavin, Victor Zhirnov, Joe E. Brewer, and George Bourianoff, "Emerging Nanoscale Memory and Logic Devices: A Critical Assessment. Computer". *Computer*. IEEE. May 2008. February 4, 2009. ‹http://www.computer.org/portal/cms_docs_computer/computer/homepage/0508/r5hutch.pdf›.

Kutnick, Dale, Peter Burris, Val Sribar, David Cearley, Will Zachmann and Jack Gold "Commentary: Timetables uncertain for new memory technologies". Cnet News. December 2000. February 4, 2009. ⟨http://news.cnet.com/Commentary-Timetables-uncertain-for-new-memory-technologies/2009-1001_3-249587.html?tag=mncol⟩.

"Memory Technology Evolution: An Overview of System Memory Technologies". Technology Brief. 8th Edition. Hewlett-Packard Development Company. April 2009. May 25, 2009. ⟨http://h20000.www2.hp.com/bc/docs/support/SupportManual/c00256987/c00256987.pdf?jumpid=reg_R1002_USEN⟩.

Rosty, George. "Bubbles: The Better Memory". *EE Times*. EE Times Online. February 4, 2009. ⟨http://www.eetonline.com/special/special_issues/millennium/milestones/bobeck.html⟩.

Software

"Computer Operating System". History. February 4, 2009. ⟨http://www.history.com/encyclopedia.do?articleId=206238⟩.

"Encyclopedia of Compilers". Compilers. February 4, 2009. ⟨http://www.compilers.net/paedia/index.htm⟩.

Lawson, Harold "Bud and Howard Bromberg. "The World's First COBOL Compilers". *Computer History Museum Lecture Series*. Computer History Museum. June 12, 1997. February 4, 2009. ⟨http://www.computerhistory.org/events/lectures/cobol_06121997/⟩.

Power, D. J., "A Brief History of Spreadsheets", DSSResources World Wide Web. version 3.6, August 30, 2004. February 4, 2009. ⟨http://dssresources.com/history/sshistory.html⟩,

"Software". The History of Computing Project. July 10, 2008. February 4, 2009. ⟨http://www.thocp.net/software/software.htm⟩.

Management

Christensen, Clayton M. *The Innovator's Dilemma: When New Technologies Cause Great Firms to Fail*. Boston, Massachusetts. Harvard Business School Press. 1997.

CHAPTER 3 — THE PACE OF TECHNOLOGY DEVELOPMENT

Articles and Papers on Technology Development

Bement, Dr. Arden L., Jr. "Energy, Environment and Economy: Can Science Help?". *Remarks*. National Science Foundation. February 4, 2009. ⟨http://www.nsf.gov/news/speeches/bement/08/alb081103_toledo.jsp⟩.

Bordogna, Dr. Joseph, "Building a New Foundation for Innovation". Office of Legislative and Public Affairs. National Science Foundation. June 2001. February 4, 2009. ⟨http://www.nsf.gov/news/speeches/bordogna/jb010618innovation.htm⟩.

Laidlaw, Frances Jean, "Acceleration of Technology Development by the Advanced Technology Program: The Experience of 28 Projects Funded in 1991". Advanced Technology Program, National Institutes of Standards. February 5, 2009. ⟨http://www.atp.nist.gov/eao/ir-6047.htm⟩.

Resetar, Susan, Beth E. Lachman, Robert Lempert, and Monica M. Pinto. *Technology Forces at Work: Profiles of Environmental Research and Development at DuPont, Intel, Mon-*

santo, and Xerox. Santa Monica, CA: Rand, 1999. Questia. 4 Feb. 2009 ‹http://www.questia.com/PM.qst?a=o&d=103791966›.

"Technology Development: From Concept through Commercialization". Pittsburgh Mineral and Environmental Technology, Inc. February 5, 2009. ‹http://www.pmet-inc.com/resources/Tech.pdf›.

"The Pace of Innovation Requires a Steep Learning Curve." *The Birmingham Post (England)* 25 July 2006: Questia. 4 Feb. 2009. ‹http://www.questia.com/PM.qst?a=o&d=5015755585›.

Technologies

Carroll, Paul. *Big Blue: The Unmaking of IBM.* Crown Publishers, Inc. New York, New York. 1993.

Cassavoy, Liane. "In Pictures: A History of Cell Phones". *PC World.* PC World Online. May 2007. February 4, 2009. ‹http://www.pcworld.com/article/131450/in_pictures_a_history_of_cell_phones.html›.

"Historical Periods in Television Technology". Federal Communications Commission. February 4, 2009. ‹http://www.fcc.gov/omd/history/tv/›.

"History of Television". History Department of the University of San Diego. February 4, 2009. ‹http://history.sandiego.edu/GEN/recording/television1.html›.

"Microwave Oven". Southwest Museum of Engineering, Communications and Computation February 4, 2009. ‹http://www.smecc.org/microwave_oven.htm›.

"Personal Computer". *The History Channel.* 2009. February 4, 2009, ‹http://www.history.com/encyclopedia.do?articleId=219014›.

Power, D. J., "A Brief History of Spreadsheets", DSSResources. August 30, 2004. February 4, 2009. ‹http://dssresources.com/history/sshistory.html›.

"What is the History of Cell Phones?". Tech Faq. February 4, 2009. ‹http://www.tech-faq.com/history-of-cell-phones.shtml›.

CHAPTER 4 — THE TECHNOLOGY PLAYERS

General

Hughes, Thomas P. *American Genesis: A Century of Invention and Technological Enthusiasm 1870-1970.* New York, New York. Viking Group, Penguin Books USA Inc. 1989.

Biographies

"Albert Einstein". Department of Physics, University of Liverpool. July 27, 2009. ‹http://www.liv.ac.uk/physics/bigbang/Einstein.html›

"Albert Einstein, Biography". From *Nobel Lectures,* Physics 1901-1921, Amsterdam, Elsevier Publishing Company, 1967. February 5, 2009. ‹http://nobelprize.org/nobel_prizes/physics/laureates/1921/einstein-bio.html›.

"Albert Einstein: Image and Impact". Center for the History of Physics. November 2004. February 5, 2009. ‹http://www.aip.org/history/einstein/›.

"Alexander Graham Bell, Biography". About.com: Inventors. February 5, 2009. ‹http://inventors.about.com/library/inventors/bltelephone2.htm›.

"Alexander Graham Bell, Biography". *Encyclopedia Britannica.* Biography.com. February 5, 2009. ‹http://www.biography.com/search/article.do?id=9205497›.

Beals, Gerald. "The Biography of Thomas Edison". Thomas Edison.com. 1999. February 5, 2009. ‹http://www.thomasedison.com/biography.html›.

Bellis, Mary. "Robert Hall". About.com: Inventors. February 5, 2009. ‹http://inventors.about.com/od/hstartinventors/a/Robert_Hall.htm›.

"Charles H. Townes, Biography". *Nobel Prizes in Physics*. Nobel.org. February 5, 2009. ‹http://nobelprize.org/nobel_prizes/physics/laureates/1964/townes-bio.html›.

"Elmer Ambrose Sperry". *Inventor of the Week*. Massachussetts Institute of Technology. February 5, 2009. ‹http://web.mit.edu/invent/iow/sperry.html›.

Haven, Kendall, and Donna Clark. *100 Most Popular Scientists for Young Adults: Biographical Sketches and Professional Paths*. Englewood, CO: Libraries Unlimited, 1999.

"John Bardeen, Biography". From *Nobel Lectures*, Physics 1971-1980, Editor Stig Lundqvist, Singapore, World Scientific Publishing Co., 1992. February 5, 2009. ‹http://nobelprize.org/nobel_prizes/physics/laureates/1972/bardeen-bio.html›.

"Karl Ferdinand Braun, Biography" From *Nobel Lectures*, Physics 1901-1921, Amsterdam, Elsevier Publishing Company, 1967. February 9, 2009. ‹http://nobelprize.org/nobel_prizes/physics/laureates/1909/braun-bio.html›.

"The Wright Brothers: Wilbur and Orville Wright". Wright-House. October 21, 2008. February 5, 2009. ‹http://www.wright-house.com/wright-brothers/Wrights.html›.

"Walter Brattain, Biography". From *Nobel Lectures*, Physics 1942-1962, Amsterdam, Elsevier Publishing Company, 1964. February 5, 2009. ‹http://nobelprize.org/nobel_prizes/physics/laureates/1956/brattain-bio.html›.

Laboratories

"About JPL: History and Archives". Jet Propulsion Laboratory (JPL) . February 5, 2009. ‹http://www.jpl.nasa.gov/about/history.cfm›.

"About PARC: Innovation Milestones". PARC. February 5, 2009. ‹http://www.parc.xerox.com/about/history/default.html›.

"About PARC: "Overview". PARC. February 5, 2009. ‹http://www.parc.xerox.com/about/default.html›.

"Bell Labs History". Alcatel-Lucent . February 5, 2009. ‹http://www.alcatel-lucent.com/wps/portal/BellLabs/History›.

"History of IBM". IBM. February 5, 2009. http://www-‹03.ibm.com/ibm/history/history/history_intro.html›.

"HP 2007 Annual Report". HP. May 25, 2009. ‹"http://media.corporate-ir.net/media_files/irol/71/71087/AR2007/index.html›.

"IBM Research History Highlights". IBM. February 5, 2009. ‹http://www.research.ibm.com/about/history.shtml›.

"Intel Corporation: 2007 Annual Report". Intel. 2008. May 25, 2009. ‹http://www.intc.com/intelAR2007/index.html›.

"Lawrence Livermore National Laboratory: History". Lawrence Livermore National Laboratory (LLNL) . February 5, 2009. ‹https://www.llnl.gov/llnl/about/make_history.jsp›.

"Naval Research Laboratory: History". Naval Research Laboratory (NRL). February 5, 2009. ‹http://www.nrl.navy.mil/content.php?P=HISTORY›.

"2008 IBM Annual Report". IBM. 2008. May 25, 2007. <http://www.ibm.com/annualreport/2008/index.shtml>.

CHAPTER 5 — THE FINANCES OF TECHNOLOGY

Data

Main Science and Technology Indicators (MSTI): 2009/10 edition. Organization for Economic Co-operation and Development. 2009. July 27, 2009. <http://www.oecd.org/document/26/0,2340,en_2649_34451_1901082_1_1_1_1,00.html>

R&D Budget and Policy Program: Guide To R&D Funding Data-Historical Data. American Association for the Advancement of Science (AAAS). 2009. January 25, 2009. <http://www.aaas.org/spp/rd/guihist.htm>.

Science and Engineering Indicators 2004. National Science Board, National Science Foundation. Arlington, Virginia. May 2004. January 25, 2009. <http://www.nsf.gov/statistics/seind04/pdfstart.htm>.

Science and Engineering Indicators 2008, (Volume 1, NSB 08-01; Volume 2, NSB 08-01A). National Science Board, National Science Foundation. Arlington, Virginia. January 2008. January 25, 2009. <http://www.nsf.gov/statistics/seind08/>

CHAPTER 6 — THE RISE OF TECHNOLOGY IN AMERICA

General Background

Beals, Gerald. "The Biography of Thomas Edison". Thomas Edison. January 28, 2009. <http://www.thomasedison.com/biography.html>.

Carlisle, Rodney. *Scientific American Inventions and Discoveries: All the Milestones in Ingenuity—From the Discovery of Fire to the Invention of the Microwave Oven.* Hoboken, NJ: Wiley, 2004.

Haven, Kendall, and Donna Clark. *100 Most Popular Scientists for Young Adults: Biographical Sketches and Professional Paths.* Englewood, CO: Libraries Unlimited, 1999.

Hovenkamp, Herbert. "The Monopolization Offense". *Ohio State Law Journal.* Volume 61 (2000). February 6, 2009. <http://moritzlaw.osu.edu/lawjournal/issues/volume61/number3/hovenkamp.pdf>.

Hughes, Thomas P. *American Genesis: A Century of Invention and Technological Enthusiasm 1870-1970.* New York, New York. Viking Group, Penguin Books USA Inc. 1989.

Rothenberg, Marc, ed. *The History of Science in the United States: An Encyclopedia.* New York: Garland, 2001.

U.S. Patent Activity Calendar Years 1790 to the Present, Table of Annual U.S. Patent Activity Since 1790. U.S. Patent and Trademark Office (USPTO). Washington, D.C. 2009. July 27, 2009. <http://www.uspto.gov/go/taf/h_counts.htm>.

CHAPTER 7 — INVENTIONS OF THE RISE

Specific Inventions

Bellis, Mary. "The History of Frozen Foods". About.com: Inventors. April 18, 2009. <http://inventors.about.com/library/inventors/blfrfood.htm>.

"Burton, Houdry, And Oil Refining". Princeton University. November 2002. April 16, 2009. ‹http://www.princeton.edu/~civ102/readings/Burton_Oil.doc›.

"George Eastman". Kodak. April 17, 2009. ‹http://www.kodak.com/US/en/corp/about_Kodak.jhtml?pq-path=2217›.

"History of the Refrigerator". The History Channel. April 18, 2009. ‹http://www.history.com/exhibits/modern/fridge.html›.

"History of the Washing Machine". The History Channel. April 17, 2009. ‹http://www.history.com/exhibits/modern/wash.html›.

"History of the Vacuum Tube". Radio Electronics. April 17, 2009. ‹http://www.radio-electronics.com/info/radio_history/valve/hov.php›.

Mieczkowski, Yanek. "The Man Who Brought Us Cadillac and Lincoln". George Mason University's History News Network. August 25, 2003. April 17, 2009. ‹http://hnn.us/articles/1646.html›.

"The Case Files: Elmer Sperry". The Franklin Institute. April 17, 2009. ‹http://www.fi.edu/learn/case-files/sperry-2524/troops.html›.

"The History of the Dishwasher". Gizmo Highway. April 2, 2009. ‹http://www.gizmohighway.com/history/dishwasher.htm›.

Compilations

Carlisle, Rodney. *Scientific American: Inventions and Discoveries.* John Wiley & Sons, Inc. Hoboken, New Jersey. 2004.

Rezende, Lisa. *Chronology of Science.* Infobase Publishing. New York, New York. 2006.

Smith, Roger. *Inventions and Inventors.* Salem Press, Inc. Hackensack, New Jersey. 2002.

CHAPTER 8 — TECHNOLOGY'S GOLDEN AGE

General Background

Hughes, Thomas P. *American Genesis: A Century of Invention and Technological Enthusiasm 1870-1970.* New York, New York. Viking Group, Penguin Books USA Inc. 1989.

Occupational Data

"AAES Reports the Engineering Salary Trends of 1994". JOM. The Minerals, Metals and Materials Society. February 15, 2009. ‹http://www.tms.org/pubs/journals/JOM/9505/Beazley-9505.html›.

"May 2007 National Occupational Employment and Wage Estimates". Bureau of Labor Statistics. February 15, 2009. ‹http://www.bls.gov/oes/current/oes_nat.htm›.

Monthly Labor Review. Bureau of Labor Statistics. Washington, D.C. (Various Dates)

Specific Government Organizations

"A Brief History of NASA". National Aeronautics and Space Administration (NASA). February 15, 2009. ‹http://www.hq.nasa.gov/office/pao/History/factsheet.htm›.

"About NIH". National Institutes of Health (NIH). February 15, 2009. ‹http://www.nih.gov/about/index.html›.

"About the NSF". National Science foundation (NSF). February 15, 2009. ‹http://www.nsf.gov/about/›.

"NIST General Information". National Institute of Standards and Technology (NIST). February 15, 2009. ‹http://www.nist.gov/public_affairs/general2.htm›.

"NOAA Legacy". National Oceanic and Atmospheric Administration (NOAA). February 15, 2009. ‹http://www.history.noaa.gov/noaa.html›.

"Origins & Evolution of the Department of Energy". Department of Energy (DOE). February 15, 2009. ‹http://www.energy.gov/about/origins.htm›.

CHAPTER 9 — DISCOVERIES AND INVENTIONS OF THE GOLDEN AGE

Specific Inventions

Bellis, Mary. "History of the Atomic Bomb and the Manhattan Project". About. com: Inventors. April 13, 2009. ‹http://inventors.about.com/od/astartinventions/a/atomic_bomb.htm›.

Bellis, Mary. "The History of Xerox". About.com: Inventors. April 3, 2009. ‹http://inventors.about.com/od/xyzstartinventions/a/xerox.htm›.

"Biography for Sam Warner". The Internet Movie Database. March 24, 2009. ‹http://www.imdb.com/name/nm0912580/bio›.

"Bread Slicer". The Great Idea Finder. April 6, 2009. ‹http://www.ideafinder.com/history/inventions/breadslicer.htm›.

Colton, Enovid, Frank Colton, Carl Djerassi. "Oral Contraceptive History — Birth Control Pills". About.com: Inventors. April 13, 2009. ‹http://inventors.about.com/library/inventors/blthepill.htm›.

"Corporal". *Redstone Arsenal Historical Information.* U.S. Army Redstone Arsenal History . April 1961. April 5, 2009. ‹http://www.redstone.army.mil/history/systems/corporal/welcome.html›.

Fredholm, Lotta. "The Discovery of the Molecular Structure of DNA — The Double Helix". Nobelprize.org. April 14, 2009. ‹http://nobelprize.org/educational_games/medicine/dna_double_helix/readmore.html›.

"Gramophone Records — Long Play Records". EDinformatics. April 2, 2009. ‹http://www.edinformatics.com/inventions_inventors/long_play_records.htm›.

Greene, Nick. "Robert Goddard Biography". About.com: Space/Astronomy. March 23, 2009. ‹http://space.about.com/od/biographies/a/robertgoddard.htm›.

Griffin, Scott. "Internet Pioneers". Master's Project . April 13, 2009. ‹http://www.ibiblio.org/pioneers/index.html›.

"Nylon History". Nylon History . March 26, 2009. ‹http://nylonhistory.org/›.

"Peter Goldmark: Biography". Answers.com. March 22, 2009. ‹http://www.answers.com/topic/goldmark-peter-carl›.

"Reminiscences of Frank Stanton (1994)". Oral History Research Office Collection of the Columbia University Libraries (OHRO/CUL). March 22, 2009. ‹http://www.columbia.edu/cu/lweb/digital/collections/nny/stantonf/transcripts/stantonf_1_14_620.html›.

Rosenberg, Jennifer. "Silly Putty". About.com: 20th Century History. April 6, 2009. ‹http://history1900s.about.com/cs/inventdiscover/a/aa122103a.htm›.

Simcoe, Robert J. "The Revolution in Your Pocket". *Invention and Technology Magazine*. American Heritage Publishing. Fall 2004. April 13, 2009. <http://www.american-heritage.com/articles/magazine/it/2004/2/2004_2_12.shtml>.

"Telling The Story of Sound Motion Pictures Through Contemporary Writings". The American Widescreen Museum. March 24, 2009. <http://www.widescreenmuseum.com/sound/sound03.htm>.

Wallerstein, Edward. "The Development of the LP". *High Fidelity Magazine*. April 1976. Volume 26, Number 4. June 17, 2009. <http://community.mcckc.edu/crosby/lphist.htm>.

"Whatever Happened to Polio?". Smithsonian National Museum of American History. April 2, 2009. <http://americanhistory.si.edu/polio/>.

Compilations

Carlisle, Rodney. *Scientific American: Inventions and Discoveries*. John Wiley & Sons, Inc. Hoboken, New Jersey. 2004.

Rezende, Lisa. *Chronology of Science*. Infobase Publishing. New York, New York. 2006.

Smith, Roger. *Inventions and Inventors*. Salem Press, Inc. Hackensack, New Jersey. 2002.

Van Dulken, Stephen. *Inventing the 20th Century*. Barnes & Noble by arrangement with New York University Press. New York, New York. 2007.

CHAPTER 10 — THE DECLINE

Statistical Data

A Companion to Science and Engineering Indicators 2008. National Science Board. National Science Foundation. Arlington, Virginia. January 2008. January 25, 2009. <http://www.nsf.gov/statistics/nsb0803/start.htm>.

Farber, David. "1990 Census Data Shows Trends For Non-Academic Scientists And Engineers". *IEEE-USA Electronic Information Bulletin*. Interesting People Message. February 16, 2009. <http://www.interesting-people.org/archives/interesting-people/199504/msg00040.html>.

"R&D Budget and Policy Program: Guide To R&D Funding Data-Historical Data". American Association for the Advancement of Science (AAAS). January 25, 2009. <http://www.aaas.org/spp/rd/guihist.htm>.

Science and Engineering Indicators 2008 (volume 1, NSB 08-01; volume 2, NSB 08-01A). National Science Board, National Science Foundation. Arlington, Virginia. 2008. January 2008. January 25, 2009. <http://www.nsf.gov/statistics/seind08/>.

"Science and Engineering Statistics". National Science Foundation . February 16, 2009. <http://www.nsf.gov/statistics/>.

General Background

Butz, William P., Gabrielle A. Bloom, Mihal E. Gross, Terrence K. Kelly, Aaron Kofner, Helga E. Rippen. "Is There a Shortage of Scientists and Engineers?" Rand Corporation. 2003. February 16, 2009. <http://www.rand.org/pubs/issue_papers/IP241/IP241.pdf>.

"Chapter 2: Higher Education in Science and Engineering". *Science and Engineering Indicators 2006*. National Science Foundation. January 2006. May 11, 2009. ‹http://www.nsf.gov/statistics/seind06/pdf_v2.htm#c2›.

Denison, D.C. "The Increasingly Short-Term CEO: Last month, 80 CEOs with an average tenure of 4.2 years left their jobs". *National Post*. Toronto, Canada. November 6, 2001.

Hughes, Thomas P. *American Genesis: A Century of Invention and Technological Enthusiasm 1870-1970*. New York, New York. Viking Group, Penguin Books USA Inc. 1989.

Kelley, Charles, Mark Wang, Gordon Bitko, Michael Chase, Aaron Kofner, Julia Lowell, James Mulvenon, David Ortiz, Kevin Pollpeter. "High-Technology Manufacturing and U.S. Competitiveness". Rand Corporation, Santa Monica, CA. March 2004. February 16, 2009. ‹http://www.rand.org/pubs/technical_reports/2004/RAND_TR136.pdf›.

"Losing the Competitive Advantage? The Challenge For Science And Technology In The United States". American Electronics Association. 2008. February 16, 2009. ‹http://www.aeanet.org/publications/idjj_CompetitivenessOverview0205.asp›.

Lucier, Chuck, Steven Wheeler, and Rolf Habbel. "The Era of the Inclusive Leader". *strategy+business* Issue 47. Booz Allen Hamilton. Summer 2007. May 11, 2009. ‹ http://www.boozallen.com/media/file/Era_of_the_Inclusive_Leader_.pdf›.

Saffo, Paul. "A Looming American Diaspora". *U.S. Airways Magazine*. May 2009. 17-18.

"The CEO Trap". *Businessweek*. December 11, 2000. February 16, 2009. ‹http://www.businessweek.com/2000/00_50/b3711001.htm›.

Wadhwa, Vivek, AnnaLee Saxenian, Richard Freeman, Alex Salkever. "Losing the World's Best and Brightest: America's New Immigrant Entrepreneurs, Part V". *Businessweek*. March 2009. May 11, 2009. ‹http://images.businessweek.com/extras/09/losing_the_worlds_best_brightest.pdf›.

Government Agencies

"About DARPA". Defense Advanced Research Projects Agency (DARPA). February 16, 2009. ‹http://www.darpa.mil/about.html›.

"About DOE". Department of Energy (DOE). February 16, 2009. ‹http://www.energy.gov/about/index.htm›.

"About JPL: History and Archives". Jet Propulsion Laboratory. February 5, 2009. ‹http://www.jpl.nasa.gov/about/history.cfm›.

"About NASA". National Aeronautics and Space Administration (NASA). February 16, 2009. ‹http://www.nasa.gov/about/›.

"Naval Research Laboratory: History". Naval Research Laboratory (NRL). February 5, 2009. ‹http://www.nrl.navy.mil/content.php?P=HISTORY›.

Industry Laboratories

"About PARC: "Overview". PARC . February 5, 2009. ‹http://www.parc.xerox.com/about/default.html›.

"Bell Labs History". Alcatel-Lucent . February 5, 2009. ‹http://www.alcatel-lucent.com/wps/portal/BellLabs/History›.

"History of IBM". IBM . February 5, 2009. ‹http://www-03.ibm.com/ibm/history/history/history_intro.html›.

CHAPTER 11 — ECONOMIC IMPACT OF A DECLINE

Data

A *Companion to Science and Engineering Indicators 2008*. National Science Board. National Science Foundation. Arlington, Virginia. January 2008. February 19, 2009. ⟨http://www.nsf.gov/statistics/nsb0803/start.htm⟩.

"Productivity Change in the Nonfarm Business Sector, 1947-2008". Bureau of Labor Statistics. February 19, 2009. ⟨http://www.bls.gov/lpc/prodybar.htm⟩.

Science and Engineering Indicators 2008 (volume 1, NSB 08-01; volume 2, NSB 08-01A). National Science Board, National Science Foundation. Arlington, Virginia. 2008. January 2008. January 25, 2009. ⟨http://www.nsf.gov/statistics/seind08/⟩.

Articles and Papers

A *National Action Plan for Addressing the Critical Needs of the U.S. Science, Technology, Engineering, and Mathematics Education System*. National Science Board. National Science Foundation, Arlington, Virginia. October 30, 2007. February 19,2009. ⟨http://www.nsf.gov/nsb/documents/2007/stem_action.pdf⟩.

Atkinson, Robert D. And Andrew S. McKay. "Understanding the Economic Benefits of the Information Technology Revolution". The Information Technology and Innovation Foundation. March 2007. February 19, 2009. ⟨http://www.itif.org/files/digital_prosperity.pdf⟩.

Brynjolfsson, Erik and Shinkyu Yang. "Information Technology and Productivity: A Review of the Literature". Published in *Advances in Computers*, Academic Press, Vol. 43, P. 179-214, 1996. February 19, 2009. ⟨http://ebusiness.mit.edu/erik/itp.html⟩.

Buderi, Robert. "Microsoft: Getting from "R" to "D"". Published in *Technology Review*. Cambridge, MA. March 2008. February 25, 2009. ⟨http://www.technologyreview.com/business/14217/?a=f⟩.

Greene, William. "Growth in Services Outsourcing to India: Propellant or Drain on the U.S. Economy?". United States International Trade Commission. Washington, D.C. January 2006. February 14, 2009. ⟨ http://www.usitc.gov/publications/332/working_papers/EC200601A.pdf⟩.

Greenspan, Alan. "Structural change in the new economy". Before the National Governors' Association, 92nd Annual Meeting, State College, Pennsylvania July 11, 2000. February 19, 2009. ⟨http://www.wzb.eu/~vitols/Seminar/New%20Economy%20Seminar/Readings%201%20pdf/greenspan.htm⟩.

"Information Technology and The New Economy". Joint Economic Committee United States Congress. July 2001. February 19, 2009. ⟨http://www.house.gov/jec/growth/it.htm⟩.

"International Science and Engineering Partnerships: A Priority for U.S. Foreign Policy and Our Nation's Innovation Enterprise (NSB-08-4)". National Science Board, National Science Foundation, Arlington, Virginia. February 14, 2008. February 25, 2009. ⟨http://www.nsf.gov/nsb/publications/2008/nsb084.pdf⟩.

Kelley, Charles, Mark Wang, Gordon Bitko, Michael Chase, Aaron Kofner, Julia Lowell, James Mulvenon, David Ortiz, Kevin Pollpeter. "High-Technology Manufacturing and U.S. Competitiveness". Rand Corporation. March 2004. July 28, 2009. ‹http://www.rand.org/pubs/technical_reports/2004/RAND_TR136.sum.pdf›.

Johnson, Simon. "The Quiet Coup". *The Atlantic.* May 2009. May 28, 2009. ‹http://www.theatlantic.com/doc/200905/imf-advice›.

"Even Corporate Execs Think Corporate America is Unethical". Knights of Columbus. February 27, 2009. August 2, 2009. ‹http://www.opposingviews.com/articles/research-even-corporate-execs-think-corporate-america-is-unethical›

"Losing the Competitive Advantage: The Challenge for Science and Technology in the United States". American Electronics Association. Washington, DC. 2005. February 14, 2009. ‹http://www.aeanet.org/Publications/idjj_AeA_Competitiveness.asp›.

Oliner, Stephen D. and Daniel E. Sichel. "Explaining a Productive Decade: An Update". Federal Reserve Bank of San Francisco. November 14, 2008. February 19, 2009. ‹http://www.frbsf.org/csip/research/200811_Oliner.pdf›.

"The Outsourcing Threat Is: a) Big b) Small c) Both". Washington Post. Washington, D.C. June 13, 2004. July 29, 2009. ‹http://www.washingtonpost.com/wp-dyn/articles/A35982-2004Jun11.html›

"We Are Still Losing The Competitive Advantage: Now Is The Time To Act". American Electronics Association. Washington, DC. 2007. March 2007. February 14, 2009. ‹http://www.hawcpa.com/pdf/We%20Are%20Still%20Losing%20The%20Competitive%20Advantage.pdf›.

Weisman, Steven R. "Powell Reassures India on Technology Jobs". New York Times. New York. March 17, 2004. July 28, 2009. ‹http://www.nytimes.com/2004/03/17/international/asia/17POWE.html›

Books

Christensen, Clayton M. *The Innovator's Dilemma: When New Technologies Cause Great Firms to Fail.* Harvard Business School Press. Boston, MA. 1997.

Chapter 12 — Relying on a Service Economy is Unacceptable

Data

Cleveland, Douglas B. "The Role of Services in the Modern U.S. Economy". U.S. Department of Commerce. January 1999. March 25, 2009. ‹http://www.ita.doc.gov/td/sif/PDF/ROLSERV199.PDF›.

Gallagher, Michael, Ph.D., Albert Link, Ph.D., Jeffrey Petrusa, B.A. "Measuring Service-Sector Research and Development, Final Report". National Institute of Standards and Technology. March 2005. March 25, 2009. ‹http://www.nist.gov/director/prog-ofc/report05-1.pdf›.

"U.S. Trade in Goods and Services — Balance of Payments (BOP) Basis". U.S. Census Bureau. March 13, 2009. March 25, 2009. ‹http://www.census.gov/foreign-trade/statistics/historical/gands.pdf›.

"2007 Economic Census". U.S. Census Bureau. March 17, 2009. March 25, 2009. ‹http://factfinder.census.gov/servlet/IBQTable?_bm=y&-geo_id=&-ds_name=EC0700CADV1&-_lang=en›.

Articles and Papers

Brauer, David. "Factors Underlying the Decline in Manufacturing Employment Since 2000". Congressional Budget Office. December 23, 2008. March 23, 2009. ⟨http://www.cbo.gov/ftpdocs/97xx/doc9749/12-23-Brief.shtml⟩.

Erceg, Christopher, Luca Guerrieri, Christopher Gust. "Trade Adjustment and the Composition of Trade". International Finance Discussion Papers Number 859. Board of Governors of the Federal Reserve System. May 2006. March 23, 2009. ⟨http://www.federalreserve.gov/pubs/ifdp/2006/859/ifdp859.pdf⟩.

Koncz & Flatness. "*Cross-Border Trade in 2007 and Services Supplied Through Affiliates in 2006* (related tables)". U.S. Department of Commerce, Bureau of Economic analysis. October 2008. March 25, 2009. ⟨http://www.bea.gov/scb/pdf/2008/10%20October/services_tables.pdf⟩.

McKenzie, Richard B. "The Emergence of the Service Economy: Fact or Artifact?". CATO Institute. March 23, 2009. ⟨http://www.cato.org/pubs/pas/pa093.html⟩.

"Service Exports". Unz and Co. March 25, 2009. ⟨http://www.unzco.com/basicguide/c8.html#typical⟩.

"The U.S. Trade Balance". The Levin Institute. March 23, 2009. ⟨http://www.globalization101.org/index.php?file=issue&pass1=subs&id=2⟩.

"Your Exports May Never Cross the Dock". The Business Forum Online. March 25, 2009. ⟨http://www.businessforum.com/exports01.html⟩.

CHAPTER 13 — RESEARCH OPPORTUNITIES ABOUND

Environmental and Public Health

Beder, Sharon. "Technological Paradigms: The Case of Sewerage Engineering". Published in *Technology Studies*, pp. 167-188. 1997, March 27, 2009. ⟨http://www.herinst.org/sbeder/sewage/technoparadigm.html⟩.

"Carbon Dioxide in the Ocean and Atmosphere". Water Encyclopedia. March 22, 2009. ⟨http://www.waterencyclopedia.com/Bi-Ca/Carbon-Dioxide-in-the-Ocean-and-Atmosphere.html⟩.

"Contract to Revolutionize Ground Water Purification". Newswise. August 13, 2007. March 26, 2009. ⟨http://www.newswise.com/articles/view/532394/⟩.

"Emerging Issues in Water and Infectious Disease". World Health Organization. 2003. March 22, 2009. ⟨http://www.who.int/water_sanitation_health/emerging/en/emerging.pdf⟩.

"Emerging Threats". Global Health Council. March 28, 2009. ⟨http://www.globalhealth.org/view_top.php3?id=229⟩.

Lamacchia, Diane. "Delving into Water Issues — LBL Earth Scientists Solve Soil and Water Contamination Problems". Lawrence Berkeley Laboratory (LBL). Spring 1993. March 26, 2009. ⟨http://www.lbl.gov/Science-Articles/Archive/water-and-soil-contamination-remediation.html⟩.

"New Materials Can Selectively Capture Carbon Dioxide, Chemists Report". Science Daily. March 22, 2009. ⟨http://www.sciencedaily.com/releases/2008/02/080214144344.htm⟩.

Paulson, Tom. "Trapping carbon dioxide could fight climate change". Seattle Post-Intelligence. November 18, 2008. March 22, 2009. <http://www.seattlepi.com/local/388399_carbonbury19.html>.

"Public Health Implications Of Exposure To Polychlorinated Biphenyls (Pcbs)". Environmental Protection Agency. March 26, 2009. <http://www.epa.gov/water-science/fish/technical/pcb99.html>.

"Studies and Research in Sustainable Farming and Food Products". German Academic Exchange Service. March 26, 2009. <http://www.daad.org.cn/Downloads/Annex_1.pdf>.

Tiemann, Mary, "Perchlorate Contamination of Drinking Water: Regulatory Issues and Regulatory Actions". Congressional Research Service, The Library of Congress. May 2008. May 26, 2009. <http://ncseonline.org/NLE/CRSreports/08Mar/RS21961.pdf>.

Tiemann, Mary. "Safe Drinking Water Act: Implementation and Issues". Congressional Research Service, The Library of Congress. August 2003. March 22, 2009. <http://www.au.af.mil/au/awc/awcgate/crs/ib10118.pdf>.

"The Orbiting Carbon Observatory and the Mystery of the Missing Sinks". Jet Propulsion Laboratory (JPL). March 22, 2009. <http://www.jpl.nasa.gov/news/features.cfm?feature=2009>.

Weiss, Kenneth R. "A Primeval Tide of Toxins". Los Angeles Times. July 30, 2006. March 26, 2009. <http://www.latimes.com/news/local/oceans/la-me-ocean-30jul30,0,952130.story?page=1>.

Energy and Transportation

Boyle, Alan. "How Far Away is Fusion?". MSNBC. June 28, 2007. March 31, 2009. <http://cosmiclog.msnbc.msn.com/archive/2007/06/28/245828.aspx>.

Bullis, Kevin. "The World's Biggest Laser Powers Up". *Technology Review*. Massachusetts Institute of Technology (MIT). March 26,2009. March 28, 2009. <http://www.technologyreview.com/energy/22347/>.

"Coal Facts 2008". World Coal Institute. March 31, 2009. <http://www.worldcoal.org/pages/content/index.asp?PageID=188>.

"Generation IV Nuclear Energy Systems". U.S. Department of Energy. March 31, 2009. <http://nuclear.energy.gov/genIV/neGenIV1.html>.

"Well-to-Wheel Energy Use and Greenhouse Gas Emissions of Advanced Fuel/Vehicle Systems — North American Analysis — Executive Summary Report". Oregon State Government. June 2001. March 28, 2009. <http://www.oregon.gov/EN-ERGY/RENEW/Biomass/docs/FORUM/163WTW_Vol1.pdf>.

"World Carbon Dioxide Emissions from the Consumption of Coal (Million Metric Tons of Carbon Dioxide), 1980-2006". *International Energy Annual 2006*. Energy Information Administration. August 17, 2008. March 31, 2009. <http://www.eia.doe.gov/pub/international/iealf/tableh4co2.xls>.

CHAPTER 14 — RESEARCHERS AND ORGANIZATIONS FOR THE FUTURE

Specific Researchers and Organizations

"About Gen-probe". Gen-probe . April 10, 2009. <http://www.gen-probe.com/about/>.

"About Ocean Power Technologies". Ocean Power Technologies website. April 11, 2009. ‹http://www.oceanpowertechnologies.com/about.htm›.

"Arcadia Biosciences". Biohealthmatics. April 10, 2009. ‹http://jobs.biohealthmatics.com/Companies/profile00160.aspx›.

Bullis, Kevin. "Making Gasoline from Carbon Dioxide". *Technology Review*. Massachusetts Institute of Technology (MIT). April 27, 2007. April 11, 2009. ‹http://www.technologyreview.com/Energy/18582/›.

Bullis, Kevin. "Solar Power at Half the Cost".). *Technology Review*. Massachusetts Institute of Technology (MIT). May 11, 2007. April 11, 2009. ‹http://www.technology-review.com/Energy/18718/›.

"CMU-RC and Dendritic Nanotechnologies launch research to purify ground water". Nanotechwire.com. August 14, 2007. April 11, 2009. ‹http://nanotechwire.com/news.asp?nid=4930›.

Emerson, Bo. "Inventor Breaks Through Again" *The Atlanta Journal-Constitution*. October 27, 2008. April 11, 2009. ‹http://www.ajc.com/metro/content/printedition/2008/10/27/breakthrough.html›.

"Michelle C. Chang". University of California, Berkeley. April 8, 2009. ‹http://chem.berkeley.edu/people/faculty/chang_m/chang_m.html›.

"Peter Corsell". The Wall Street Green Trading Summit. April 8, 2009. ‹http://www.wsgts.com/speakers.php›.

"Peter L. Corsell, 30". *Technology Review*. Massachusetts Institute of Technology (MIT). April 8, 2009. ‹http://www.technologyreview.com/tr35/Profile.aspx?Cand=T&TRID=698›.

"Ronggui Yang". University of Colorado at Boulder. April 8, 2009. ‹http://spot.colorado.edu/~yangr/›.

"Ronggui Yang, 34". *Technology Review*. Massachusetts Institute of Technology (MIT). April 8, 2009. ‹http://www.technologyreview.com/tr35/Profile.aspx?Cand=T&TRID=750›.

"Safe Drinking Water". U.S. International Trade Commission. April 10, 2009. ‹http://www.pghsi.com/pghsi/safewater/›.

Savage, Neil. "Making Gasoline from Bacteria". *Technology Review*. *Technology Review*. Massachusetts Institute of Technology (MIT). August 1, 2007. July 30, 2009. ‹http://www.technologyreview.com/business/19128/page1/›

Singer, Emily. "A Better Biofuel: A California biotech company is engineering microbes to produce cheap biofuels that could outcompete ethanol". *Technology Review*. Massachusetts Institute of Technology (MIT). April 3, 2007. April 8, 2009. ‹http://www.technologyreview.com/Biotech/18476/›.

"Speakers Bios and Abstracts", The Puerto Rico Louis Stokes Alliance for Minority Participation. April 8, 2009. ‹http://www.prlsamp.org/what_is_prlsamp/student_activities/harvard/speakers_bios_abstracts.pdf›.

"Theodore Betley, 31". *Technology Review*. Massachusetts Institute of Technology (MIT). April 8, 2009. ‹http://www.technologyreview.com/tr35/Profile.aspx?Cand=T&TRID=684›.

"Top 10 New World-Changing Innovations of the Year". *Popular Mechanics.* November 2008. April 10, 2009. ⟨http://www.popularmechanics.com/science/research/4286850.html?page=7⟩.

"Vic Knauf". Arcadia Biosciences. April 10, 2009. ⟨http://www.arcadiabio.com/bio_knauf.php⟩.

Wald, Matt. "TR10: Traveling-Wave Reactor". *Technology Review.* Massachusetts Institute of Technology (MIT). March/April 2009. April 11, 2009. ⟨http://www.technologyreview.com/read_article.aspx?ch=specialsections&sc=&id=22114 ⟩.

"Yes, You Can Make a Million". *Kiplinger.com.* April 11, 2009. ⟨http://www.kiplinger.com/magazine/archives/2007/03/millionaire.html⟩.

Zimmer, Carl. "Scientist of the Year: Jay Keasling". *Discover.* November, 2006. April 3, 2009. ⟨http://discovermagazine.com/2006/dec/cover⟩.

CHAPTER 15 — EPILOGUE

A National Action Plan for Addressing the Critical Needs of the U.S. Science, Technology, Engineering, and Mathematics Education System. National Science Board. National Science Foundation. Washington, DC. October 30, 2007. February 25, 2009. ⟨http://www.nsf.gov/nsb/documents/2007/stem_action.pdf⟩.

Losing the Competitive Advantage: The Challenge for Science and Technology in the United States. American Electronics Association. Washington, DC. 2005. February 25, 2009. ⟨http://www.aeanet.org/Publications/idjj_AeA_Competitiveness.asp⟩.

"R&D Budget and Policy Program". American Association for the Advancement of Science (AAAS). March 23, 2009. May 28, 2009. ⟨http://www.aaas.org/spp/rd/⟩.

Research and Development: Essential Foundation for U.S. Competitiveness in A Global Economy — A Companion to Science and Engineering Indicators — 2008. National Science Board. National Science Foundation. Washington, DC. January 2008. February 25, 2009. ⟨http://www.nsf.gov/statistics/nsb0803/start.htm⟩.

Rosenblatt, A. "The Attractions of Technology [Engineering/Technology Survey – Professionals and Students]". *Spectrum,* IEEE. February 2004. July 30, 2009. ⟨ http://www.fmlink.com/News/ArchivedArticles/IEEEsurv.15745.html⟩

Vergano, Dan. "TV, Films Boldly Go Down Scientific Path". *USA Today.* March 30, 2009. July 30, 2009. ⟨ http://www.usatoday.com/life/movies/news/2009-03-25-hollywood-science_N.htm⟩.

INDEX

Made in the USA
Charleston, SC
15 January 2010